International Safeguards for Children in Sport

Safeguarding should be a central concern for any sports organisation working with children or young people. This significant new study examines the development, implementation and impact of the International Safeguards for Children in Sport, a set of guidelines drawn up by a working group of international organisations committed to child protection which lays out the measures that need to be taken to ensure children are kept safe from harm.

Including critical perspectives and in-depth real-life case studies, this book looks beyond perpetrator, victim and abuse to focus on the development of a systematic safeguarding culture. The first study to adopt a global perspective on safeguarding in sport, it draws on the insights of researchers and practitioners to discuss best practise for child welfare, organisational reform, policy implementation and directions for future research.

International Safeguards for Children in Sport: Developing and Embedding a Safeguarding Culture is important reading for all those working directly with children through the provision of sport in schools and communities, as well as for students and researchers of the sociology of sport.

Daniel Rhind is a Chartered Psychologist and a Senior Lecturer in Social Psychology at Brunel University, UK. Daniel's research focuses on understanding the development and maintenance of (un)healthy and (in)effective relationships in sport. He was the Principle Investigator for the research project reported in this book. He makes regular contributions to national and international media on issues related to safeguarding in sport. Daniel's research has been funded by a range of organisations including the Oak Foundation, International Inspiration, the Daiwa Foundation, the Change Foundation, the Football Association, the Rugby Football Union, the International Tennis Federation, the Commonwealth Secretariat and the European Commission.

Frank Owusu-Sekyere is a Research Assistant and Doctoral Student in Sport and Exercise Sciences at Brunel University, UK. Having been awarded a First Class Honours degree at Brunel, he went on to complete a Graduate Diploma in Psychology at Middlesex University where he was awarded a Distinction. In 2012, Frank returned to Brunel as a Master's student of Sports and Exercise Psychology completing the course with a Distinction. Frank's area of interest is Safeguarding and Child Athlete Welfare. To date, his research has focused specifically on Emotional Abuse in Youth Sport and Safety culture. Frank also has extensive experience working as a Football Coach, Youth Mentor and Community Development Officer.

Routledge Research in Sport, Culture and Society

www.routledge.com/sport/series/RRSCS

International Safeguards for Children in Sport

Developing and Embedding a Safeguarding Culture

Daniel Rhind and Frank Owusu-Sekyere

Routledge
Taylor & Francis Group
LONDON AND NEW YORK

First published 2018
by Routledge
2 Park Square, Milton Park, Abingdon, Oxon OX14 4RN

and by Routledge
711 Third Avenue, New York, NY 10017

Routledge is an imprint of the Taylor & Francis Group, an informa business

British Library Cataloguing-in-Publication Data
A catalogue record for this book is available from the British Library

Library of Congress Cataloging-in-Publication Data
A catalog record for this book has been requested

ISBN: 978-0-415-79017-8 (hbk)
ISBN: 978-1-315-21354-5 (ebk)

Typeset in Sabon
by Apex CoVantage, LLC

Contents

Figures and tables

Figures

Tables

Acknowledgements

The research team would like to take this opportunity to sincerely thank everyone who made this project possible. We thank the Oak Foundation and International Inspiration for funding this important research. We thank all members of the Founders Group for their on-going support and feedback throughout this project. We also thank all of the pioneers and everyone involved in the case studies. We were inspired by this global coalition who are working together to safeguard children. Last, but certainly not least, we would like to thank Celia Brackenridge, OBE, whose work in this field has inspired this research project. Thank you for your mentorship and guidance, which are deeply treasured.

Chapter 1

Introduction

This book outlines the research project that informed the development, implementation and evaluation of the International Safeguards for Children in Sport. These Safeguards outline the measures that should be put in place by any organisation providing sports activities. The project involved working with 32 organisations throughout a three-year piloting process. This included organisations who work directly with children through the provision of sport for a variety of outcomes (e.g., sport for development (SfD), physical activity or elite performance). It also involved organisations who worked indirectly with children through collaboration with these delivery organisations (e.g., International Federations, Governments or funding providers).

The participants recognised the importance of conducting research alongside the Safeguards project, as illustrated by the following participant quotes:

> "It is a very good experience that we have research integrated from the start of the project. Through this process we can actually feedback messages from the ground on what are the challenges for us, the real genuine challenges."
>
> (National Deliverer, Asia)

> "I really appreciate your work around this project. It is very exciting and I think that it is going to be so valuable for so many kids and people going forward."
>
> (National Governor, North America)

Participants also highlighted that there is a real momentum around safeguarding in sport, both within and beyond their organisations:

> "The nicest part of it is that when you start to talk about the need for child protection you get a lot of nodding heads and people saying that this is an organisational issue and an issue that we need to take seriously. You know, so there is some sort of core commitment to the issue."
>
> (Local Deliverer, Europe)

> "The Safeguards have only been met by positive responses. I really like the fact that everyone is banding together with all of the different stakeholders from grass roots to the highest levels. There really seems to be a drive behind this and everybody agrees that it is important. This may be the most important thing. What we are trying to do is to use SfD and peace. This cannot be achieved at all if sport is not clean and not a good tool in itself."
>
> (International Deliverer, Africa)

The launch of the Safeguards has also been welcomed by a range of leading figures in sport around the world:

> "As an international footballer and founder of a grassroots soccer school in Mozambique, I've witnessed first-hand just how powerful sport can be in transforming children's lives. Children can only excel through sport if they play in a safe and inclusive environment. The implementation of these Safeguards will ensure that many more children around the world will be inspired by sport and protected from harm."
>
> (Manuel Bucane (Tico Tico), international footballer and founder of a grassroots soccer school)

> "I started cycling about the same time I started to walk, as a result of my father being a keen cyclist. Sport was an important part of my own childhood, and I believe children the world over have the right to take part in sporting activities that have a positive effect in their life. I welcome the newly launched International Safeguards which will help to keep children safe both here in the UK and around the world."
>
> (Victoria Pendleton, CBE, Olympic Champion Cyclist)

> "I began swimming when I was five years old, so sport has been part of my life since I was very young. I remember being inspired by watching the 2004 Athens Paralympic Games and so it was a dream come true for me when just four years later I won gold medals at the Beijing Olympics. I strongly believe that all children should have the chance to take part in a way that helps them to benefit from sport while being kept safe at the same time."
>
> (Ellie Simmonds, OBE, Paralympic Champion swimmer)

> "I very much welcome the Safeguards to make sport safer. I know how the power of sport can improve lives but also what the horrible impact can be when things go wrong. The more organisations can do to make sport safe the greater the world of sport will be. Participating in sport should be a positive, empowering experience. We all need to embrace these Safeguards and make sport safe for children."
>
> (Amanda Dlamini, International Footballer)

> "Staff and volunteers who provide sports activities can end up being a real lifeline for children – which is why is it essential that all sports organisations have safeguarding measures in place and most importantly a team of people on-board that feel enable to take action and do so willingly. These new Safeguards set out the key steps that every organisation can take – right from the recruitment stage to developing policies and procedures to ensure children's safety, well-being and protection across all sports."
>
> (Anne Tiivas, Director of the Child Protection in Sport Unit)

> "All children have the right to participate in sport in a safe and enjoyable environment; it is a crucial part of a happy, healthy childhood. UNICEF UK is one of a number of organisations that has worked on trialing these standards with sporting organisations so we can be confident that they will enable everyone involved in sport to stop and think about the risks to children and have appropriate measures in place to prevent abuse."
>
> (Liz Twyford, Sports Programme Specialist, UNICEF UK)

Trinidad and Tobago Sports Hall of Fame member, former professional footballer Shaka Hislop and ESPN football analyst has added his support for the Safeguards, noting that this was a significant milestone in the efforts to make sport safer for children worldwide. Shaka endorsed the safeguards and called on those responsible for the administration of sport for children and young people across the globe to adopt the safeguards as a demonstration of their commitments to preserve the integrity of sport and to ensure that children enjoy the positive benefits of sport participation.

The launch of these Safeguards represents a key step forward on a journey that began over 20 years ago through the pioneering work of Professor Celia Brackenridge OBE. Brackenridge was the first to systematically study abuse in sport, despite significant resistance, to contribute a series of seminal publications (Brackenridge & Rhind, 2014). Other key steps on this journey include the series of expert statements published by the International Olympic Committee (IOC) on issues including sexual harassment and abuse in sport and training the elite child athlete (Mountjoy, Rhind, Tiivas, & Leglise, 2015). The IOC have also included safeguarding as an integrated component of the Youth Athletic Development Model (Mountjoy et al., 2015). Likewise, the United Nations Office for Sport for Development and Peace (UNOSDP) identified the protection of children from all forms of harm as a strategic priority in 2009. The United Nations Children's Fund (UNICEF) commissioned a review of the available empirical research and policy initiatives on safeguarding in sport (Brackenridge, Kay, & Rhind, 2012). This review highlighted the need for a global set of standards to safeguard children in sport as well as a lack of systematic data on measures to safeguard children, particularly in the Global South (Brackenridge et al.,

2012). These developments have contributed to the internationalisation of safeguarding in sport.

1.1 Why do we need safeguarding in sport?

On first reading, this may appear to be a moot question. After all, as the participants pointed out:

> "In theory, nobody is opposed to protecting children."
>
> (International Governor)

> "[Y]ou are not going to have a programme if you cannot protect the child, it is that core of an issue."
>
> (Local Deliverer)

However, there is still value in outlining the arguments which justify the need for safeguarding in sport. The first of these rationales is that abuse does happen in sport. Sport, like any other social institution such as a school, church or care home, puts people in positions of trust and power that can be used to develop abusive relationships (Alexander, Stafford, & Lewis, 2011; Vertommen et al., 2016). Though in comparison to schools, religious institutions and hospitals, sporting organisations have received comparatively less scrutiny (Brackenridge & Rhind, 2014). Indeed, it has been said that "[t]he institution of sport was, at one time, a cultural and political island, defined as separate and free from the rest of society, with Cinderella status." (Brackenridge & Rhind, 2014, p. 329). As abuse happens in sport, in all forms, contexts and competitive levels, it is thus important that safeguards are put in place.

The second rationale concerns the fundamental protection of children's rights as outlined in the United Nations Convention on the Rights of the Child (UNCRC, 1989). This has formed an important facilitator of change as those who engage with children regularly are showing an increasing willingness to consider children's rights (Gilbert, Parton, & Skivenes, 2011). The UNCRC (1989) contains articles with specific relevance to sport. For example, Article 31 states that "Children have the right to relax and play, and to join in a wide range of cultural, artistic and other recreational activities." Furthermore, Article 19 sets out ". . . to protect the child from all forms of physical or mental violence, injury or abuse, neglect or negligent treatment, maltreatment or exploitation, including sexual abuse." It also calls on state parties to take all appropriate measures for the protection of children, including while in the care of others. Sport and exercise represents a context within which a child's rights may be violated. Rights advocates have therefore argued that every child has the right to play safely, in an enabling and protective environment. Effective safeguarding should therefore help to both protect and promote children's rights in sport.

The third rationale is linked to the children's' rights perspective and is the moral argument that one has an ethic of care (Brackenridge, 2001). When faced with ethical and moral issues in sport, one makes a judgment regarding the strength of feeling about any potential wrongdoing. As such, safeguarding can be seen as 'the right thing to do.' One could argue that we have a moral duty to ensure that any children can interact with an organisation in a safe environment that is characterised by healthy and effective relationships. This argument can be strengthened by the very powerful stories of those who have been abused in sport (e.g., Kennedy, 2016).

A fourth rationale focuses on matters of self-interest. This relates to arguments that encourage people to safeguard children because this will help them to meet their own interests. This rationale can concern the individual directly, such as through legal, regulatory or contractual obligations. Failing to meet such obligations may jeopardise an individual's job security, career progress or reputation. It can also indirectly serve self-interest through factors related to the organisation. Safeguarding may help to achieve other goals related to the children's performance or participation rates. There are also broader organisation arguments such as potential links between safeguarding, whether or not funding is received, and the reputation of the organisation in the public and in the media. Indeed, it has been argued that in some countries, progress has not been prompted by legislation or a moral obligation, but instead, by high-profile cases of abuse covered by domestic media (Lang & Hartill, 2015).

1.2 What is the contribution of this book?

This research makes a significant contribution to the literature in two key areas: the application of a systems approach and the use of a global sample. Existing literature on abuse in sport has tended to focus on the individual or the interpersonal approach. The individual approach primarily focusses on the experiences and perceptions of perpetrators and survivors of abuse. The interpersonal approach tends to focus on understanding the relational dynamics involved in safeguarding and abuse. The use of the individual and interpersonal approaches were based on the assumption that sport would be safest for children if it focused on regulating the individuals that gain access to children through sport, increasing the awareness of those already in the sport, and ensuring that the relationships between adults and children are appropriate (Boocock, 2002). This focus on individual and interpersonal aspects may not capture all of the salient factors which can serve to safeguard children.

As awareness of the limitations of these existing approaches increased, so too did the recognition of a need to also consider various organisational structures that bring consistency, standardisation and transparency to safeguarding. For example, Hartill and Lang (2014) acknowledge the multifaceted organisational factors which can influence the success of safeguarding initiatives. Similarly, Jacobs, Smits, and Knoppers (2016) highlighted how the institutional contexts can normalize and rationalize child abuse in sport. East (2012) states that systems, structures and tools should be utilised to build upon the strengths of the individual and interpersonal approaches. Brackenridge, Kay, and Rhind (2012) also state that even where elements such as codes of conduct exist, children are still at risk when the systems that should accompany and reinforce them are absent or inadequate. Therefore, in the recognition that sport may have focused too much on getting the right people, as opposed to getting sport right (Brackenridge & Rhind, 2014), there is a move towards a systems approach to safeguarding children in sport.

Abusive relationships can be facilitated or prevented by a complex network of individual, interpersonal and organisational factors. It is therefore clear that in order to achieve effective safeguarding, a similarly comprehensive strategy, based on a systems approach, is merited. Brackenridge and Rhind (2014) argued that "systemic organisational elements . . . are likely to lead to more sustainable prevention and, ultimately, safer sport for all" (p. 333). The present research is therefore based on a systems approach through exploring what should be in place to safeguard children and which factors influence the effective implementation of these measures.

The present research is also the first to adopt a global perspective on safeguarding in sport. Brackenridge, Kay, and Rhind (2012) highlighted the lack of research on safeguarding in sport that has focused on the Global South. This means that there remained a significant gap in the literature. It is clear that the over-generalisation of research to different contexts than that on which the research was focused is going to lack the necessary reliability, validity or trustworthiness to be theoretically or practically useful. Davies Banda has worked and coached in Zambia and Botswana and has conducted research on HIV/AIDS and sport development projects. He argues:

> "There is a need for research in issues of abuse in this [sport for development] sector due to the vulnerability of the participants that attend sports sessions organized by sport-for-development NGOs. This vulnerability is mainly to do with power relations – abuse is always about the misuse of power by those who have more power within the organisation . . . The vulnerable mostly are the orphans who depend entirely on financial support from such NGOs to fund their school expenses. Abuse or violence does happen to such young people. . .[There is a] lack of systematic policies and procedures for NGOs to vet those that apply as volunteers with the organisations. On the part of the NGO, there is also fear of losing the 'faithful' volunteers if such suspect that they are being investigated for a child abuse allegation."
>
> (Banda, 2007 in Brackenridge, Kay, & Rhind, 2012, p. 57)

Since the Brackenridge et al. (2012) review, there has been a significant expansion in the number of countries in which safeguarding research has been conducted and reported in peer-reviewed publications. For example, the edited book by Lang and Hartill (2015), included perspectives from Japan, South Africa and China. However, studies have primarily focused on a single country (e.g., Mori, Rhind, & Gervis, 2015) or a small number of geographically similar countries (Vertommen et al., 2016). There are a limited number of European projects, such as that on preventing sexual harassment and abuse (Chroni et al., 2012), which have taken a broader perspective. However, the current research is the first to adopt a global approach through including organisations working in North and South America, Europe, Africa, Asia and Oceania.

1.3 The structure of this book

The specific objective of this book is to report the development, implementation and impact of the International Safeguards. It is a research monograph. The structure is an expanded version of a typical empirical journal paper. As such, the opening section defines the key terms related to this project (Chapter 2) before research on the prevalence and risk factors of maltreatment in sport are summarized (Chapter 3). The development of the International Safeguards (Chapter 4) and then the finalised International Safeguards for Children in Sport are presented (Chapter 5). The methods employed in the present research (Chapter 6) are described before the impact of the project is assessed (Chapters 7 and 8). A new model of the factors which influence the implementation of these Safeguards is then explained (Chapter 9) with all of the pillars which comprise this model being outlined (Chapters 10–17). Finally, the key messages are reiterated along with the researchers' reflections and ideas for future research (Chapter 18).

This book will be relevant for post-graduate students who are studying for a taught masters or research degree (e.g., PhD, MPhil) related to safeguarding. It will also be of interest to academics researching issues related to safeguarding in sport. The themes are of relevance to anyone working to safeguard children within organisations and hence it will have wider appeal beyond sport in other sectors (e.g., social work, schools, churches, law). With regards to taught courses, it would be useful reading for students studying undergraduate and post-graduate courses in sports science, international development, social work and organisational psychology.

References

Alexander, K., Stafford, A., & Lewis, T. L. (2011). *The experiences of children participating in organised sport in the UK*. Edinburgh, UK: NSPCC Child Protection Research Centre.

Boocock, S. (2002). The child protection in sport unit. *Journal of Sexual Aggression*, *8*(2), 99–106.

Brackenridge, C. H. (2001). *Spoilsports: Understanding and preventing sexual exploitation in sport*. London, UK: Routledge.

Brackenridge, C. H., Kay, T., & Rhind, D. J. A. (Eds.). (2012). *Sport, children's rights and violence prevention: A source book on global issues and local programmes*. London, UK: Brunel University Press.

Brackenridge, C. H., & Rhind, D. (2014). Child protection in sport: Reflections on thirty years of science and activism. *Social Sciences*, *3*, 326–340.

Chroni, S., Fasting, K., Hartill, M., Knorre, N., Martin, M., Papaefstathiou, M., Rhind, D., Rulofs, B., Toftegaard Stockel, J., Vertommen, T., & Zurc, J. (2012). *Prevention of sexual and gender harassment and abuse in sport: Initiatives from Europe and beyond*. Berlin: German Sports Youth.

East, J. (2012). The causes of violence in sport: Who is to blame? In C. Brackenridge, T. Kay, & D. Rhind (Eds.), *Sport, children's rights and violence prevention: A sourcebook on global issues and local programmes* (pp. 18–24). London, UK: Brunel University Press.

Gilbert, N., Parton, N., & Skivenes, M. (2011). *Child protection systems: International trends and orientations*. New York, NY: Open University Press.

Hartill, M., & Lang, M. (2014). "I know people think I'm a complete pain in the neck": An examination of the introduction of child protection and "Safeguarding" in English sport from the perspective of national governing body safeguarding lead officers. *Social Sciences*, *3*, 606–627.

Jacobs, F., Smits, F., & Knoppers, A. (2016). 'You don't realize what you see!': The institutional context of emotional abuse in elite youth sport. *Sport in Society*, *20*(1), 126–143.

Kennedy, S. (2016). *Why I didn't say anything*. Toronto: Insomniac Press.

Lang, M., & Hartill, M. (2015). *Safeguarding, child protection and abuse in sport: International perspectives in research, policy and practice*. Oxfordshire, UK: Routledge.

Mori, K., Rhind, D. J. A., & Gervis, M. (2015). The present state of abuse or corporal punishment involving children and sports authority figures: The necessity for a child protection system in sports in Japan. *Annals of Fitness and Sports Science*, *50*, 17–24.

Mountjoy, M., Rhind, D., Tiivas, A., & Leglise, M. (2015). Safeguarding the child athlete in sport: A review, a framework and recommendations for the IOC youth athlete development model. *British Journal of Sports Medicine*, *49*, 883–886.

United Nations General Assembly. (1989). *United Nations rights of the child*. Retrieved from www.unicef.org.uk/what-we-do/un-convention-child-rights/

Vertommen, T., Veldhoven, N. S., Wouters, K., Kampen, J. K., Brackenridge, C. H., Rhind, D., Neels, K., & Van Den Eedea, F. (2016). Interpersonal violence against children in sport in the Netherlands and Belgium. *Child Abuse and Neglect*, *51*, 223–236.

Chapter 2

Defining key terms

The present chapter seeks to define the key terms that will underpin the rest of this book. Those terms include: the child, childhood and child maltreatment. In order to understand child maltreatment in a sporting context, a framework for child maltreatment will be outlined. The approaches to preventing child maltreatment in sport will then be defined, which will differentiate child protection from safeguarding, and discuss the three types of safeguarding in sport.

2.1 Defining the child and childhood

Historically, children were understood as miniature and as an inadequate representation of their parents (Hart, 1991). With a lack of understanding of child development issues, parents and guardians were given the freedom to assess their child's competencies, and interpret what was appropriate for them to do or endure (Hart, 1991). Therefore, up to the 16th century, children were politically powerless and had no rights to recognise their unique vulnerabilities (Miller-Perrin & Perrin, 2013). Although research, activism and changes in public opinion meant that during the 16th, 17th and 18th centuries, significant developments were made to differentiate children from adults, recognising their status as not just small adults, but developing people with physical and psychological limitations that make them typically more vulnerable and malleable in nature (Brackenridge, 2001; Hart, 1991; Miller-Perrin & Perrin, 2013).

With a growing appreciation for the developmental stages of childhood, several considerations emerged regarding children and the period of childhood. For example, the precise vulnerabilities of the child, and the facilitators and hindrances to their healthy development. To date, ideas on such matters have differed on the grounds of the specific historical timeframe, political and ideological stance, geographical location and cultural contexts (Brackenridge, 2001). This has been especially hindered by fundamental disagreements in the definition and time frame of childhood. Therefore, in a bid to ensure global congruency, the United Nations have defined the child as a human below the age of 18 years old (United Nations General Assembly, 1989).

Though this definition has afforded a great deal of political conformity, it has not necessarily settled debates on the matter. The definition and implications of childhood are still inconsistently defined in different countries and cultures (Piper, Garratt, & Taylor, 2013). This may reflect differing degrees of awareness or differences in the extent to which the UN definition is valued. Consequently, the UN definition of a child provides a degree of conformity in theory, though it does not necessarily do so in practice and it is unlikely to be recognised and appreciated in the same manner globally (Piper, Garratt, & Taylor, 2013).

2.2 Problematising child maltreatment

Notwithstanding its global incongruence, the recognition of childhood as a unique and significant time of human development has been central to the problematisation of child maltreatment. Child maltreatment was brought to prominence by seminal work such as the *Battered Child Syndrome* (Garbarino, Guttmann, & Seeley, 1986; Miller-Perrin & Perrin, 2013), which heightened awareness of child abuse. This book discussed abuse as a matter of public concern, rather than a preference in parenting style. Similarly, high-profile scandals in countries like Canada, Scotland, Australia and the USA also increased the feeling that something was to be done to ensure that children are offered protection from various forms of harm (Parton, 2006).

Increasing understanding and awareness of the various forms of harm that children may be subjected to led to the most significant global development for the protection of children from harm, the United Nation Convention on the Rights of the Child (UN General Assembly, 1989). This legally binding international treaty ratifies children's rights globally in a wide variety of matters, most pertinently to this book, their right to be protected from violence, abuse, exploitation and neglect. It compels agreeing governments and nations to ensure there is adequate legislation, policies and practices in place for the protection of children from harm, while providing a framework to assess their success in such matters.

Similar to the UN's definition of childhood, the impact of this treaty is subject to varying levels of awareness and perceptions of significance globally. Additionally, not all governments throughout the world have signed the treaty. Somalia and the USA are not bound to the treaty at the time of writing. Though with most countries being signees, the UNCRC can be described as the most significant and applicable legislation for the protection of children globally. It has enshrined the protection of children as a fundamental human right for the child.

2.3 Defining and categorising child maltreatment: conceptual issues

With increasing recognition of childhood and the need to have specific measures in place for the protection of children, various strategies and policies have been developed globally (Parton, 2006). However, their content and application has differed on the grounds of the cultural and ideological differences of those developing and implementing them. Empirical evidence of this is offered by Ferrari who explored the child raising practices of 150 participants of differing ethnic and cultural backgrounds. Using a multitude of peer reviewed questionnaires, Ferrari measured; gender role attitudes, the value placed on children, attitudes towards family, the experience of childhood maltreatment, warmth towards their children and punitive behaviour towards their children. The study also measured participant's perceptions of the severity of several child maltreatment vignettes. Findings suggested that there are significant differences in the child rearing attitudes and behaviours of differing ethnic groups on matters such as: understanding and definition of maltreatment, attitude towards physical punishment and perceptions of the severity of certain types of child maltreatment (Ferrari, 2002). Such findings are significant as they reflect the divergence of views which may subsequently impact the extent to which people subscribe to global, international or national legislation and policy on child maltreatment. So, while Crooks and Wolfe argue that maltreatment should be considered a parent term for other forms of ill treatment (e.g. abuse, violence & neglect), and define maltreatment as "... volitional acts that result in or have the potential to result in physical injuries or psychological harm" (2007, p. 640), a debate remains on the extent to which a settled and all-encompassing definition may be possible.

The antithesis of such attempts to develop a settled and stable definition of child maltreatment holds that maltreatment should be considered a relative matter that is determined by ideological stances and cultural norms as it is a "... socially constructed phenomenon that reflect the values of a particular culture at a particular time" (Parton, Thorpe, & Wattam, 1997, p. 71). Indeed, empirical evidence has been offered that suggests that cultural differences can be so substantial that normalised practices in one culture, may be considered maltreatment in another. For example, Westby states that while it is considered typical practice for North Americans to allow infants and young children to sleep in their own room and bed, some cultures may deem this neglect. Conversely, while some cultures may deem it good practice to sleep in the same bed as an infant child, many North Americans would argue that this is at best inappropriate behaviour (Westby, 2007). However, it is also arguable that differences in views should not merely be accepted as inevitable and constant. Especially as they can lead to global, national or regional conflict between affording civil liberties, and the uniform protection of children (Westby, 2007). This may cause large disparities in the quality of child maltreatment prevention work globally, and violations of the UNCRC may be justified by suggestions that certain types or degrees of child maltreatment are culturally acceptable. Thus, there is potential for an entirely relative approach to cause culturally rationalised maltreatment, the development of a dangerous cultural deficit framework and the ultimate inconsequentiality of the UNCRC (Westby, 2007).

Considering these potential negative implications, the popular view is that maltreatment should not be considered culturally relevant. With this, Westby argues that "children's interests are best served by adopting an absolutist approach . . . focusing on the experience of the child rather than the intent of the caregivers" (2007, p. 144). Further, Chan, Elliott, Chow, and Thomas (2002) suggest that maltreatment should be determined by the acts of individuals and their outcomes, rather than intent, culturally derived or not. With this stance, those in positions of power are urged to categorise cultural practices as either beneficial, neutral, potentially harmful or harmful (Koramoa, Lynch, & Kinnair, 2002). With this categorisation, Koramoa and colleagues state that in order to avoid cultural supremacy, which may lead to the systematic dilution of cultural practices, socially and developmentally beneficial acts should be promoted, neutral acts should be understood and respected, people should be educated on potentially harmful acts and measures should be put in place to prevent unequivocally harmful acts.

The effectiveness of this more absolutist approach remains subject to effective implication. Questions may still be raised over who determines what is harmful, and precisely how harmful is defined. Such questions typically raise concerns over cultural supremacy, and the potential for the dominant views of global powerhouses to take precedence. These concerns are exacerbated by research on maltreatment tending to experience a bias towards Western, developed and/or Global North countries, with significant gaps in the knowledge base of child maltreatment in North and sub-Saharan Africa, Asia and the Caribbean (Rhind, Brackenridge, Kay, & Owusu-Sekyere, 2016). Thus, critics may argue that developing a globally accepted definition and categorisation of child maltreatment is, at best, an on-going mission and, at worst, utopian.

Considering these issues, it is certainly arguable that further work is required, and global conformity, particularly in practice, should not be assumed. Though it should not be discounted that significant progress has been made to present globally representative definitions and categorisations of child maltreatment. Arguably the most noteworthy of those is offered by the World Health Organisation (WHO) who state that maltreatment refers to;

> "All forms of physical and/or emotional ill-treatment, sexual abuse, neglect or negligent treatment or commercial or other exploitation, resulting in actual or potential harm to the child's health, survival, development or dignity in the context of a relationship of responsibility, trust or power."
>
> (Butchart, Putney, Furniss, & Kahane, 2006, p. 59)

With this definition, the present book takes the stance that although maltreatment is frequently used interchangeably with similar terms such as abuse and violence (Porter, Antonishak, & Reppucci, 2006), it should instead be considered an all-encompassing term that includes and considers the following;

- Abuse – Acts of commission or omission which lead to children experiencing harm (Rhind et al., 2016);
- Violence – The intentional use of force or power, threatened or actual, against oneself, another person, or against a group or community, that results either in or has a high likelihood of resulting in injury, death, psychological harm, maldevelopment or deprivation (WHO, 2002);
- Harm – Negative physical and/or emotional impact or consequences (Rhind et al., 2016).

Therefore, maltreatment should be considered inclusive of acts of omission, commission, and exploitation which may be direct, indirect, intentional or unintentional (Parton, Thorpe, & Wattam, 1997; Raakman, Dorsch, & Rhind, 2010). This is categorised further when placed into a sport specific framework for child maltreatment.

2.4 A sport-specific framework for child maltreatment in sport

The traditional understanding of child maltreatment in sport is that it consists of four types of maltreatment; sexual abuse, physical abuse, emotional abuse and neglect (David, 2005; Raakman et al., 2010). Contemporary research has identified various other forms of maltreatment which may exist in sport. This includes: child labour, discrimination and institutional maltreatment (Stirling, 2009). Therefore, within sport, there is currently a broadened scope of maltreatment types that are understood and offered attention. With this growing understanding of the range of maltreatment types that may exist in sport, there is scope for a more encompassing framework of child maltreatment in sport. This has been offered by Stirling (2009).

Stirling's Framework of Child Maltreatment in Sport (2009) distinguishes relational maltreatment from non-relational maltreatment. In doing so, relational maltreatment is defined as maltreatment that occurs ". . . within the context of a critical relationship role, in which the relationship has significant influence over an individual's sense of safety, trust, and fulfilment of needs" (Stirling, 2009, p. 1092). This may be coaches, medical staff, teammates and parents. It includes neglect and maltreatment of a sexual, emotional and physical nature.

Conversely, non-relational maltreatment is described as maltreatment that does not occur within the contexts of a significant relationship (Stirling, 2009). This includes maltreatment in which the perpetrator is not necessarily an individual, but possibly an institution. It also recognises incidents in which the perpetrator is a stranger to the child. Stirling argues that it is possible for non-relational maltreatment to take the form of the more traditional forms of maltreatment (e.g., physical abuse) (2009), though it is typically broader forms of maltreatment (e.g., corruption, child labour and child trafficking). This may involve the sport or sporting organisation, but may not necessarily occur in the competitive sporting environment. Furthermore, it is now recognised that maltreatment is frequently experienced indirectly by the child (i.e. performed in the presence of, but not aimed at the child in question) (Raakman, 2010), which may cause comparable harm to personal and direct experiences of maltreatment (Omli & LaVoi, 2009).

Conceptual and ideological differences on matters such as the definition of childhood, child maltreatment and its constituent terms (such as abuse and violence), mean that there is unlikely to be uniform agreement on the applicability of this framework globally. This inevitable incongruence in views is unfortunate as such disagreement has been discussed as the greatest challenge of safeguarding work (Porter, Antonishak, & Reppucci, 2006). It has also been discussed as hindering the ability to replicate studies and generalise findings (Stirling, 2009). Nonetheless, this framework is arguably the most comprehensive overview of child maltreatment in sport to date (Stirling, 2009). Its expansion beyond the traditional approach enables the inclusion of a multitude of maltreatment types which are commonly overlooked. This may be further developed as the framework makes no claims of being a static or exhaustive one.

2.5 Preventing child maltreatment: child protection and safeguarding

With increasing recognition of children's rights and the need to protect children from maltreatment, differing strategies for the prevention of child maltreatment have emerged. These developments have been made at government level and are not exclusive to sport. However, the approaches used in sport have mirrored those used in wider society and by national governments (Brackenridge, 2001). Therefore, it is necessary to consider differing approaches from this perspective, before discussing their application to sport. Gilbert has presented two previously dominant approaches for the prevention of child maltreatment (2012). These approaches differ on the grounds of their underpinning theory on how and why maltreatment occurs, how it may be discovered and the role of influential organisations (e.g., governing bodies).

The first approach to preventing child maltreatment is referred to as 'child protection.' This position holds that maltreatment occurs as a result of pathological and unscrupulous individuals being entrusted with the care of children (Gilbert, 2012). Thus, the focus of this approach is on ensuring that those who are afforded closeness to children through trusted organisations are thoroughly checked (e.g., via criminal record checks and references). Furthermore, this approach attempts to offer additional protection to those who have been assessed as being particularly vulnerable, either due to the nature of their exposure to potential perpetrators, or factors that may heighten their vulnerability to maltreatment. Within the child protection approach, government and governing bodies are mainly reactive in nature and although pre-emptive strategies may be put in place and mandated (e.g., criminal record checks), state involvement typically occurs in response to cases of maltreatment. Particularly those that require legal investigation and have criminal implications (Gilbert, 2012).

The second approach focuses on 'family services' (Gilbert, 2012). This position posits that maltreatment as a negative consequence of the psychological, social and economic issues faced by those with the responsibility to care for a child (Gilbert, 2012). With this stance, governments and governing organisations are pre-emptive and the prevention of maltreatment is achieved by focussing on empowerment. Therefore, governments and governing organisations aim to work collaboratively offering support, guidance and therapy to both children and those responsible for their care.

Gilbert's (2012) findings suggest that the child protection approach was previously dominant in countries such as the United Kingdom, the USA, Canada and Australia during the 1990s. Conversely, during this time, the family services approach was dominant in European countries such as Denmark, Sweden and Germany. Into the 21st century, a new, broadened approach emerged. Underpinned by advocacy and international developments in policy and research, this approach reflected those with a child protection approach adopting elements of the family services approach, and vice versa, giving birth to the 'child development' approach (Gilbert, 2012). The child development approach considers that maltreatment may occur either as a result of pathological and unscrupulous individuals, or as a consequence of psycho-socio-economic issues. It aims to provide preventative and reactive elements, and is typified by its broad and all-encompassing nature which aims to prevent maltreatment to all children.

This new broader approach to preventing child maltreatment has arguably become the most popular in general society and in sport. It is reflected in the increasingly popular term, safeguarding. This is the reasonable "actions taken to ensure all children and young people are safe from harm" (Hayhurst, Kay, & Chawansky, 2016, p. 73). Though this is often incorrectly used as a synonym for child protection (Lang & Hartill, 2015), this is in stark contrast to child protection, which can be defined as a "set of activities that are required for specific children who are at risk of/or are suffering from significant harm" (Hayhurst, Kay, & Chawansky, 2016, p. 73).

Reorientations in influential countries such as England and the USA have encouraged many countries to also adopt this approach (Melton, 2009, as cited in Lang & Hartill, 2015). In some instances, this influence may occur through education orientated partnerships, or by funders, grant and award bodies who make safeguarding policy, procedures and practices conditions of any agreements. Thus, there is a growing perception that safeguarding is the gold standard of the prevention of child maltreatment (Lang & Hartill, 2015). This is not an undisputed claim. Some have rejected the preventative-surveillance state, lamenting its potential to erode civil liberties at the expense of giving children rights (Parton, 2006, 2008), while concerns are also raised about the resources and infrastructure required to adequately administer a more all-encompassing approach (Laird, 2013; Parton, 2008). Nonetheless, safeguarding has grown as one of, if not the most valued and popular approach to protecting children from maltreatment in sport.

2.6 Safeguarding in, around and through sport

There are a wide variety of organisations in sport for whom safeguarding is a consideration. Those organisations can be split into two broad categories; deliverers (e.g., sports clubs, community-based SfD organisations and schools) and governors (e.g., International Federations, Government departments or programme funders). Within these categories there are even more divergences that may influence the organisation's precise strategy towards safeguarding children. Factors include, but are not limited to the organisations location, resources, mission, authority and their nature of engagement with children (Brackenridge & Rhind, 2014). In recognition of this, three specific types of safeguarding have been identified, reflecting the way an organisation may attempt to safeguard children.

Safeguarding in sport

Safeguarding in sport explicitly focusses on the protection of children from harm during training and competition. During this time, children are deemed the responsibility of the organisation and care is taken to manage the environment and those with contact of the child during this time. Safeguarding in sport typically focusses on relational types of maltreatment (e.g., abuse from coaches, parents or spectators) and is typically adopted by those sporting organisations who are concerned with the advancement of sport and sporting performance (Brackenridge & Rhind, 2014).

Safeguarding around sport

Safeguarding around sport focusses on matters that are peripheral to sport, but may influence or be influenced by sport (Brackenridge & Rhind, 2014). For example, forced displacement which may occur because of mega sporting events (Rhind et al., 2016; Brackenridge et al., 2014). This approach is typically used by governing or sport related children's service agencies, whose ambitions to prevent child maltreatment are more extensive than sport or sporting performance (Brackenridge & Rhind, 2014).

Safeguarding through sport

Safeguarding through sport focusses on the use of sport to accomplish humanitarian objectives such as peace building and post disaster development (Brackenridge & Rhind, 2014). When safeguarding through sport, sport is merely the vehicle through which actual or potential harm in society may be addressed. This may be used by delivery or governing organisations, though it is typically used in SfD where an organisation's mission is to promote the development of individuals or communities. When safeguarding through sport, sport is used as a mechanism through which children's rights can be promoted or protected (Rhind et al., 2016).

2.7 Summary

This chapter has defined and categorised the key terms that will underpin this book. The United Nations definition of a child was used, which states that a child is a human below the age of 18 years old (United Nations General Assembly, 1989). This formed the basis for the definition of child maltreatment. Having discussed various conceptual issues, child maltreatment was defined as;

> "All forms of physical and/or emotional ill-treatment, sexual abuse, neglect or negligent treatment or commercial or other exploitation, resulting in actual or potential harm to the child's health, survival, development or dignity in the context of a relationship of responsibility, trust or power."
>
> (Butchart et al., 2006, p. 59)

Maltreatment was then placed into sport specific contexts, and Stirling's comprehensive framework of child maltreatment in sport was used (2009). This framework differentiates relational maltreatment from non-relational maltreatment, while accounting for recent findings, such as the significance of indirect forms of abuse (Raakman, Dorsch, & Rhind, 2010). With safeguarding defined as the reasonable ". . . actions taken to ensure all children and young people are safe from harm" (Hayhurst et al., 2016, p. 73), three types of safeguarding were discussed: safeguarding in, through and around sport.

References

Brackenridge, C. H. (2001). *Spoilsports: Understanding and preventing sexual exploitation in sport*. London, UK: Routledge.

Brackenridge, C. H., & Rhind, D. (2014). Child protection in sport: Reflections on thirty years of science and activism. *Social Sciences, 3*, 326–340.

Butchart, A., Putney, H., Furniss, T., & Kahane, T. (2006). *Preventing child maltreatment: A guide to taking action and generating evidence*. Geneva, Switzerland: World Health Organisation.

Chan, J. S., Elliott, J. M., Chow, Y., & Thomas, J. I. (2002). Does professional and public opinion in child abuse differ? An issue of cross-cultural policy implementation. *Child Abuse Review, 11*, 359–379.

Crooks, C. V., & Wolfe, D. A. (2007). Child abuse and neglect. In E. J. Mash & R. A. Barkley (Eds.), *Assessment of childhood disorders* (4th ed., pp. 1–17). New York, NY: Guilford Press.

David, P. (2005). *Human rights in youth sport: A critical review of children's rights in competitive sports*. New York, NY: Routledge.

Ferrari, A. M. (2002). The impact of culture upon child rearing practices and definitions of maltreatment. *Child Abuse and Neglect, 26*, 793–813.

Garbarino, J., Guttmann, E., & Seeley, J. (1986). *The psychologically battered child*. San Francisco, CA: Jossey-Bass.

Gilbert, N. (2012). A comparative study of child welfare systems: Abstract orientations and concrete results. *Children and Youth Services Review, 34*, 532–536.

Hart, S. N. (1991). From property to person status: Historical perspective on children's rights. *American Psychologist, 46*(1), 53–59.

Hayhurst, L., Kay, T., & Chawansky, M. (2016). *Beyond sport for development and peace: Transnational perspectives on theory and practice*. Oxon, UK: Routledge.

Koramoa, J., Lynch, M. A., & Kinnair, D. (2002). A continuum of childrearing: Responding to traditional practices. *Child Abuse Review, 11*, 411–421.

Laird, S. (2013). *Child protection: Managing conflict, hostility and aggression*. Bristol, UK: Policy Press.

Lang, M., & Hartill, M. (2015). *Safeguarding, child protection and abuse in sport: International perspectives in research, policy and practice*. Oxfordshire, UK: Routledge.

Miller-Perrin, C. L., & Perrin, R. D. (2013). *Child maltreatment: An introduction* (3rd ed.). Thousand Oaks, CA: Sage.

Omli, J., & LaVoi, N. M. (2009). Background anger in youth sport: A perfect storm? *Journal of Sport Behaviour, 32*, 242–260.

Parton, N. (2006). *Safeguarding childhood: Early intervention and surveillance in a late modern society*. Basingstoke, UK: Palgrave/Macmillan.

Parton, N. (2008). The 'Change for children' programme in England: Towards the 'Preventive-surveillance state'. *Journal of Law and Society, 35*, 166–187.

Parton, N., Thorpe, D., & Wattam, C. (1997). *Child protection: Risk and the moral order*. Basingstoke, UK: Macmillan Press.

Piper, H., Garratt, D., & Taylor, B. (2013). Child abuse, child protection and defensive 'touch' in PE teaching and sports coaching. *Sport, Education and Society, 18*, 583–598.

Porter, M. R., Antonishak, J., & Reppucci, N. D. (2006). Policy and applied definitions of child maltreatment. In M. Feerick, J. Knutson, P. Trickett, S. Flanzer, & K. Snow (Eds.), *Child abuse and neglect: Definitions, classifications, and a framework for research* (pp. 331–341). Baltimore, MD: Brooks Publishing.

Raakman, E., Dorsch, K., & Rhind, D. (2010). The development of a typology of abusive coaching behaviours within youth sport. *International Journal of Sports Science and Coaching*, *5*(4), 503–515.

Rhind, D., Brackenridge, C. H., Kay, T., & Owusu-Sekyere, F. (2016). Child protection and SDP: The post-MDG agenda for policy, practice and research. In L. Hayhurst, T. Kay, & M. Chawansky (Eds.), *Beyond sport for development and peace: Transitional perspectives on theory policy and practice* (pp. 72–86). Oxon, UK: Routledge.

Stirling, A. E. (2009). Definition and constituents of maltreatment in sport: Establishing a conceptual framework for research practitioners. *British Journal of Sports Medicine*, *43*, 1091–1099.

United Nations General Assembly. (1989). *United Nations rights of the child*. Retrieved from www.unicef.org.uk/what-we-do/un-convention-child-rights/

Westby, C. E. (2007). Child maltreatment: A global issue. *Language, Speech and Hearing Services in Schools*, *38*, 140–148.

World Health Organisation. (2002). *World report on violence and health: Summary*. Geneva, Switzerland: World Health Organisation.

Chapter 3

Prevalence and risk factors of child maltreatment in sport

A growing body of research has been conducted in a range of countries demonstrating the prevalence of child maltreatment in sport. This chapter will outline the current state of knowledge through summarising the available empirical evidence. The various risk factors which have been associated with child maltreatment in sport will be described and then a new model of these risk factors is proposed.

3.1 Evidence of relational maltreatment in sport

During the 1980s, cases of sexual, physical and emotional maltreatment in sport began to be publicised. This inspired the scientific study of maltreatment in sport with abuse, exploitation and violence emerging as a topic of significant interest by the start of the 1990s (Brackenridge, 2001). Much progress has been made in these areas, and research has expanded to consider many more forms of maltreatment (Brackenridge & Rhind, 2014). Though a large proportion of the field remains dedicated to the relational forms of maltreatment that initially inspired the area of research (e.g., sexual abuse). This is consistently validated by contemporary findings of prevalence and popular cases of serious abuse which have continued to emerge into the 21st century.

This research is rarely globally representative. Some evidence does exist from countries as wide ranging as Japan, South Africa, Brazil and Slovenia (Lang & Hartill, 2015), though studies tend to emanate from developed countries that are typically in the global north (e.g., the USA, the United Kingdom and Canada). This is somewhat concerning, as it is not necessarily the case that such findings are transferable to other cultural, legal, political and economic contexts (Rhind, Brackenridge, Kay, & Owusu-Sekyere, 2016). Therefore, it becomes difficult to ensure that calls for the intensification of safeguarding strategies (e.g., Brackenridge et al., 2012), are responded to in a manner that reflects the needs, concerns and realities of developed, developing, Global North and Global South countries. In recognition of this, the following section provides a brief review of some of the evidence of relational maltreatment in sport. This seeks to be as representative as possible, though in the absence of research it is acknowledged that such findings do not necessarily reflect the realities of all countries and cultures.

3.1.1 Sexual exploitation

Sexual exploitation is an umbrella term that describes varying types and degrees of sexual maltreatment (Brackenridge, 2001; Brackenridge, Bishop, Moussali, & Tapp, 2008; Brackenridge & Fasting, 2005). This has been outlined by Brackenridge in the Sexual Exploitation Continuum (Brackenridge, 2001). This framework identifies three forms of sexual exploitation; sexual discrimination, sexual harassment and sexual abuse (Brackenridge, 2001).

Sexual discrimination describes processes or practices in which individuals are discriminated against on the grounds of gender (Brackenridge, 2001). This form of sexual exploitation unfairly prejudices one demographic, while servicing the needs of another (Brackenridge, 2001). Sexual discrimination is present at all points of the sexual exploitation continuum. Therefore, it may occur along with other forms of sexual exploitation, or in isolation, reflecting institutional or individual behaviour. Examples include differences in pay, working conditions or the availability of gender-specific facilities.

Though it is notoriously difficult to define (Fasting, 2005), sexual harassment involves unwanted sexual attention (Fasting & Brackenridge, 2005). At this point of the continuum, discrimination is accompanied by a misuse of power which results in behaviour such as stalking, sexual jokes and lewd comments (Brackenridge, Bishop, Moussali, & Tapp, 2008; Brackenridge & Fasting, 2005). In practice, this is extremely difficult to differentiate from sexual abuse, which also involves a misuse of power, but it differs in the extent to which the victim is forced to acquiesce with the perpetrators sexual behaviour (Brackenridge, Bishop, Moussali, & Tapp, 2008; Brackenridge & Fasting, 2005).

Sexual abuse is "[a]ny sexual interaction with person(s) of any age that is perpetrated against the victims will, without consent or in an aggressive, exploitative, manipulative or threatening manner" (Ryan & Lane, 1997, p. 3). This may occur simultaneously or consecutively with other forms of sexual exploitation (Brackenridge & Fasting, 2005), but is commonly the most extreme and personally invasive form of sexual exploitation. Examples include rape, groping or sexual violence. Therefore, in contrast to sexual harassment, the victim has been groomed, coerced or forced to comply with the sexual desires of the perpetrator (Fasting & Brackenridge, 2009; Brackenridge, 2001). This is despite the absence of consent, or the inability of consent to be given (Leahy, Pretty, & Tenenbaum, 2002).

3.1.2 Evidence of sexual exploitation in sport

The most renowned cases of child maltreatment in sport have been of a sexual nature. For example, former British Olympic Swimming coach Paul Hickson was convicted of fifteen counts of sexual exploitation against teenage swimmers (Brackenridge, 2001), and Canadian Ice Hockey Coach Graham James was convicted for sexual abuse of former youth athletes, including the well-known Sheldon Kennedy (Donnelly, Kerr, Heron, & DiCarlo, 2016). These popular cases caused a 'moral panic' which awakened the public and those in the field to issues of child maltreatment in sport (Brackenridge, 2001). This has subsequently inspired research on sexual exploitation, in countries as varied as: Australia (Leahy, Pretty, & Tenenbaum, 2002), the USA (Volkwein, Schnell, Sherwood, & Livezey, 1997), Canada (Kirby & Greaves, 1996), Norway (Fasting, Brackenridge, & Sundgot-Borgen, 2004), the UK (Benedict & Klein, 1997; Alexander, Stafford, & Lewis, 2011), Nigeria (Elendu & Umeakuka, 2011) and Denmark (Nielsen, 2001).

In these studies, prevalence often varies depending on factors such as the victim's gender, sport, competitive level and the location of the study. Previous research provides significant evidence of sexual exploitation in sport. For example, in the UK, Alexander, Stafford, and Lewis (2011) found that 29% of former youth athletes from organised sport had experienced sexual harassment (n = 6124). In a recent study with over 4,000 former youth athletes in the Netherlands and Belgium, 17% of women and 11% of men reported experiencing at least one form of sexual exploitation in sport (Vertommen et al., 2015). Similarly, in a mixed-methods study with 107 former youth athletes at various levels in Australia, over 35% of respondents reported experiencing at least one form of sexual harassment (McPherson et al., 2015).

Inconsistencies in prevalence literature often occur due to differences in definition, sampling, response rate and trustworthiness (Fasting, 2005). They are also impacted by the willingness of participants to report their experiences, an issue that especially impacts males who may be less likely to report their experiences due to a fear of losing their masculine identity (Hartill, 2013; Parent & Bannon, 2012). Further, the field is dominated by research from developed countries, and less evidence is offered of sexual exploitation in developing countries. Therefore, it is almost impossible to cite a precise figure of prevalence. Although considering the evidence which has been provided, and continues to emerge, it can be argued that sexual exploitation is at the very least, a significant issue for children in sport.

3.1.3 Physical abuse

Physical abuse is the exposure to actual or significant risk of physical harm, trauma or injury (Matthews, 2004). Despite commonly being discussed synonymously with violence, it is a broader term that involves both incidences in which physical contact has taken place and incidences in which no physical contact has taken place (Stirling, 2009). Examples of physical abuse that involves physical contact include: punching, kicking and slapping children. Conversely, examples of physical abuse in which no physical contact has taken place include: denying access to water, denying access to bathroom facilities and forcing the child to inflict pain on themselves. Such actions are regarded as physical abuse, in so far as they are acts of volition, regardless of an intention to cause harm (Chan, Elliott, Chow, & Thomas, 2002).

3.1.4 Evidence of physical abuse in sport

Evidence of physical abuse in sport has been offered by previous research. For example, 4,043 participants took an online questionnaire on their experiences in sport at different competitive levels in Holland and Belgium. Of this sample, 11% of participants reported experiencing physical violence (Vertommen et al., 2016). In Australia, 34% of 93 former youth athletes reported experiencing physical abuse, such as being pushed and shoved (McPherson et al., 2015). In the United Kingdom, 24% of 6,000 former youth athletes reported experiencing physical abuse (Alexander et al., 2011) and 20% of all safeguarding allegations relate to physical abuse (Rhind, McDermott, Lambert, & Koleva, 2015).

These studies have found evidence of the more direct forms of physical abuse. Evidence has also been offered of the indirect forms of physical abuse, such as the use of inappropriate training in youth sports. In a study with 231 young athletes from Japan, Sweden and the USA, 35% of young athletes experienced symptoms of significant overtraining (Raglin, Sawamura, Alexiou, Hassmen, & Kentta, 2000). Evidence from Taiwan following the analysis of 119 youth athletes suggests that such inappropriate and insensitive training regimes can cause serious muscle injury in children (e.g., Rhabdomyolysis) and, in some instances, may even require hospitalisation (Lin, Lin, Wang, & Leu, 2005). Such findings have inspired articles from other countries, such as China, where concern has been raised over the severity and potential harm of elite youth training programmes (Hong, 2004).

In spite of these studies, it is important to note that there is significantly less research on physical abuse, in comparison to other forms of maltreatment (e.g. sexual exploitation). The main reason that has been offered for this is that sport consistently struggles to negotiate the dichotomy between intense, yet physically beneficial practice and abusive practice (Oliver & Lloyd, 2015). Therefore, it is argued that there is often a poor ability to identify, and an unhealthy tolerance of, physical abuse (Coakley, 2007; Alexander et al., 2011). This may even extend to the development of a sporting or organisational culture in which abuse is normative and thus unlikely to be reported. Considering this, it must be noted that even with the evidence that does exist, it is likely that the genuine extent of physical abuse in sport may be masked or significantly underplayed (Brackenridge, Bringer & Bishop, 2005).

3.1.5 Emotional abuse

Emotional abuse is "[a] repeated pattern of behaviour or extreme incidents that convey to children that they are worthless, flawed, unloved, unwanted, endangered or of value only in meeting another's needs" (American Professional Society on the Abuse of Children (ASPAC), 1995, p. 2). This includes behaviours such as: belittling, humiliating, shouting, scapegoating, rejecting, isolating, threatening and ignoring (Garbarino, Guttmann, & Seeley, 1986; Gervis & Dunn, 2004). These behaviours may be accidental or non-accidental, while they may also be acts of commission, or omission (Glaser, 2002; O'Hagan, 1995). Additionally, for emotional abuse to be present, these behaviours must be performed repetitively, typifying the nature of the relationship between the victim and the perpetrator, while also provoking a negative emotional response in the child (Gervis & Dunn, 2004; O'Hagan, 1995).

3.1.6 Evidence of emotional abuse in sport

Unfortunately, very little evidence of emotional abuse has been offered outside of developed countries such as the United Kingdom, the USA, Canada and Australia, although it is noted that an element of emotional abuse exists in all other forms of abuse (APSAC, 1995; Shaffer, Yates, & Egeland, 2009). Therefore, emotional abuse may be the most common form of abuse in youth sport. This is somewhat reflected in the results of empirical research. For example, in the UK, 75% of over 6,000 male and female participants reported experiencing emotionally abusive behaviours in various types and competitive levels of organised youth sport (Alexander et al., 2011). Likewise, from a sample of 652 safeguarding cases, research found evidence to suggest that over 20% of safeguarding cases relate to behaviours which may be considered emotionally abusive (e.g., humiliation, bullying and racist insults) (Rhind et al., 2015). Evidence is also offered from Australia, where approximately 54% of former youth athletes reported being deliberately humiliated at least once, 30% reported being bullied in their primary sport and 18% testified to being shouted and/or sworn at regularly (McPherson et al., 2015).

Previously, in researching emotional abuse, research focussed on the relationship between the athlete and their instructor or coach. For example, Gervis and Dunn's (2004) retrospective study with former elite youth athletes in the UK found that all ten participants had experienced performance detriments and feelings of rejection and worthlessness after experiencing prolonged emotional abuse from their coaches. Similarly, after a qualitative study with fourteen former elite-level youth swimmers in Canada, all participants discussed experiencing emotional abuse from their coaches, and its significant emotional and physical effects (Stirling & Kerr, 2008). Recent research suggests that other individuals in the sporting environment can be perpetrators of emotional abuse, such as parents and peers. Indeed, some research has found that the most common perpetrators are peers (Alexander et al., 2011).

3.1.7 Neglect

Neglect is the only form of maltreatment that is identified solely by an absence of action. Glaser defines it as a failure to provide reasonable care (2002), where reasonable care describes recognised and undisputed societal standards that relate to food, shelter, protection and affection (Crooks & Wolfe, 2007). Therefore, neglect relates to the failure to provide, in accordance to the physical and/or emotional demands of the child. In sport, this may occur in the form of; physical, educational, emotional and social (Stirling, 2009).

3.1.8 Evidence of neglect in sport

Neglect overlaps with various other forms of maltreatment. For example, emotional neglect may be considered emotional abuse, while physical neglect may be considered a form of physical abuse. Therefore, depending on one's position on the suggestion that emotional abuse exists in all other forms of maltreatment, it can be argued that neglect is merely a subcategory, or precise type of emotional abuse. This may explain why Stirling argues that there are extremely few dedicated studies of neglect in sport (2009). Though some studies have found evidence of neglect when treating it as a potential standalone type of maltreatment.

When Rhind et al. reviewed 652 safeguarding cases in sport, 1.2% of cases related to neglect (2015). Similarly, after analysing 132 case files in Football in the UK, Brackenridge et al. (2005) found that approximately 4% of cases included neglect. McPherson et al. (2015) conducted a study in Australia and found that up to 9% of former youth athletes were regularly ignored. The body of research which has specifically focused on neglect remains limited and hence there is scope for further studies in this area.

3.2 Evidence of non-relational maltreatment

As research on child maltreatment is growing, so is the recognition of the range of maltreatment types in sport (Brackenridge & Rhind, 2014).

Therefore, despite the understandable lack of research on non-relational maltreatment in comparison to relational maltreatment, some evidence of the prevalence of non-relational maltreatment in sport has been offered by previous research (Stirling, 2009). Some studies have conflated maltreatment that exists within and outside of a significant relationship when presenting evidence of child maltreatment (e.g., Volkwein et al., 1997), though research that exclusively discusses non-relational maltreatment has been produced on topics such as institutional maltreatment, bullying and hazing, and virtual maltreatment. The following section provides a brief review of what may be considered the most prevalent forms of non-relational maltreatment in sport; institutional maltreatment and hazing.

3.2.1 Institutional maltreatment

Institutional maltreatment is the exploitative, abusive, discriminatory or neglectful actions of a child serving organisation which exposes children to, or significantly increases their chances of experiencing maltreatment (Stirling, 2009). This form of maltreatment is intertwined with the organisation's practices and regular functioning. Therefore, institutional maltreatment is systematic, and it may not necessarily be possible to identify one sole perpetrator. Examples of this include failures to meet basic standards of care or differential treatment on the grounds of matters such as sexuality or sporting ability (Stirling, 2009). Such actions may cause harm directly or, through the organisation's neglect, expose the child to harm indirectly.

Research on institutional maltreatment is very much in its infancy (Stirling, 2009). One reason for this is that it is possible for institutional maltreatment to take place in the form of those types of maltreatment that are traditionally considered relational maltreatment. For example, an organisation may systematically enable, encourage or condone coaching practices which are physically abusive. Though with institutional maltreatment growing in notoriety, some studies have emerged. One area of interest is the various forms of institutional maltreatment that occur in relation to mega sporting events. This has been discussed by Brackenridge, Rhind and Palmer-Felgate (2015) who highlighted concerns related to child labour, displacement, child sexual exploitation and human trafficking affecting children following mega sporting events. Though the weaknesses of the existing evidence were discussed as a difficulty, they cited several examples of institutional maltreatment which relate to mega sporting events. For example:

- The 720,000 people forcibly displaced before the 1988 Seoul Olympic Games for infrastructure development which increased poverty, divided families and forced children to witness their parents being beaten and their houses being destroyed (Brackenridge et al., 2015)

- Child labour, which may involve the manufacturing of goods to be sold during events, the construction of stadia or street selling (Brackenridge et al., 2015)
- The 'housing' of street children in prisons before the South Africa 2007 FIFA Preliminary Draw, exposing them to violence, rape and possible HIV infection (Brackenridge et al., 2015)

Examples of other work in this field include that of child rights organisation Terre Des Hommes, who have recently launched the Children Win campaign to address such issues. This campaign considers sexual exploitation, forced eviction and displacement, along with child labour that occurs as a result of institutional maltreatment. Based on seventy interviews with participants from non-governmental organisations, government departments and local sporting organisations, it has been suggested that the risk of child labour, trafficking, sexual exploitation and unsafe displacement significantly increases as a result of mega sporting organisations (Brackenridge et al., 2015).

In a similar study in 2014 in Brazil, findings suggested that the risk of institutional maltreatment to children increases dramatically during the construction phase of mega sporting events (Rotteveel, 2014). Findings from this study suggested that at this stage of mega sporting events, children are more likely to be separated from their families during displacement, and are thus forced to provide for themselves through means such as crime and/or prostitution. Coupled with this, organisations may facilitate or increase the chances of children experiencing maltreatment by failing to adequately vet those brought in for work before, during or after the event (Rotteveel, 2014). Consequently, despite the evidence of institutional child maltreatment remaining in its infancy, it can be said that evidence does exist and is emerging of the presence of institutional maltreatment towards children in sport.

3.2.2 Hazing

Hazing describes humiliating or dangerous acts that individuals are forced to perform so that they may be considered a member of a group (Stirling, 2009). These acts are considered hazing regardless of the individual's willingness to take part. They occur as a result of a disparity of power that is exploited by existing group members (Stirling, 2009). Though hazing is often used interchangeably with bullying, it does not necessarily occur in a prolonged fashion, while within the hazing process, the motivation to comply is born explicitly from a desire to be considered a member of the group.

Hazing can be considered a form of various other forms of maltreatment. For example, it may be viewed as institutional maltreatment when it is systematic, embedded in the organisation's induction process and ritualistically performed before individuals may be accepted as a member. Similarly, it may also be considered emotional abuse where the hazing process is prolonged (e.g., over a season, or in the new member's first year as a member). For these reasons, overlaps exist, and evidence of hazing in sport is not always found in studies that focus on hazing exclusively.

Much of the evidence on hazing in sport originates from North America (Fields, Collins, & Cornstock, 2010). One example from the USA found that 17% of 12th grade high school athletes (n = 1105) had been victims of hazing (Gershel, Katz-Sidlow, Small, & Zandieh, 2003). Other, similar studies have found prevalence of over 80% (Hoover, 1999) and 48% (Hoover & Pollard, 2000), while Hoover found evidence to suggest that experiences of hazing may occur before the age of nine years old (1999). Therefore, despite the potential for hazing to be a sub-category of other forms of maltreatment, and the lack of global representation in research on hazing, Stirling argues that hazing may be the most common form of non-relational maltreatment (2009).

3.3 General risk factors for child maltreatment in sport

Where risk factors are discussed in the literature, they tend to be considered from the perspective of one particular form of maltreatment. This may reflect the unique nature of each type of maltreatment. Though within the literature, there are some regularly occurring themes which may be considered general risk factors of child maltreatment in sport. Those regular themes include: the power of the perpetrator (usually the coach), the closeness of the coach athlete relationship, the vulnerability of the child and negative or neglectful attitudes towards children's wellbeing (Brackenridge & Rhind, 2014; Fasting & Sand, 2015; Brackenridge, 2001; Stirling & Kerr, 2008; Gervis & Dunn, 2004). With these considerations, and findings of research on various forms of maltreatment, a configuration of general risk factors may be compiled.

A set of general risk factors may be developed from arguably the most comprehensive framework of risk factors for child maltreatment in sport which has been offered by Brackenridge (2001). Discussing sexual exploitation, Brackenridge argued that there are three main risk factors: the coach, the child and the sport. The coach risk factors include their suitability for working with children and the power that they may hold. Though these factors have been consistently discussed within the literature (e.g., Gervis & Dunn, 2004), recent evidence suggests that almost anyone may be a perpetrator of child maltreatment in sport (Alexander et al., 2011; Rhind et al., 2015). This includes parents, medical staff and peers. Therefore, when discussing general risk factors, the coach may be expanded to 'perpetrator.'

This also enables the inclusion of maltreatment which may not necessarily be traced back to one individual, but an organisation as a whole.

The child's psychological and physiological development is generally discussed by research as a general risk factor. Not only does this increase their vulnerability (Brackenridge, 2001), but it may also increase their likelihood to internalise, accept or even justify maltreatment (Tibbert, Andersen, & Morris, 2015; Brackenridge, 2001). Another group that is of significant interest is bystanders. Bystanders are individuals who witness one or more incidents of maltreatment, but make no effort, or an inadequate effort, to ensure perpetrators are brought to justice and that maltreatment ceases (Brackenridge, 2001). They may be considered risks as they may enable, exacerbate or help to prolong both the incidence of maltreatment and harm, particularly as children may feel helpless and be less likely to report further incidents (Brackenridge, Kay, & Rhind, 2012). This risk factor can be expanded as a term to include those who do not necessarily witness abuse, but are aware, and equally make no or inadequate effort to ensure perpetrators are brought to justice and that maltreatment ceases. An example of this includes recipients of allegations who fail to deal with the information given to them appropriately

The last risk factor discussed by Brackenridge is the sport (2001). This includes normative cultural ideas (e.g., perceptions of the appropriateness of coach athlete relationships) and structural elements (e.g. the hierarchical system). This has consistently been discussed as a crucial risk factor in various forms of maltreatment. Findings also suggest that this risk factor may exacerbate other risk factors. For example, Brackenridge, Kay and Rhind (2012) discussed the potential for organisations to develop a 'bystander culture' which facilitates or enables witnesses of maltreatment to maintain ignorance. While Tibbert, Andersen and Morris (2015) have presented evidence that children may become encultured, accepting abuse as normal or even necessary for success. Although this risk factor did not include the physical environment. That is the play or competitive environments that children are placed in that may predispose them to harm. Though maltreatment has been defined in this book as volitional, children being forced or encouraged to play in unsafe physical environments can be considered neglect, or volitional inaction from those responsible for ensuring the area is safe and appropriate. A summary of the various categories of risk factors is presented in Table 3.1.

When risk factors are present, they tip the balance of probability towards the possibility of child maltreatment in sport (as depicted in Figure 3.1). This model is called the Seesaw Model of Safeguarding. This analogy emphasises the inter-play between factors which safeguard children and those which increase risk. Therefore, safeguarding is tasked with tipping the balance of probability in favour of the protection of children in order to minimise the

Table 3.1 General risk factors of child maltreatment in sport

Risk Factors	*Description*
Perpetrators	Enactors of child maltreatment (e.g., coaches, peers, parents and spectators).
The Child	The physical and psychological characteristics of the child.
Bystanders	Those whose inaction or inadequate action enables, exacerbates or helps to prolong maltreatment.
Physical Environment	Suitability for sporting activity and latent risk of harm.
The Sport	Cultural and structural elements of the sport (e.g., reporting procedure).

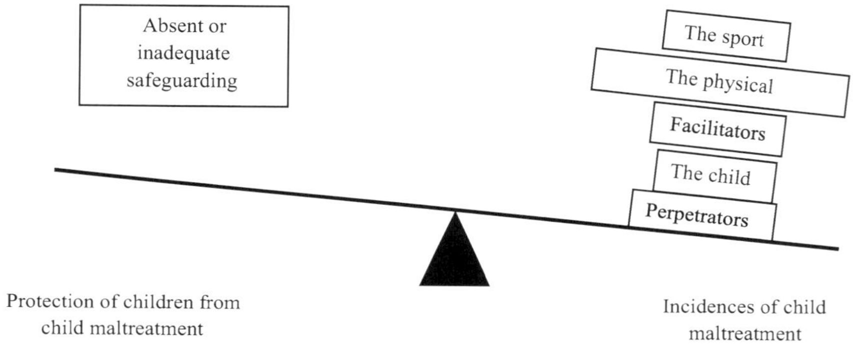

Figure 3.1 The seesaw model of safeguarding

probability that these risk factors will result in actual incidences of child maltreatment in sport.

3.4 Summary

This chapter has presented evidence of relational and non-relational forms of maltreatment in sport. Though it is recognised that more research is required, particularly to address global disparities in the evidence base, it is argued that various forms of maltreatment exist in sport. Based on these findings, a new Seesaw Model of Safeguarding was presented.

References

Alexander, K., Stafford, A., & Lewis, T. L. (2011). *The experiences of children participating in organised sport in the UK*. Edinburgh, UK: NSPCC Child Protection Research Centre.

American Professional Society on the Abuse of Children. (1995). *Psychosocial evaluation of suspected psychological maltreatment in children and adolescents*. Chicago, IL: American Professional Society on the Abuse of Children.
Benedict, J., & Klein, A. (1997). Arrest and conviction rates for athletes accused of sexual assault. *Sociology of Sport Journal*, *14*(1), 86–94.
Brackenridge, C. H. (2001). *Spoilsports: Understanding and preventing sexual exploitation in sport*. London, UK: Routledge.
Brackenridge, C. H., Bishop, D. T., Moussali, S., & Tapp, J. (2008). The characteristics of sexual abuse in sport: A multidimensional scaling analysis of events described in media reports. *International Journal of Exercise and Sport Psychology*, *6*, 385–406.
Brackenridge, C., Bringer, J., & Bishop, D. (2005). Managing cases of abuse in sport. *Child Abuse Review*, *14*, 259–274.
Brackenridge, C. H., & Fasting, K. (2005). The grooming process in sport: Narratives of sexual harassment and abuse. *Auto/Biography*, *13*(1), 33–52.
Brackenridge, C. H., Kay, T., & Rhind, D. J. A. (Eds.). (2012). *Sport, children's rights and violence prevention: A source book on global issues and local programmes*. London, UK: Brunel University Press.
Brackenridge, C. H., & Rhind, D. (2014). Child protection in sport: Reflections on thirty years of science and activism. *Social Sciences*, *3*, 326–340.
Brackenridge, C. H., Rhind, D., & Palmer-Felgate, S. (2015). Locating and mitigating risks to children associated with major sporting events. *Journal of Policy Research in Tourism, Leisure & Events*, *7*(3), 237–250.
Chan, J. S., Elliott, J. M., Chow, Y., & Thomas, J. I. (2002). Does professional and public opinion in child abuse differ? An issue of cross-cultural policy implementation. *Child Abuse Review*, *11*, 359–379.
Coakley, J. J. (2007). *Sports in society: Issues & controversies*. London, UK: McGraw-Hill Higher Education.
Donnelly, P., Kerr, G., Heron, A., & DiCarlo, D. (2016). Protecting youth in sport: An examination of harassment policies. *International Journal of Sport Policy and Politics*, *8*(1), 33–50.
Elendu, I. C., & Umeakuka, O. A. (2011). Perpetrators of sexual harassment experienced by athletes in southern Nigerian universities. *South African Journal for Research in Sport, Physical Education and Recreation*, *33*, 53–63.
Fasting, K. (2005). *Research on sexual harassment and abuse in sport*. Retrieved from www.researchgate.net/publication/255570351_Research_on_Sexual_Harassment_and_Abuse_in_Sport
Fasting, K., & Brackenridge, C. (2009). Coaching, sexual harassment and education. *Sport, Education and Society*, *14*(1), 21–35.
Fasting, K., Brackenridge, C., & Sundgot-Borgen, J. (2004). Prevalence of sexual harassment among Norwegian female elite athletes in relation to sport type. *International Review for the Sociology of Sport*, *39*(4), 373–386.
Fasting, K., & Sand, T. S. (2015). Narratives of sexual harassment experiences in sport. *Qualitative Research in Sport, Exercise and Health*, *7*(5), 573–588.
Fields, S. K., Collins, C. L., & Comstock, R. D. (2010). Violence in youth sports: Hazing, brawling and foul play. *British Journal of Sports Medicine*, *44*, 32–37.
Garbarino, J., Guttmann, E., & Seeley, J. (1986). *The psychologically battered child*. San Francisco, CA: Jossey-Bass.

Gershel, J. C., Katz-Sidlow, R. J., Small, E., & Zandieh, S. (2003). Hazing of suburban middle school and high school athletes. *Journal of Adolescent Health*, *32*(5), 333–335.

Gervis, M., & Dunn, N. (2004). The emotional abuse of elite child athletes by their coaches. *Child Abuse Review*, *13*(2), 215–223.

Glaser, D. (2002). Emotional abuse and neglect (psychological maltreatment): A conceptual framework. *Child Abuse and Neglect*, *26*, 697–714.

Hartill, M. (2013). Concealment of child sexual abuse in sports. *Quest*, *65*(2), 241–254.

Hong, F. (2004). Innocence lost: Child athletes in china. *Sport in Society*, *7*(3), 338–354.

Hoover, N. C. (1999). *Initiation rites and athletics: A national survey of NCAA sports teams. Final report*. New York, NY: Alfred University.

Hoover, N. C., & Pollard, N. J. (2000). *Initiation rites in American high schools: A national survey. Final report*. New York, NY: Alfred University.

Kirby, S., & Greaves, L. (1996). Foul play: Sexual abuse and harassment in sport. Paper presented to the *Pre-Olympic Scientific Congress*, Dallas, TX, July 11–14.

Lang, M., & Hartill, M. (2015). *Safeguarding, child protection and abuse in sport: International perspectives in research, policy and practice*. Oxfordshire, UK: Routledge.

Leahy, T., Pretty, G., & Tenenbaum, G. (2002). Prevalence of sexual abuse in organised competitive sport in Australia. *Journal of Sexual Aggression*, *8*(2), 16–36.

Lin, A. C., Lin, C., Wang, T., & Leu, J. (2005). Rhabdomyolysis in 119 students after repetitive exercise. *British Journal of Sports Medicine*, *39*(1), 3.

Matthews, D. D. (2004). *Child abuse sourcebook*. Detroit, MI: Omnigraphics.

McPherson, L., Long, M., Nicholson, M., Cameron, N., Atkins, P., & Morris, M. E. (2015). Children's experience of sport in Australia. *International Review for the Sociology of Sport*, *52*, 1–18.

Nielsen, K. J. (2001). The forbidden zone: Intimacy, sexual relations and misconduct in the relationship between coaches and athletes. *International Review for the Sociology of Sport*, *36*(2), 165–182.

O'Hagan, K. P. (1995). Emotional and psychological abuse: Problems of definition. *Child Abuse and Neglect*, *14*, 449–461.

Oliver, J. L., & Lloyd, R. S. (2015). Physical training as a potential form of abuse. In M. Lang & M. Hartill (Eds.), *Safeguarding, child protection and abuse in sport* (pp. 163–171). Oxfordshire, UK: Routledge.

Parent, S., & Bannon, J. (2012). Sexual abuse in sport: What about boys? *Children and Youth Services Review*, *34*, 354–359.

Raglin, J., Sawamura, S., Alexiou, S., Hassmên, P., & Kenttä, G. (2000). Training practices and staleness in 13–18 year-old swimmers: A cross cultural study. *Paediatric Exercise Science*, *12*, 61–70.

Rhind, D., Brackenridge, C., Kay, T., & Owusu-Sekyere, F. (2016). Child development and SDP: The post-MDG agenda for policy, practice and research. In L. Hayhurst, T. Kay, & M. Chawansky (Eds.), *Beyond sport for development and peace: Transnational perspectives on theory policy and practice* (pp. 72–86). Abingdon, Oxon: Routledge.

Rhind, D., McDermott, J., Lambert, E., & Koleva, I. (2015). A review of safeguarding cases in sport. *Child Abuse Review*, *24*, 418–426.

Rotteveel, J. (2014). Sexual exploitation of children in Brazil: Putting a spot on the problem. Den Haag, The Netherlands: Terre des Hommes.
Ryan, G. D., & Lane, S. L. (1997). *Juvenile sexual offending: Causes, consequences, and correction*. San Francisco, CA: Jossey-Bass.
Shaffer, A., Yates, T. M., & Egeland, B. R. (2009). The relation of emotional maltreatment to early adolescent competence: Developmental processes in a prospective study. *Child Abuse and Neglect*, *33*(1), 36–44.
Stirling, A. E. (2009). Definition and constituents of maltreatment in sport: Establishing a conceptual framework for research practitioners. *British Journal of Sports Medicine*, *43*, 1091–1099.
Stirling, A. E., & Kerr, G. A. (2008). Elite female swimmers' experiences of emotional abuse across time. *Journal of Emotional Abuse*, *7*(4), 89–113.
Tibbert, S. J., Andersen, M. B., & Morris, T. (2015). What a difference a "Mentally toughening" year makes: The acculturation of a rookie. *Psychology of Sport and Exercise*, *17*, 68–78.
Vertommen, T., Veldhoven, N. S., Hartill, M. J., & Eede, V. E. (2015). Sexual harassment and abuse in sport: The NOC*NSF helpline. *International Review for the Sociology of Sport*, *50*(7), 822–839.
Vertommen, T., Veldhoven, N. S., Wouters, K., Kampen, J. K., Brackenridge, C. H., Rhind, D., & Van Den Eedea, F. (2016). Interpersonal violence against children in sport in the Netherlands and Belgium. *Child Abuse and Neglect*, *51*, 223–236.
Volkwein, K. A. E., Schnell, F. I., Sherwood, D., & Livezey, A. (1997). Sexual harassment in sport: Perceptions and experiences of American female student-athletes. *International Review for the Sociology of Sport*, *32*(3), 283–295.

Chapter 4

Developing the International Safeguards

This chapter discusses the background and development process of the International Safeguards. This includes the creation of the Founders Group and the initial draft version of the International Standards. The key changes which were made in developing the final version of the International Safeguards are described. This includes the change of the name from Standards as well as the simplification of the content.

4.1 Background

The formalisation and internationalisation of safeguarding in sport during the first decade of the 21st century facilitated a growing recognition of the criticality of this issue. This ensured that the safeguarding of children in sport became an increasingly significant concern for organisations that worked within sport. However, prior to the present project, organisations tended to address safeguarding in silos, in the absence of a coordinated and global approach. In 2012, it was in the shadow of the Olympic flame in London that the spark of an idea first ignited the concept of the International Safeguards. During a meeting between representatives of UNICEF UK and the National Society for the Prevention of Cruelty to Children (NSPCC), it was stated that all children, in any situation, of all castes, tribes, genders and abilities, should have the opportunity to participate in, enjoy and develop through safe, well delivered sport and physical activity. This principle then inspired the creation of a Founders Group through which organisations working in sport came together with the unifying aim to work collaboratively towards achieving this ultimate goal.

4.2 The Founders Group

The International Safeguarding Children in Sport Founders Group was established in 2012. This group met at least every three months to oversee the project. They have had a total of 20 meetings to date, and they continue to meet as the momentum of the project continues to build. The Founders Group contains representatives from the following organisations:

- *International Inspiration* – At the time of this project, UK Sport's independent international development charity partner, working through partners around the globe to support their programme design and implementation as well as to facilitate capacity building.
- *UK Sport* – Providing expertise in the elite sport context as well as international development in and through sport.
- *Keeping Children Safe* – A network of organisations working together to promote measures to safeguard children within the international development context.
- *The Child Protection in Sport Unit (CPSU)* – Providing expertise on safeguarding in sport within the UK context. The CPSU is a national charity funded by Sport England and the NSPCC. The standards developed by the CPSU provided the foundation for the International Safeguards.
- *Swiss Academy for Development (SAD)* – Managed an online platform for the sport and development community. This represents an important resource through which organisations can share experiences and materials.
- *UNICEF UK* – Providing expertise on global strategies relevant to the protection and promotion of children's rights.
- *Commonwealth Secretariat* – Has important links with Governments around the world and hence represented an important champion for safeguarding in sport in this context.
- *Right to Play* – An international sport for development agency that provided expertise on child protection for organisations working in this sector around the world.
- *WomenWin* – A network of organisations promoting girls' empowerment through sport.
- *Comic Relief* – A charitable organisation that provides funding for projects related to sport for development.
- *Beyond Sport* – Organises events to promote collaborations between organisations working in the sport for development sector, such as the annual Beyond Sport Summit.
- *Caribbean Sport for Development Agency (CSDA)* – Leading advocate and activist for sport for development in the Caribbean region, supporting sporting agencies in their delivery and organisation of sport.

4.3 The draft international standards

The Founders Group worked together to develop a draft set of International Standards, which were relevant to the international context. The initial version was based on the Child Protection in Sport Unit's Standards which had been developed through working with sports organisations in the United Kingdom. This initial draft version was then further developed to reflect discussions with members of the Founders Group and representatives from other interested organisations at the Beyond Sport Summit, held in London in 2012. The purpose of these standards was to;

- Help create a safe sporting environment for children wherever they participate and at whatever level.
- Provide a benchmark to assist sports providers and funders to make informed decisions.
- Promote good practice and challenge practice that is harmful to children.
- Provide clarity on safeguarding children to all involved in sport.

The draft Standards were:

1. Have a written policy on keeping children safe
2. Have procedures, personnel and systems to support safeguarding
3. Assess and minimise risks to children
4. Have written guidelines on behaviour towards children
5. Promote Equity – ensuring ALL children are safeguarded
6. Communicate the 'keep children safe' message
7. Provide education and training for keeping children safe
8. Engage with advice and support
9. Work with partners to meet the Standards
10. Involve children in the development, review and implementation
11. Monitor and evaluate compliance and effectiveness of safeguarding measures

4.4 Revising the standards

In the first year of the research project, the researchers collected data which informed the revision of the International Standards. Based on the aims and objectives that are outlined in Chapter 6, feedback was collected from the participants using a range of sources including: interviews, online discussions, virtual learning sets and a meeting at the Beyond Sport Summit in Philadelphia in 2013. This resulted in significant changes to the Standards, which was subsequently transformed into the International Safeguards for Children in Sport, or the "Safeguards." These changes are outlined in the rest of this chapter.

4.4.1 Changing from Standards to Safeguards

Due to the wide range of interpretations of terms such as child protection and safeguarding, coupled with the variety of contexts and cultures in which the participant organisations are operating, there was a lack of consensus regarding what the Standards should be called. The strength of opinions regarding the different possibilities demonstrates the importance of packaging this project in a way which will promote buy-in and ownership of organisations with varying missions (e.g., sport for development, sport for competition) and sizes (e.g., local, national and international). Some participants liked the term Standards:

> "Well, I think that they are standards. I think that it is a good thing. I think that they should be called standards and it is absolutely fine if some of us fall short some of the time. That is only human, you know. So as long as we can show that we are trying. It is not due to lack of intent or effort, you know. So for us, you know, that is not an issue."
>
> (National Deliverer)

> "In terms of the name, I think that Standards is good. It is very straightforward and I think that everyone understands what that means."
>
> (Local Deliverer)

The strength of this term is that it implies that these various actions need to be enacted, that a standard for attainment is set or fixed. However, with this benefit comes the potential drawback of a perceived rigidity of approach:

> "In terms of the word Standards, it is a very high expectation when I hear the word and it seems as though you need to meet it. So I am thinking here that maybe it could be the core principles of safeguarding for development organisations. We could change the word so that it does not make people feel like this is a must and there is no flexibility at all for your country and still it is something that you have to do. We do not want to lose that sense of urgency or that sense of importance but we do not want to put too much pressure on people globally."
>
> (International Governor)

> "The question you need to ask is whose Standards? If we are talking about global then that does not necessarily work."
>
> (National Governor)

As an alternative, participants suggested 'guidelines':

> "I prefer the term guidelines. Standards sort of imply that this is the only way in which things can be done. It is important that people adapt them to their context."
>
> (National Governor)

> "In terms of the name, guidance makes it less mandatory. We want them to understand that it is going to take time and it will be a process."
>
> (International Governor)

However, there was also some opposition to guidelines with a preference for principles:

> "Principles, definitely principles. I have to run from guidelines. I think that principles are what underlie everything. They can underlie throughout the world in any society and in any context. Once you are into standards or guidelines you are very determinate. In fact, what organisations need are a set of principles which they can work from. That is what we need in all kinds of areas of our work."
>
> (Local Deliverer)

Other participants reported success through adopting a systems approach to safeguarding:

> "The approach that I have adopted is around frameworks. To say, right, these are the core competencies, these are the things that you are trying to get to. How you get there may differ because the circumstances that they are working in and the resources that they have will vary significantly."
>
> (International Governor)

> "Look at the International coach education systems, which is global. That was initially called Standards and a number of partners did not like the word Standards. We changed it to systems because it was a systems-driven process dependent on the organisation who was delivering it and what kind of system they had in place. System also alludes to infrastructure and a change of infrastructure as opposed to guidelines which may not be perceived as compulsory. So Safeguarding Systems maybe?"
>
> (National Governor)

Based on this feedback, two key changes were made to the draft Standards. Firstly, the name was changed to the International Safeguards for Children in Sport. The use of Safeguards as opposed to Standards was viewed to be a name which would help to overcome the perceived resistance to the term Standards. Secondly, the concept of providing a framework was adopted by ensuring that there was flexibility within the International Safeguards to allow people to tailor implementation to the specific characteristics of the given settings. The focus was on facilitation rather than dictation. In other words, the project became about helping people to safeguard children and championing those making progress as opposed to telling people what they had to do. This approach was under-pinned by a clear set of principles which were also outlined along with the International Safeguards.

4.4.2 Simplification

There was support for a general simplification of the presentation and language. This is not a simplification of the Standards and their content, however, which is viewed as being merited:

> "In terms of the number of Standards, it is a huge cauldron of issues in child protection and I would rather stay with the 11 and ensuring that we are covering everything. Then, say in a couple of years down the line, these things can be clumped, perhaps, I would be more comfortable with something like that. I would rather this than sitting here now and saying right, what can we leave out. You know, I do not think that this is an appropriate approach to the issue."
>
> (National Deliverer)

> "For me it is not the number of Standards but how they are presented. As far as I am concerned, the simplification of all of this would be a big bonus."
>
> (National Governor)

Simplification therefore referred to the way in which the Standards are packaged and communicated as opposed to removing any of the content. Participants also felt that there was scope for simplification to be achieved through grouping the Standards:

> "When we work with our organisations we tend to group the Standards to say that they are in three or four areas. A list of 11 can be rather overwhelming and represent a barrier to engagement."
>
> (National Governor)

Based on this feedback, two further changes were made to the International Safeguards. Firstly, the language was simplified throughout with clearer examples being included. The need for the implementation guide was emphasised to help people understand how their organisation can work towards the International Safeguards, irrespective of their current situation in relation to safeguarding. Secondly, the number of Safeguards were reduced from eleven to eight, as this was viewed as being more manageable. Table 4.1 provides a summary of these revisions.

In terms of the more substantial changes, the Standards related to education and training as well as communication were merged. The topic of

Table 4.1 A summary of the changes from the draft Standards to the International Safeguards

Original Draft Standards	*Finalised International Safeguards*	*Explanation of Changes*
Have a written policy on keeping children safe	Developing Your Policy	Simplified language
Have procedures, personnel and systems to support safeguarding	Procedures for Responding to Safeguarding Concerns	Simplified language
Assess and minimise risks to children	Minimising Risks to Children	Simplified language
Have written guidelines on behaviour towards children	Guidelines for Behaviour	Simplified language
Promote Equity – ensuring ALL children are safeguarded		Embedded throughout the other Safeguards
Communicate the 'keep children safe' message	Recruiting, Training and Communicating	Merged with the inclusion of recruitment
Provide education and training for keeping children safe		
Engage with advice and support	Advice and Support	Simplified language
Work with partners to meet the standards	Working with Partner	Simplified language
Involve children in the development, review and implementation		Embedded throughout the other Safeguards
Monitor and evaluate compliance and effectiveness of safeguarding measures	Monitoring and Evaluating	Simplified language

recruitment was also specified in the title of the new Safeguard as this was viewed as a key issue. This helped to emphasise the need for safeguarding measures from the point at which individuals are joining an organisation, through their induction and training to ensuring that there is an on-going dialogue about safeguarding. Furthermore, the Standards related to equity and involving children were removed. This in no way diminished the critical significance of these topics. On the contrary, the content of each of these Standards were embedded throughout the other Safeguards through the inclusion of specific items addressing these points in all of the other Safeguards. It was felt that this would help to ensure that equity and involving children were key priorities in all aspects of work related to the safeguarding of children in an organisation. They are an integral part of safeguarding as opposed to additional elements.

4.5 Summary

This chapter has described the background and development process of the International Safeguards. This included the organisations who inspired the initial idea, and those who regularly met to oversee the project through the Founders Group. The chapter outlines the International Standards, while also presenting and explaining the desire to simplify and use more suitable terminology which underpinned the change from the International Standards to the International Safeguards.

Chapter 5

The International Safeguards

5.1 Final version of the international safeguards for children in sport

After the first year of the pilot process, the finalised version of the International Safeguards for Children in Sport was published. The International Safeguards were officially launched by Amanda Dlamini (International Football player), in October 2014 during the Beyond Sport Summit in Johannesburg, South Africa. The International Safeguards are presented throughout the following pages.

International safeguards

These Safeguards aim to outline the things that should be put in place by any organisation providing sports activities to children and young people. The Safeguards should be viewed as guides, which facilitate an organisation's journey towards safeguarding children rather than an end in themselves.

They reflect international declarations, the United Nations Convention on the Rights of the Child, relevant legislation, government guidance, existing child protection/safeguarding standards and good practice. They have been informed by research conducted by Brunel University with a diverse range of perspectives from different countries and stakeholder groups during an extensive piloting phase.

These Safeguards represent collective good practice at a point in time and will be subject to periodic review to ensure they reflect developments within safeguarding practice.

The eight Safeguards are:

1. Developing Your Policy
2. Procedures for Responding to Safeguarding Concerns
3. Advice and Support
4. Minimising Risks to Children

5 Guidelines for Behaviour
6 Recruiting, Training and Communicating
7 Working with Partners
8 Monitoring and Evaluating

The Safeguards aim to:

- Help create a safe sporting environment for children wherever they participate and at whatever level.
- Provide a benchmark to assist sports providers and funders to make informed decisions.
- Promote good practice and challenge practice that is harmful to children.
- Provide clarity on safeguarding children to all involved in sport.

The Safeguards are based on the following principles:

- All children have the right to participate, enjoy and develop through sport, in a safe and inclusive environment, free from all forms of abuse, violence, neglect and exploitation.
- Children have the right to have their voices heard and listened to. They need to know who they can turn to when they have a concern about their participation in sport.
- Everyone, organisations and individuals, service providers and funders, has a responsibility to support the care and protection of young people.
- Organisations providing sports activities to children and young people have a duty of care to them.
- There are certain factors that leave some children more vulnerable to abuse, and steps need to be taken to address this.
- Children have a right to be involved in shaping safeguarding policy and practice
- Organisations should always act in the best interests of the child.
- Everyone has the right to be treated with dignity and respect and not be discriminated against based on gender, race, age, ethnicity, ability, sexual orientation, beliefs, religious or political affiliation.
- The processes and activities for the creation, development and implementation of safeguarding measures should be inclusive.

Please note that whilst these Safeguards have been developed in relation to children (aged under 18 years old). they can also provide a valuable framework for good practice in relation to other groups such as vulnerable adults.

Safeguard 1: Developing Your Policy

What – Any organisation providing or with responsibility for sports activities for children and young people under the age of 18 should have a safeguarding policy. This is a statement of intent that demonstrates a commitment to safeguard children involved in sport from harm and provides the framework within which procedures are developed.

Why – A safeguarding policy makes clear to all what is required in relation to the protection of children and young people. It helps to create a safe and positive environment for children and to show that the organisation is taking its duty of care seriously. It also takes account of specific factors that may leave some children more vulnerable.

- You have a safeguarding policy which is clearly written and easy to understand.
- The policy clearly describes your understanding and definitions of all forms of harm.
- The policy covers your organisation's commitment to safeguard children in all aspects of your work.
- The policy is clear that all children have equal rights to protection.
- This policy is officially endorsed by staff at the highest level of your organisation.
- Staff at the highest level of the organisation have the responsibility to oversee the implementation of the policy.
- All staff, volunteers, carers or other representatives have signed up to the policy.
- Your organisation has consulted with children, parents/carers and staff as part of the initial development and/or on-going review of your policy.

Safeguard 2: Developing a System to respond to safeguarding concerns

What – Procedures describe the operational processes required to implement organisational policy and provide clear step-by-step guidance on what to do in different circumstances. They clarify roles and responsibilities, and lines of communication. Effective systems are required which help to process any complaints or concerns and support any victims of violence. You should build on existing systems and understand your role with regards to relevant national systems and legislation.

Why – For safeguarding to be effective, procedures have to be credible for children. Procedures help to ensure a prompt response to concerns about a child's safety or well-being. They also help you to comply with and implement legislation and guidance. Violence against children is distressing and can be difficult to deal with. Organisations have a duty to ensure that advice and support is in place to help people to play their part in safeguarding children.

- There are clear procedures in place that provide step-by-step guidance on what action to take if there are concerns about a child's safety or well-being, both within and external to the organisation.
- There is an identified member of staff in your organisation responsible for leading on safeguarding.
- Your organisation provides children and young people with information about their rights and about who they can turn to if they are worried, in a process which empowers them.
- Your organisation has made information available to children and their parents/carers, about what is likely to happen following a disclosure, in a format and language that can be easily understood by everyone.
- Your organisation has a process for dealing with complaints in a fair and transparent way that includes an appeals process.
- All incidents, allegations and complaints are recorded, monitored and stored securely.
- Your organisation has consulted with children, parents/carers and staff as part of the initial development and/or ongoing review of your response system.

Safeguard 3: Advice and Support

What – Arrangements made to provide essential information and support to those responsible for safeguarding children. Children and young people are advised on where to access help and support.

Why – You have a duty to ensure advice and support is in place to help people to play their part in safeguarding children such that they know who they can turn to for help.

- Contacts are established at a national and/or local level with relevant child protection agencies, NGOs and community groups providing support on child protection.
- Your organisation ensures that staff members with special responsibilities for keeping children safe have engagement with specialist advice, support and information Children are provided with advice and support on keeping themselves and one another safe.
- Your system acknowledges that children with additional vulnerabilities (for example, a disability) may face extra barriers to getting help.
- Parents/carers in the wider community are provided with information, advice and support on safeguarding children.

Safeguard 4: Minimising Risks to Children

What – Measures to assess and minimise the risks to children.

Why – Some people, who work or seek to work in sport in a paid or voluntary capacity, pose a risk to children. Children are also at risk when placed in unsuitable places or asked to participate in unsuitable activities, including age-inappropriate activities, over-training and through unrealistic expectations being placed on them. It is possible to minimise these risks by putting safeguards in place.

- Risk assessments are available and conducted for activities, transport, accommodation and spaces.
- Steps are taken to minimise any risks identified through a risk assessment.
- If the risks are assessed to be too significant then the activity does not go ahead.
- Training is available to help staff and volunteers recognise the additional risks some children are exposed to, because of their race, gender, age, religion, disability, sexual orientation, social background or culture.

Safeguard 5: Guidelines on Behaviour

What – Codes of conduct to describe what an acceptable standard of behaviour is and promote current best practice.

Why – Children's sport should be carried out in a safe, positive and encouraging atmosphere. Standards of behaviour set a benchmark of what is acceptable for all.

- Your organisation has written guidelines for behaviour (codes of conduct) which contain statements about treating people with dignity, respect, sensitivity and fairness.
- Your organisation has guidance and expectations around activities that include time spent away from home, including placing children in the care of others and overnight stays.
- Where organisations are involved in placing children in the care of others, frequent meetings are held with the child to discuss their experiences.
- Your organisation has guidance around working with children who have a disability.
- Your organisation has guidance around the appropriate use of information technology and social media to make sure that children are not put in danger and made vulnerable to exploitation.
- Your organisation has guidance on positive ways of managing the behaviour of children that do not involve physical punishment or any other form of degrading or humiliating treatment and are age and gender appropriate.
- Your organisation has guidance on expected and acceptable behaviour of children towards others, particularly other children (for example, a learning agreement).
- There are clear consequences for not following the guidelines on behaviour that are linked to organisational disciplinary procedures.
- The highest level of the organisation has the responsibility to ensure that the guidelines are followed.
- Your organisation has consulted children, parents/carers and staff as part of the initial development and/or on-going review of your organisation's guidelines on behaviour.

Safeguard 6: Recruiting, Training and Communicating

What – Recruiting appropriate members of staff, creating opportunities to develop and maintain the necessary skills and communicating regarding safeguarding.

Why – Everyone in contact with children has a role to play in their protection. They can only do so confidently and effectively if they are aware, have the necessary understanding of and the opportunity to develop, practice and implement key skills. Organisations providing sporting activities for children have a responsibility to provide training and development opportunities for staff and volunteers.

- Job descriptions contain statements about treating people with dignity, respect, sensitivity and fairness.
- The recruitment process includes an interview, character/employment references and a background check in line with local legislation.
- All staff, volunteers and other relevant people have been trained on safeguarding and child protection, including how to report concerns.
- The highest level of the organisation has the responsibility to oversee the implementation of the training.
- All staff, volunteers and relevant people with special responsibilities for safeguarding have access to regular additional training and specialist support.
- Your organisation has consulted with children, parents/carers and staff as part of the initial development and/or on-going review of your organisation's recruitment, training and development.

Safeguard 7: Working with Partners

What – Action taken by the organisation to influence and promote the adoption and implementation of measures to safeguard children by partner organisations.

Why – A number of sports organisations have both a strategic and a delivery role in relation to children and young people. Where organisational partnership, membership, funding or commissioning relationships exist or develop with other organisations, the organisation should use its influence to promote the implementation of safeguarding measures. The organisation should provide or signpost support and resources in relation to implementing adequate safeguarding measures. The organisation should actively promote the adoption of the International Safeguards for Children in Sport.

- Your organisation has worked with partners/members to ensure that there are shared expectations around safeguarding Your organisation has worked with partners/members to agree how to share learning about making sport safer for children.
- Your organisation has shared written guidance on current best practice in relation to working with children (for example, sharing the International Safeguards for Children in Sport).
- Your organisation's safeguarding policy represents an essential part of any partnership/membership agreements.
- Your organisation publicises information about your policy to your community, partners and members.
- Your organisation works to sensitise your communities to the importance of safeguarding children.

Safeguard 8: Monitoring and Evaluation

What – The on-going monitoring of compliance and effectiveness, involving all relevant groups.

Why – Organisations need to know whether safeguarding is effective and where improvements and adaptations are needed or recognise patterns of risk.

- There are systems in place to monitor and evaluate the effectiveness of your organisation's:
  - policy
  - system for responding to safeguarding concerns
  - advice and support
  - systems to minimise the risks to children
  - guidelines for behaviour
  - recruitment, training and communication
  - work with partners to safeguard children
- The highest level of the organisation has the responsibility to oversee the implementation of the monitoring and evaluation system.
- Your organisation has consulted with children, parents/carers and staff as part of the initial development and/or on-going review of your monitoring and evaluation system.

5.2 Key steps on the safeguarding journey

The following steps will guide your journey through each of the Safeguards. They should facilitate an organisation to reflect on their current system and inform their efforts towards ensuring the safety of children.

Step1: Foundation level

- The Safeguards are used to raise awareness of the need to minimise the risks faced by children in your organisation and inform discussion around the next steps towards implementation.

Step 2: Preparing to implement

- The Safeguards are used to conduct a review to identify current strengths and weaknesses in relation to minimising the risks faced by children in your organisation.

Step3: Action planning

- There is a written plan which details the steps which will be taken to implement the Safeguards, who is responsible for these actions and a time-scale as to when these actions will be completed.

Step 4: Implementation

- You have implemented the strategies and systems outlined within each of the Safeguards.

Step 5: Maintaining and Embedding

- The system is reviewed on a regular basis (at least every three years) and is further developed based on the experiences of children, parents/carers and staff.

5.3 Dissemination of the International Safeguards

Since its inception, the research team and members of the Founders Group have presented the International Safeguards at a variety of workshops, conferences and international meetings. Some examples of these presentations are listed below:

- Beyond Sport Summit, Philadelphia, United States of America – September 2013
- Redefining Normal Conference, Trinidad, Caribbean – May 2014
- Beyond Sport Summit, Johannesburg, South Africa – October 2014
- Sport for Development symposium, Brunel University, London, England – June 2015
- European Congress of Sport Sciences, Malmo, Sweden – June 2015
- Child Protection in Sport Conference, Tokyo, Japan – November 2015

- Beyond Sport Summit, London, United Kingdom – December 2015
- Invited presentation, Northumbria University, England – January 2016
- Webinar to the International Child Protection Network of Canada, online – April 2016
- Invited presentation, Loughborough University, England – April 2016
- Beyond Sport Summit, London, United Kingdom – October 2016
- Sports and Exercise Medicine Conference, London, United Kingdom – March 2017
- Policy Cohesion Expert Round Table, Commonwealth Secretariat, London, United Kingdom – April 2017
- Child Protection and Well-being Conference, Glasgow, Scotland – April 2017
- NSPCC How Safe Are Our Children Conference, London, United Kingdom – June 2017
- Safe Sport International Conference, Madrid, Spain – April 2018
- British Association for the Study and Prevention of Child Abuse and Neglect Conference, Warwick, United Kingdom, April 2018

The following publications have also been produced as a result of, or in relation to the International Safeguards Project:

Mountjoy, M., Rhind, D. J. A., Tiivas, A. & Leglise, M. (2015). Safeguarding the child athlete in sport: A review, a framework and recommendations for the IOC youth athlete development model. *British Journal of Sports Medicine*, *49*, 883–6.

Rhind, D. J. A. (2016). Safeguarding in Sport. In Commonwealth Advisory Body on Sport, *Policy guidance to Commonwealth Governments on protecting the integrity of sport*. London: CABOS.

Rhind, D. J. A., Brackenridge, C., Kay, T. & Owusu-Sekyere, F. (2016). Child protection and SDP: the post-MDG agenda for policy practice and research. In L. M. C. Hayhurst, T. Kay & M. Chawansky (Eds.). *Beyond Sport for Development and Peace*. London: Routledge.

5.4 Endorsement of the International Safeguards

As a result of such dissemination and advocacy, the International Safeguards have grown rapidly in popularity and have been endorsed by significant organisations and networks in sport. The number of organisations who have demonstrated a commitment to working towards the International Safeguards in their organisation has grown beyond the 32 organisations who participated in the research, to a total of 82 (as of 2017). This positive response to the International Safeguards includes National Governing Bodies (NGBs), International Federations (IFs) and Non-Governmental Organisations (NGOs). Some of the more notable endorsements are cited below.

- The safeguards have been publicly endorsed by the Association of IOC Recognised International Sports Federations (ARISF), which issued a press release following the ARISF Council meeting during the Sport Accord Convention where they discussed the importance of keeping sport safe for children. ARISF took the decision to promote the Safeguards for Children in Sport to its 35 Member Federations.

- The Commonwealth Secretariat and the Commonwealth Advisory Body for Sport (CABOS) have promoted safeguarding as a key pillar of the integrity agenda. The International Safeguards have been promoted as good practice to the Sports Ministers of all 53 member states.
- The International Netball Federation (INF) has developed an international policy based on their involvement in the initiative which promotes the International Safeguards as good practice to all of their 70+ member governing bodies. The INF requires their members to prioritise safeguarding and they won the Sport Accord 'Spirit of Sport' award in 2015 in recognition of their work to safeguard children.
- The International Sailing Federation has also adopted a safeguarding policy for all of their member organisations.
- Oceania World Rugby is committed to working towards the safeguards and have promoted them internally to their members.
- The US Olympic Committee (which is a member of a Virtual Learning Set) has dedicated $10 million US to develop an athlete protection infrastructure. This work is being supported by the International Safeguards and their involvement in this project.
- The Special Olympics is revising their Coach Training modules to incorporate the principles of the International Safeguards.
- A Safeguarding Toolkit was hosted by the International Platform on Sport and Development. This provided online access to relevant project resources. These pages were viewed over 25,000 times during the research period.
- The number of Virtual Learning Sets (VLS) grew from six to nine, and these continue to meet to support one another beyond the end of the three-year piloting phase.

5.5 The UNICEF Safeguarding in Sport Award

One significant social change that the International Safeguards has already contributed to is the development of The UNICEF Safeguarding in Sport Award. Leading on from the 2014 launch, the 2015 Beyond Sport Summit marked the inauguration of this award. The Beyond Sport Summit is the largest global event which brings together organisations who are working to promote social change through sport. The 2015 award received 35 high-quality entries which demonstrated the wide range of innovative ways in which organisations were engaging with the International Safeguards to safeguard children in, around and through sport.

The 2015 award was given to Moving the Goalposts (MTG) ". . . in recognition of their youth-led approach to safeguarding, which was applauded by the Beyond Sport Judging Panel as making the delivery of sport safer for all." Particularly good practice was identified with respect to the way in which the development and implementation of safeguarding policy and procedures which was led by the young girls and women with whom they worked. This resonated particularly with the judging panel and the Founders Group as involving children in is embedded throughout the International Safeguards. Rachel Muthoga, the Executive Director of MTG, said:

> "Child protection and safeguarding are really close to the heart of what MTG does as an organisation. Our team work tirelessly to advocate for the rights of children and to ensure young women and girls have access to safe and inclusive sport so it was a great honour to be recognised for our work in that field."

The success of the award in 2015 ensured that the UNICEF Safeguarding in Sport Award was retained for the Beyond Sport Summit in 2016. This time the award was given to the CPSU. The award was given in recognition of the CPSU's collaborations with statutory and sports organisations over the past 15 years. This world-leading approach of multi-agency working to safeguard children is now highlighted as good practice from which other organisations are now learning and working to replicate. Anne Tiivas, the Director of the CPSU, said:

> "As a unit, we work with over 200 organisations across the UK to safeguard children and young people. This award sends a message to all these sports organisations to be proud of what we have achieved together to ensure children have a safe and enjoyable experience when taking part in sport."

It is expected that this award will continue to be given out in future Beyond Sport Summits. It represents a very important symbol of the growth of interest and activity related to safeguarding in sport. It also represents an important opportunity to recognise and champion those individuals and organisations who are doing great work in this area. The winners of this award and the nominees are key role models who can advocate for the importance of safeguarding and show other organisations how progress can be made. They can also help to highlight that good safeguarding has a range of positive outcomes from which other organisations can benefit through engaging with the International Safeguards.

5.6 Summary

This chapter has presented the aims, principles and key steps of the International Safeguards that have been created to guide all organisations in their safeguarding journey. The eight Safeguards, which have been presented in detail, are:

1 Developing Your Policy
2 Procedures for Responding to Safeguarding Concerns
3 Advice and Support
4 Minimising Risks to Children
5 Guidelines for Behaviour
6 Recruiting, Training and Communicating
7 Working with Partners
8 Monitoring and Evaluating

Evidence of the impact that the International Safeguards are already having has been presented in the form of the endorsements, dissemination and the development of the International Safeguarding in Sport Awards.

Chapter 6

Research objectives and methods

6.1 The research project

In July 2013, a team of researchers at Brunel University were commissioned by International Inspiration on behalf of the Founders Group to conduct a three-year research project to evaluate a trial of the International Safeguards. The aim of this research was to answer the overarching research question: Are the Safeguards appropriate for global adoption to keep children safe while participating in sport?"

6.1.1 Research objectives

The following objectives were adopted:

1 Support the working group to finalise the draft Safeguards, drawing on the input of organisations involved in piloting the Safeguards.
2 Analyse the baseline information collected from the Self-Audit process for the organisations involved in piloting the Safeguards.
3 Understand and document the challenges and experiences of a representative sample of organisations piloting the Safeguards.
4 Provide representative case studies of how organisations implement the Safeguards.
5 Provide recommendations on the external support required to implement the Safeguards.
6 Produce an implementation guide for organisations or make recommendations to a trainer/consultant to facilitate developing a guide.

6.1.2 Research questions

The following research questions were derived from the research objectives:

RQ1: Are the draft Safeguards appropriate for global adoption?
RQ2: Where are the participant organisations now and at the end of the pilot in relation to the Safeguards?

RQ3: What profile of activation do the various stakeholder groups demonstrate and how does this change with the implementation of the Safeguards?
RQ4: What are the challenges and experiences of the participating organisations during the pilot?
RQ5: What can be learned from selected case studies of the pilot experience?
RQ6: What should be included in an implementation guide for organisations seeking to adopt the Safeguards?

6.2 Our philosophical approach

Within the social sciences, people are both the conductors and the subjects of research (Robson, 2002). Therefore, conclusions of such research are not only determined by the characteristics of the people being observed, but also by the characteristics and perspectives of the observer (Robson, 2002; Patton, 2015). With that in mind it is crucial that researchers are aware of and make clear their own inherent beliefs, assumptions and worldviews. This helps the researcher to construct their study in a manner that consistently and adequately pursues valued knowledge that is harmonious with their underpinning philosophies (Patton, 2015). This also sets the contexts for the reader, providing clarity on the researcher's stance on interpreting the findings of the study.

The amalgamation of a researcher's beliefs in the quest for knowledge can be referred to as an individual's philosophy of science (Ponterotto, 2002). Inclusive in this is one's views on ontology (the nature of reality), epistemology (what knowledge is and how it may be attained), axiology (the role of personal values in research), rhetorical structure (the language and presentation of research) and methodology (the process and procedure of research) (Ponterotto, 2002; Cresswell, 1998; Ponterotto & Grieger, 2007). This impacts the means through which the researcher pursues the development of knowledge as they select a research paradigm that is representative of their views. A paradigm is a "Basic belief system or worldview that guides investigators in choices of method not only in ontologically and epistemologically fundamental ways" (Guba & Lincoln, 1994, p. 105).

This project valued relativism and subjectivity, asking participants to make sense of their experiences. The methodology also showed appreciation for the varying contexts in which these experiences took place. It was acknowledged that this construction of knowledge was contributed to by the researchers, who guided the participants thinking and interpreted the information they provided. Therefore, it can be said that in line with Guba and Lincoln's (2005) classification of research paradigms, the present project sits within the Constructivism paradigm. This paradigm states that social realities are contextual, subjective and multiple perceptions of reality may exist (Guba & Lincoln, 2002; Ponterotto, 2002; Robson, 2002). Constructivists make no assertions that these realities represent absolute truth, arguing that "Truth is a matter of best-informed and most sophisticated construction on which there is consensus at a given time" (Schwandt, 1994, p. 128). Nonetheless, knowledge is deemed to be equally valid from context to context and is co-created as the researcher interacts with the participant to uncover meaning (Ponterotto, 2002).

6.3 Research design

What differentiates a paradigm from others is about more than the methods used (Morgan, 2007). Nonetheless, some methodological approaches are suited to particular paradigms as they allow the researcher to pursue knowledge that is valued by their chosen paradigm in a manner that pays respects to its ontological and epistemological assumptions. For this reason, the present thesis adopted the traditional approach to collect data within a Constructivism paradigm, using qualitative and dialectal processes (Aliyu, Bello, Kasim, & Martin, 2014; Guba & Lincoln, 1994; 2005).

Qualitative research is "[a] form of social inquiry that focusses on the way that people interpret and make sense of their experiences" (Sparkes & Smith, 2014, p. 14). This is used to understand the social realities of participants without manipulation (Robson, 2002; Patton, 2015). This can be achieved by inquiring about what is significant to those that have experienced the phenomenon in question and by conducting research within its natural settings. This helps the researcher "[t]o gain a level of knowledge that penetrates the experience" (Charmaz, 2004, p. 984). In doing so, qualitative researchers use purposive sampling, prioritise the collection of textual data and rely on the quotes of experienced participants which are presented in the form of overarching themes (Cresswell, 2007).

In focussing on meanings, context, subjectivity and processes, qualitative research adopts idiographic (individualistic) and emic (unique) assumptions (Sparkes & Smith, 2014). This makes the use of qualitative research well suited to social science research that is conducted within a Constructivist paradigm as it allows for the presentation of many expressions of reality, without any presumptions of categorisation. Qualitative research also provides an effective means to understand the process of social phenomenon, not just its outcomes (Sparkes & Smith, 2014).

There is a sizeable and rapidly growing literature about programme evaluation. Current thinking encourages researchers to address both the process and outcomes of a change programme and not to focus solely on outcomes (Coalter, 2007; Pawson, 2006). As a result, this project was conducted longitudinally, and ensured that data were collected at the start and end of the project as well as periodically throughout the process of implementing the International Safeguards. This is in line with the recommendations of researchers who have called for such an approach in evaluative social research to overcome the potential limitations of collecting data at one moment in time (Brackenridge et al., 2005). People's attitudes towards safeguarding are likely to fluctuate over time and hence a longitudinal approach can help to capture the direction and intensity of any such changes. It also assumes that any change will not necessarily be linear or causal in nature. Conducting research over a longer period of time also allowed the researchers to build rapport with the participants through ensuring that it was genuinely a collaborative project at each stage of the process.

6.4 Ethical considerations

The moral duty of researchers to ensure that their research protects its participants from harm is well documented (Jones, Brown, & Holloway, 2013). Ethical considerations must be made at various points in the research process, including when choosing the topic, gaining access to participants, retrieving data and when writing and disseminating findings. The majority of these ethical considerations can be anticipated before the data collection commences. One of the most significant ethical issues considered before the collection of data was the potential for the research itself to uncover or experience abuse or harm to children. The interest of the present research was such that the researchers did not specifically ask for participants to disclose accounts of maltreatment. However, there remained the potential for such disclosures to be made. For this reason, prior to any data collection, information on appropriate reporting mechanisms internally and externally were identified for the given context. This was not always a formal organisation for the protection of children and may have been the wider police force or social services.

Before a formal application was made for ethical approval, the present research benefitted from an initial consultation with the Chair of the Brunel University ethics committee. This consultation helped to mould the methods and procedures used to collect data, and hence informed the researcher's application for ethical approval. Participant information sheets and informed consent forms were developed. These documents emphasised the participant's right to anonymity, confidentiality and to withdraw their involvement and data from the project at any time. These points were reiterated prior to any data being collected. Whether or not a pioneer organisation took part in the research had no impact on their involvement in the broader International Safeguards project and this point was emphasised both at the recruitment and data collection phases. Participants were also given pseudonyms to ensure anonymity. The identity of the participating organisations was also typically kept anonymous, apart from the case studies for which some organisations gave their consent to be named.

This research was approved by the Brunel University Research Ethics Committee prior to the commencement of data collection. Although the project had attained ethical clearance, ethics can be both procedural, in regards to gaining ethical approval, and practice based in regards to managing issues that may emerge during data collection. For this reason, ethics were still strongly considered throughout the research and were discussed at every research meeting.

6.5 Participants

An important indicator of change is the experience of key change agents. The researchers therefore engaged with the key change agent within the pioneer organisations. It was important to understand their experiences as these participants were in a position to facilitate and symbolise the implementation of the International Safeguards. Each of the 49 organisations who had volunteered to pilot the International Safeguards was contacted to provide an overview of the aims and nature of the research. An informed consent form was then sent to any organisations who showed an interest in taking part in the research. All of the 32 interested organisations signed and return this form. Each organisation was classified as either a 'Deliverer' (N = 16) or 'Governor' (N = 16):

- Deliverer organisations are those who work directly with children (e.g., sports clubs at all competitive levels or a sport for development programme).
- Governors work with partner or member organisations who in turn work directly with children (e.g., Governments, Funders or Federations).

This distinction was made to ensure that a wide range of key stakeholders were represented in this project. It was also expected that deliverer and governor organisations may have different experiences of working towards the International Safeguards as a result of the level at which their role was focused. In order to maintain anonymity, the details given regarding the participants and their organisations are limited in this book. However, quotes are labelled to give a sense of the individual's role, the purpose of the organisation (i.e., deliverer or governor) and their context (e.g., local, national or international).

6.6 Sources of data

Data were collected from five main sources throughout the project: group discussions, interviews, virtual learning sets, site visits and a Self-Audit Tool. Each of these methods is now explained.

Group Discussions (N = 4) – Meetings were held as part of the annual Beyond Sport Summit. This was viewed as a key event to which the majority of participants would already be attending. It was deemed important to meet face-to-face each year to build and maintain rapport with the participants as well as the momentum of the project. The first meeting took place in Philadelphia (2013) and focused on clarifying expectations and confirming participation in the project. Interim meetings were held in Johannesburg (2014) and London (2015) to discuss the participants' experiences with specific reference to any challenges and successes. A final meeting was held in London (2016) to review the project and to discuss the progress that had been made towards the International Safeguards. Each meeting began with a presentation from the research team. This was followed by small group discussions with the key points then being fed back to the group as a whole. The research team made notes on these discussions which then fed into the on-going analysis of the project.

One-to-One Interviews (N = 64) – Interviews were conducted with each of the participants to gain in-depth data regarding their experiences. The researchers sought to "[o]btain the perspectives, feelings and perceptions of the participant(s)" (Holloway, 1997, p. 94). Each participant was formally interviewed on two occasions. The first interview took place between six and 12 months of the project with the second interview being conducted between 30–36 months. An interview schedule was developed based on relevant theory and literature (e.g., Brackenridge et al., 2005). The interviews were flexible "as appropriate to the emergent relationship that is formed between the interviewer and the interviewee" (Patton, 2015, p. 433). For this reason, the interviews used a semi-structured approach. As a result, the interviews had the orderliness of the structured interview type, in the form of a prescribed set of questions. However, the interviewer was not limited to asking those questions in a strict order and was given the freedom to modify the content and order of questions based on the researcher's perceptions of what seems most appropriate during the dialogue (Robson, 2002). Furthermore, the researcher was able to ask follow-up questions and deviate from the interview guide, making it a truer social meaning making act (Sparkes & Smith, 2014; Robson, 2002). Interviews were conducted either face-to-face or via Skype or telephone. They ranged in length from 35–105 minutes. These formal interviews were supplemented by informal interactions throughout the project to share on-going experiences (e.g., via an e-mail or through a discussion at the Beyond Sport Summit).

Virtual Learning Sets (VLS: N = 72) – Participating organisations were assigned into six small groups. Allocations were made based on the purpose and size of the organisation as well as the time zone of the participant to facilitate virtual meetings. Each VLS was co-ordinated by a member of the International Safeguards Working Group. The VLS co-ordinator had experience relevant to safeguarding children in the context in which their group's organisations were operating (e.g., elite sport, sport for development etc.). These VLS were conducted every three months (i.e., a total of 12 throughout the project) via Skype to discuss experiences and share good practice. The co-ordinator sent a summary of each discussion to the research team. These discussions were supplemented by an online discussion forum through which participants could ask questions or share their experiences of challenges or promising practice.

Self-Audit (N = 64) – This tool facilitates self-reflection through organisations considering the extent to which each aspect of the Safeguards is in place. The self-audit is designed to be used on a regular basis for organisations to monitor their progress towards the Safeguards and to evaluate the impact of their safeguarding efforts. The participants completed the self-audit at the start of the project and this represented the baseline. The self-audit was completed again at the end of the project to facilitate an analysis of where any changes had taken place.

Case Studies (N = 6) – The researchers also conducted a more in-depth analysis of 6 of the 32 pioneer organisations. These cases were selected using maximum variation sampling (Patton, 2015). The researchers identified the following characteristics that were used to select the sample: organisational size (local, regional or international), location(s) and mission (e.g., coach education, governance or sports delivery). The priority was not that each characteristic of each criterion is represented, instead that each case represents a unique constellation of the predetermined criteria. This sampling method values heterogeneity based on the belief that themes that emerge from great variation are of particular value in capturing core experiences (Patton, 2015). This is useful in providing high-quality and detailed descriptions of each case, along with its ability to highlight any important shared patterns that are given increased significance having arrived out of heterogeneity (Patton, 2015; Sparkes & Smith, 2014).

Each pioneer organisation was assessed for suitability on the basis of what Sparkes and Smith (2014) state are the three key factors in the sampling process; availability, accessibility and theoretical interest. Theoretical interest was the priority and it was deemed essential to ensure that each organisation represented a unique context in which the International Safeguards had been piloted. Therefore, where duplicates existed, in regard to organisational size, type, or location, the researchers determined which organisation to include based on initial perceptions of their relevance and distinctiveness. However, in some instances the researchers also had to consider selection based on the other two key factors of the sampling process; accessibility and availability (Sparkes & Smith, 2014). Where accessibility and availability were considered, the researchers focussed on whether there were any practical constraints to including particular organisations within the analysis. The most prominent considerations were the extent to which the organisation could wholly and feasibly facilitate the research within a time frame that was amenable to both parties, and whether this could be achieved in a manner that was deemed relatively resource efficient, considering the projects limited budget. Organisations that were deemed appropriate to include in the research based on those three criteria were sent an e-mail inviting their organisation to become a case study. The participant within the case study organisation acted as an important gatekeeper (Holloway, 1997). These gate keepers were valuable in terms of advocating for the research, facilitating access to the organisation and as well as helping to introduce the researchers to potential interviewees (Jones, Brown, & Holloway, 2013; Reeves, 2010).

6.7 Data analysis

Qualitative data requires analysis to describe, interpret, explain and/or evaluate it (Matthews & Ross, 2010). Qualitative data analysis brings order to the data by organising, categorising and looking for relationships within the data set. It was viewed as a dynamic and iterative process (Holloway & Wheeler, 2010), which ensured that it was both a complex and time-consuming process (Jones, Brown, & Holloway, 2013). All of the qualitative data was transcribed verbatim and analysed using the stages of thematic analysis outlined by Braun and Clarke (2006).

The first stage is the familiarisation process. At this stage, the researchers immersed themselves in the data so that they are familiar with the depth and breadth of the content. In order to do this, the researchers read through the transcription several times. At this stage, notes were taken, to be considered in more detail at a later stage. Transcription is a way to begin the familiarisation process and a key phase of the interpretative analysis of data. Therefore, care was taken to ensure that the transcript retained all verbal information in a manner that was true to its original presentation.

The second stage involved generating initial codes. The researchers manually worked through printouts of each interview to determine both semantic and latent features of the data. The third stage began once all data had been coded and codes had been collated. The researchers sorted through each of the codes attempting to place each code into groups with similar codes that represented a particular aspect of the data. This involved the researcher going to and from unsorted group of codes, attempting to find the best groupings. The researcher followed Braun and Clarke's suggestion that themes that do not fit anywhere may be temporarily housed in miscellaneous to be housed elsewhere later or to be discarded (2006).

Following the development of themes, stage four involved the review and refinement of those themes. In accordance with Braun and Clarke, this occurred in two phases (2006). The first phase involved checking that the codes form a coherent pattern, or if the ordering of themes are problematic themselves. Themes were then analysed across the whole data set and with theoretical guidance, themes were evaluated for accurate reflection of the phenomenon globally. This phase also involved reviewing the data to establish if any codes may have been missed. In stage five, the researchers defined each theme. Braun and Clarke describe this as "identifying the essence of what each theme is about" (2006, p. 92), as the researcher considers how that theme fits within the phenomenon of question. This required the researcher to interpret the codes, rather than merely paraphrase the data, and to rely upon the notes developed in stage two as codes were initially developed.

The sixth and final stage is the presentation of the final set of findings. Within Braun and Clarke's process, the development of themes can be conducted using the graphic representation of themes in the form of a thematic map (2006). This is a way of organising a thematic analysis which facilitates the depiction of the structure of the themes, sub-themes and codes (Attride-Stirling, 2001). At this stage, the researcher refined the thematic map and labelled them accordingly.

6.8 Establishing trustworthiness

Researchers using fixed research designs traditionally seek to establish the quality of their research on the grounds of validity and reliability (Robson, 2002). Discrepancies between these types of research and more flexible, field-based, qualitative research means that it is with great difficulty that the quality of research can be assessed using these criteria (Sparkes & Smith, 2014). For example, the reliability and replicability that one would seek to evidence in a fixed quantitative research would not be possible within flexible qualitative social sciences research. This is because social life has elements which are particular to a given setting, and identical circumstances cannot be re-created (Robson, 2002). For these reasons, the relevance of popular research quality measures such as reliability and validity to flexible qualitative research is disputed (Patton, 2015; Robson, 2002). This has resulted in the field generally using the term trustworthiness to establish the quality of more flexible, qualitative research (Robson, 2002; Denzin & Lincoln, 2005). Denzin and Lincoln (2005) propose that qualitative research should follow the parallel criteria of trustworthiness, which consists of credibility, transferability, dependability and confirmability.

Pitney and Parker (2009) describe credibility as "whether research findings capture what really happened" (p. 62). This is a parallel term to what is traditionally understood as internal validity (Sparkes & Smith, 2014). Credibility was established through prolonged engagement with the participants over a three-year period. With respect to the case studies, the use of maximum variation sampling further enhanced the credibility of the research through enabling a more embedded approach to data collection in a diverse range of settings.

Transferability is a parallel convention to external validity, describing the extent to which the findings of a particular study can be extrapolated and applied to other contexts (Sparkes and Smith, 2014). In order to achieve this, the researchers sought to use thick descriptions of each theme. This includes contextual information which assists the reader to understand the extent to which the details described may be transferred to other organisations, situations, countries and people.

Dependability is parallel to the convention of reliability, in that it is concerned with the stability of the data over time' (Denzin & Lincoln, 2005). Dependability can be demonstrated through a clear audit trail (Sparkes & Smith, 2014). The present project did this by keeping a full record of all activities completed during the study as suggested by Robson (2002). This included keeping a record of interviews, field notes, a journal and details of the coding process. This allowed the researchers to demonstrate a logical, trace able and documented process (Sparkes & Smith, 2014).

Confirmability is the parallel convention of objectivity. This describes the assurance that the data and interpretations of research have considered and minimised the potential impact of researcher bias (Denzin & Lincoln, 2005). This was achieved through the researchers adopting a disciplined sense of reflexivity. In doing so, the researchers were able to identify the perspectives and potential biases brought to the research and consider how they may impact the way they analyse, interpret and report the findings (Sparkes and Smith, 2014). Through this approach, the researchers adhered to Walcott's (1995) recommendation to

> "covet your biases, display them openly, and ponder how they can help you formulate both the purposes of your investigation and how you can proceed with your investigation. With biases firmly in place, you won't have to pretend to complete objectivity."
>
> (p. 165)

Through adopting a reflective axiology, the researchers remained mindful of their biases and their potential impact upon the research, thus helping to ensure its trustworthiness.

6.9 Summary

This chapter has provided an overview of the aims, objectives and methods employed in this research project. The chapter has presented the research questions, and outlined the philosophical approach taken to answer those questions. Having discussed the ethical considerations of the research project, the recruitment of participants, sources of data and data analysis process were presented. This chapter concluded by outlining the methods used to attain and maintain trustworthiness.

References

Aliyu, A. A., Bello, M. U., Kasim, R., & Martin, D. (2014). Positivist and non-positivist paradigms in social science research: Conflicting paradigms or perfect partners? *Journal of Management and Sustainability*, *4*(3), 79–95.

Attride-Stirling, J. (2001). Thematic networks: An analytic tool for qualitative research. *Qualitative Research*, *1*(3), 385–405.

Brackenridge, C. H., Pawlaczek, Z., Bringer, J. D., Cockburn, C., Nutt, G., Pitchford, A., & Russell, K. (2005). Measuring the impact of child protection through activation states. *Sport, Education and Society*, *10*(2), 239–256.

Braun, V., & Clarke, V. (2006). Using thematic analysis in psychology. *Qualitative Research in Psychology*, *3*, 77–101.

Charmaz, K. (2004). Premises, principles, and practices in qualitative research: Revisiting the foundations. *Qualitative Health Research*, *14*(7), 976–993.

Coalter, F. (2007). *A wider social role for sport? Who's keeping the score?* Abingdon, UK: Routledge.

Cresswell, J. W. (1998). *Qualitative inquiry and research design: Choosing among five traditions*. Thousand Oaks, CA: Sage.

Creswell, J. W. (2007). *Qualitative inquiry and research design: Choosing among five approaches*. Thousand Oaks: Sage.

Denzin, N. K., & Lincoln, Y. S. (Eds.). (2005). *The SAGE handbook of qualitative research* (3rd ed.). London, UK: Sage.

Guba, E. G., & Lincoln, Y. S. (1994). Competing paradigms in qualitative research. In N. K. Denzin & Y. S. Lincoln (Eds.), *Handbook of qualitative research* (pp. 105–117). Thousand Oaks, CA: Sage.

Guba, E. G., & Lincoln, Y. S. (2005). Paradigmatic controversies, contradictions and emerging confluences. In N. K. Denzin & Y. S. Lincoln (Eds.), *The Sage handbook of qualitative research* (3rd ed., pp. 191–213). Thousand Oaks, CA: Sage.

Holloway, I. (1997). *Basic concepts for qualitative research*. Oxford, UK: Blackwell Science.

Holloway, I., & Wheeler, S. (2010). *Qualitative research in nursing and healthcare*. Oxford, UK: Blackwell.

Jones, I., Brown, L., & Holloway, I. (2013). *Qualitative research in sport and physical activity*. London, UK: Sage.

Matthews, B., & Ross, L. (2010). *Research methods: A practical guide for the social sciences*. Harlow, UK: Pearson Longman.

Morgan, D. L. (2007). Paradigms lost and pragmatism regained. *Journal of Mixed Methods Research*, *1*(1), 48–76.

Patton, M. Q. (2015). *Qualitative research and evaluation methods* (4th ed.). London, UK: Sage.

Pawson, R. (2006). *Evidence-based policy: A realist perspective*. London, UK: Sage.

Pitney, W., & Parker, J. (2009). *Qualitative research in physical activity and the health professions*. Champaign, IL: Human Kinetics.

Ponterotto, J. G. (2002). Qualitative research methods: The fifth force in psychology. *The Counselling Psychologist*, *30*(3), 394–406.

Ponterotto, J. G., & Grieger, I. (2007). Effectively communicating qualitative research. *The Counselling Psychologist*, *35*(3), 404–430.

Reeves, C. L. (2010). A difficult negotiation: Fieldwork relations with gatekeepers. *Qualitative Research*, *10*, 315–331.
Robson, C. (2002). *Real world research* (2nd ed.). Oxford, UK: Blackwell Publishing.
Schwandt, T. A. (1994). Constructivist, interpretivist approaches to human inquiry. In N. K. Denzin & Y. S. Lincoln (Eds.), *Handbook of qualitative research* (pp. 118–127). London, UK: Sage.
Sparkes, A. C., & Smith, B. (2014). *Qualitative research methods in sport, exercise and health*. London, UK: Routledge.
Walcott, H. (1995). *The art of fieldwork*. London, UK: Sage.

Chapter 7

Assessing impact

The Self-Audit Tool

7.1 The Self-Audit Tool

Through this project, the research team and Founders Group have developed and implemented the Self-Audit Tool (SAT). It is based on work undertaken by George Varnava with the Forum on Children and Violence for the National Children's Bureau. It is an approach which has been used by Keeping Children Safe and the National Society for the Prevention of Cruelty to Children (NSPCC).

The SAT facilitates self-reflection through respondents considering the extent to which their organisation has made progress towards each aspect of the Safeguards. Within each Safeguard, the relevant criteria are displayed. Respondents are asked to decide if their organisation has each safeguard and its specific criteria either; in place (A), partially in place (B) or not in place (C). This helps organisations to identify areas of strength as well as areas in which there is scope for improvement. The SAT can be used on a regular basis for organisations to monitor their progress towards the Safeguards and to evaluate the impact of their safeguarding efforts. The SAT was revised during the research project to ensure that it accurately reflected the finalised content of the International Safeguards. The SAT is also aligned with the Implementation Guides which are explained in more detail in Chapter 14. These help organisations to interpret their data and to use it to develop their plan for moving towards the International Safeguards. It also represents a tool which can be used in future projects to expand our understanding of the antecedents and correlates of effective safeguarding for children in sport.

7.2 Assessing impact using the Self-Audit Tool

Participants completed the self-audit at the start of the project in 2013 and again at the end of the project in 2016. These data were compared to assess any progress that had been made towards the International Safeguards. It is important to explain that over the last three years, the International

Safeguards have been subject to an ongoing content review which has resulted in changes to its structure and content. To ensure the self-audit tool provides an adequate assessment of the International Safeguards, it has also been updated to reflect the up-to-date version of the Safeguards. Consequently, one cannot make an exact comparison between the self-audit data collected as a baseline in 2013 and the data collected during 2016 using the updated version of the self-audit. Nonetheless, many of the individual items of the self-audit tool remained similar and hence a comparison between selected criteria is possible. Therefore, a comparison can be made between the responses given on equivalent criteria given during 2013 and 2016. The overall percentage of criterion 'in place' were calculated for each organisation. The mean percentages are displayed in Table 7.1 for deliverers (The 16 participating organisations which work directly with children, governors (The 16 participating organisations which support or govern other organisations who work directly with children) and the group as a whole. Though we must acknowledge that this approach has limitations, it does offer some insight into any progress that had been made towards the International Safeguards during this Project.

The data are now presented with respect to each of the eight International Safeguards with any key changes being identified.

7.2.1 Safeguard 1: Developing Your Policy

The number of organisations with a policy in place increased from 56% to 93% during the project. The SAT data therefore suggest that significant progress had been made regarding Safeguard 1. It may be that developing a policy to safeguard children within an organisation is a Safeguard for which progress is more readily made relative to the other Safeguards. It may also be that developing a policy is a logical first step for organisations who are at the start of their safeguarding journey. The content of the rest of the Safeguards can then be grounded in this policy which outlines the organisation's values and commitment towards safeguarding children.

At the baseline, Deliverers (63%) were more likely to already have a policy in place than Governors (38%). By 2016, the vast majority of Deliverers (89%) and all of the Governors had developed and implemented a policy for safeguarding children. The progress made by the Governors is particularly notable. As these organisations did not directly work with children, the relevance of having their own safeguarding policy was not always acknowledged. However, the fact that all of these organisations had a policy in place by 2016 demonstrates that this was seen as an important step forward and a mechanism through which the organisation's commitment and approach to safeguarding could be emphasised to the partner organisations which these governors supported, funded or governed.

Table 7.1 A comparison of the self-audit data from the start and end of the project

	2013 *Start of the project*	*2016* *End of the project*
Safeguard 1: Developing Your Policy		
Deliverers	63%	89%
Governors	38%	100%
Total	56%	93%
Safeguard 2: Procedures for Responding to Safeguarding Concerns		
Deliverers	26%	44%
Governors	25%	33%
Total	26%	40%
Safeguard 3: Advice and Support		
Deliverers	37%	44%
Governors	25%	33%
Total	33%	40%
Safeguard 4: Minimising Risks to Children		
Deliverers	58%	67%
Governors	13%	33%
Total	44%	53%
Safeguard 5: Guidelines for Behaviour		
Deliverers	37%	78%
Governors	38%	50%
Total	37%	67%
Safeguard 6: Recruiting, Communicating and Training		
Deliverers	47%	56%
Governors	25%	67%
Total	41%	60%
Safeguard 7: Working with Partners		
Deliverers	53%	67%
Governors	0%	67%
Total	37%	67%
Safeguard 8: Monitoring and Evaluating		
Deliverers	37%	67%
Governors	38%	38%
Total	37%	53%

7.2.2 *Safeguard 2: Procedures for Responding to Safeguarding Concerns*

The number of organisations with procedures in place increased from 26% to 40% during the project. Some progress had therefore been made towards this Safeguard. Fully implementing effective procedures is likely to take time, and hence this may explain why further progress had not been made by the end of the research project. It is also important to highlight that the

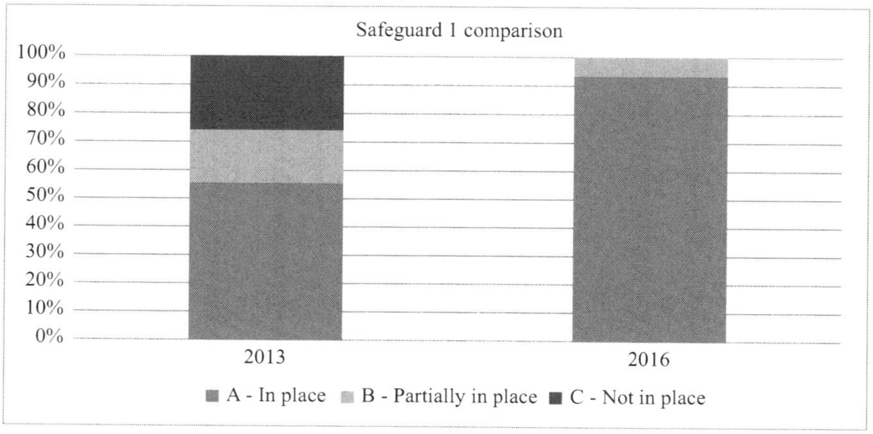

Figure 7.1 Safeguard 1 comparison

number of organisations who reported having nothing at all in place did fall from 26% to 13%. Therefore, although procedures were not fully in place, some progress had been made towards implementation.

At the baseline, Deliverers (26%) and Governors (25%) reported similar profiles. Both Deliverers (44%) and Governors (33%) were able to make some progress towards this Safeguard during the project. More progress was therefore made by organisations who work directly with children. However, there remains scope for more work in this area in terms of supporting organisations to either develop their own procedures or to at least have effective partnerships with other organisations to manage situations in which safeguarding concerns are disclosed. Partnerships may be of particular importance to relatively small organisations, and hence this aspect has clear links with Safeguard 7.

7.2.3 Safeguard 3: Advice and Support

The number of organisations with Advice and Support in place increased from 33% to 40% during the project. As with Safeguard 2, fully implementing effective mechanisms for advice and support is likely to take time, and hence this may explain why further progress had not been made by the end of the research project. Whilst this Safeguard was not fully in place for most organisations, some progress had been made. This is illustrated by the fact that the number of organisations who reported having nothing at all in place did fall from 37% to 13%. Therefore, although Advice and

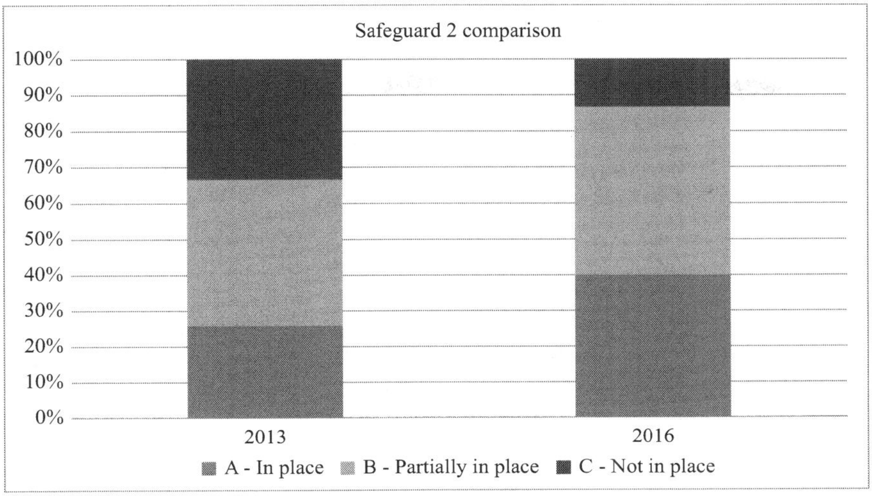

Figure 7.2 Safeguard 2 comparison

Support were not fully in place, some progress had been made towards implementation.

At the baseline, Deliverers (37%) and Governors (25%) reported similar profiles. Both Deliverers (44%) and Governors (33%) were able to make some progress towards this Safeguard during the project. Progress was often made, particularly for smaller organisations, by developing relationships with partners through Safeguard 7 who provided advice and support, thus helping to build capacity.

7.2.4 *Safeguard 4: Minimising Risks to Children*

The number of organisations with processes in place to minimise risks to children increased from 44% to 53% during the project. This suggests that limited progress had been made in terms of having this safeguard fully in place. The concept of identifying and mitigating risk through a proactive approach may be significantly different to the reactive approach adopted in some organisations who respond to safeguarding after a concern has been highlighted. Such a cultural change may take time to become fully embedded.

At the baseline, Deliverers (58%) were more likely to already have processes in place than Governors (13%). By 2016, Deliverers (67%) and Governors (33%) had made some progress towards this Safeguard. Importantly,

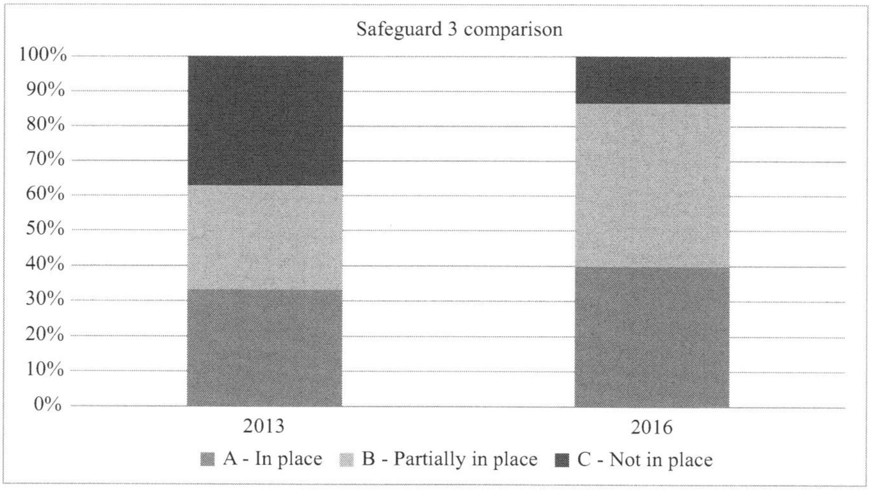

Figure 7.3 Safeguard 3 comparison

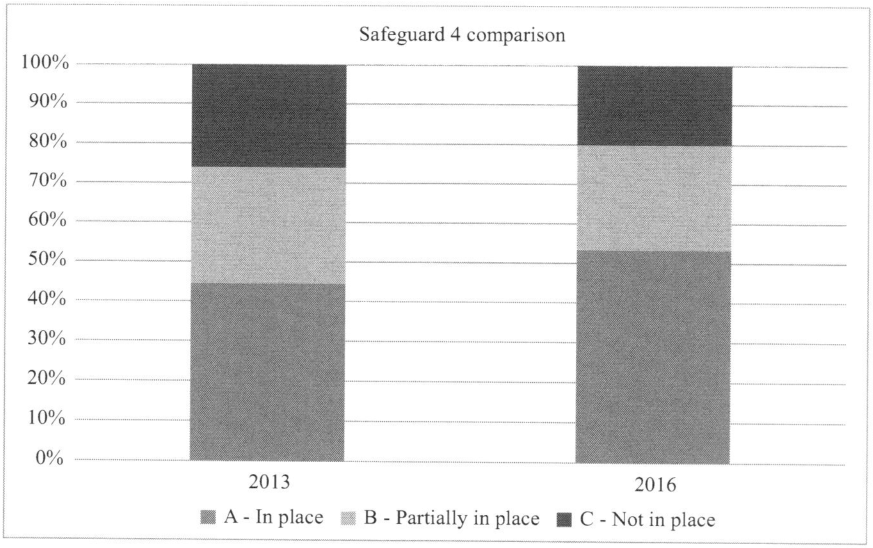

Figure 7.4 Safeguard 4 comparison

the Governors with nothing at all in place fell from 63% in 2013 to 33% in 2016 further demonstrating that some progress had been reported.

7.2.5 *Safeguard 5: Guidelines for Behaviour*

The number of organisations with Guidelines for Behaviour in place increased from 37% to 67% during the project. The SAT data therefore suggest that significant progress had been made regarding Safeguard 5. As explained with respect to developing a policy, it may be that developing guidelines is an area in which progress is more readily made relative to the other Safeguards. It may also be that developing such guidelines is perceived to be more logical and achievable for organisations early in their safeguarding journey. It is also noteworthy to highlight that 19% of all organisations had nothing at all in place in 2013. By 2016, process had been made such that all 32 organisations had at least partially implemented this Safeguard.

At the baseline, both Deliverers (37%) and Governors (38%) had similar profiles. Both Governors (50%) and, in particular, Deliverers (78%) made progress towards this Safeguard. It may be that organisations who directly work with children can see the immediate relevance of having guidelines in place and hence this resulted in them prioritising and making progress in this area.

7.2.6 *Safeguard 6: Recruiting, Communicating and Training*

The number of organisations with processes for Recruiting, Communicating and Training staff on Safeguarding increased from 41% to 60% during

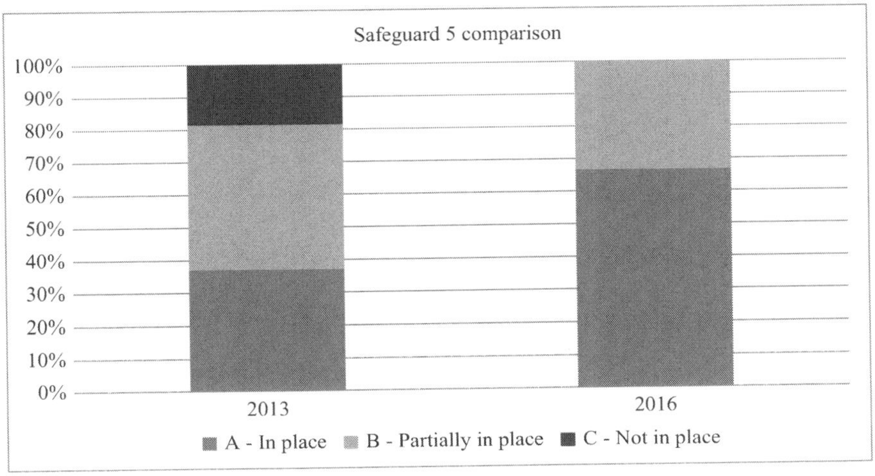

Figure 7.5 Safeguard 5 comparison

the project. The SAT data therefore suggests that some progress had been made regarding Safeguard 6. Significantly, 41% of all organisations had nothing at all in place in 2013. By 2016, only 7% of organisations reported that they still had nothing in place. Whilst these systems were not yet fully embedded, these data do suggest that participants reported that these were now partially in place.

When comparing the different types of organisation, Governors made particularly significant progress with the percentage of items being in place increasing from 25% to 67% during the project. Deliverers also reported making progress with the figure for these organisations increasing from 47% to 56%. Overall, it was evident that more organisations had systems in place to recruit and provide safeguarding training for staff. It was with respect to facilitating on-going communication about safeguarding where there was scope for future progress to be made.

7.2.7 Safeguard 7: Working with Partners

The number of organisations who actively worked with partners on issues related to safeguarding children increased from 37% to 67% during the project. Significantly, 22% of all organisations had nothing at all in place in 2013. By 2016, this figure reduced to 0%, demonstrating that all organisations had at least partially implemented a plan to work with partners to safeguard children. This progress was particularly facilitated by the nature of this collaborative project which encouraged the sharing of resources, experiences and contacts amongst the participating organisations. The importance

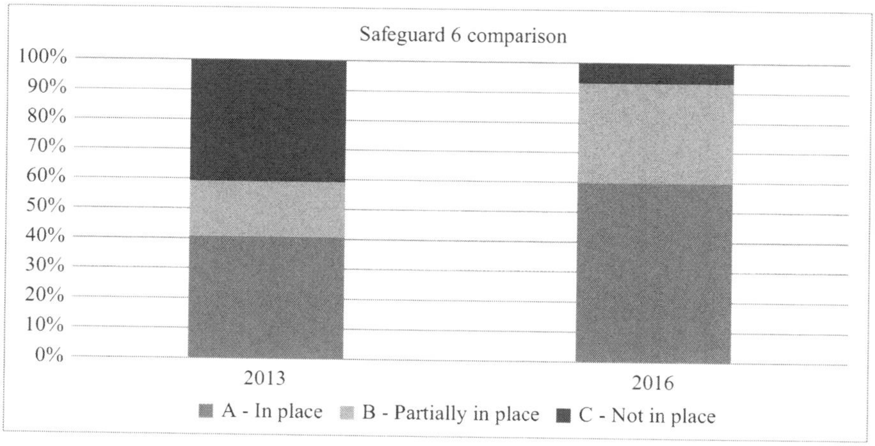

Figure 7.6 Safeguard 6 comparison

of developing such networks was emphasised and this is discussed further in Chapter 17.

With respect to the different types of organisation, Governors made particularly significant progress from 0% to 67%. This is indicative of an important change in approach amongst these organisations from one of working in isolation to one of working in partnership. This change was also reflected in the data from the Deliverers who also made progress from 53% to 67%. It was often through considering the items in Safeguard 7 that participants were able to find solutions and make progress with respect to items in other Safeguards.

7.2.8 *Safeguard 8: Monitoring and Evaluating*

The number of organisations which had procedures for monitoring and evaluating their Safeguards increased from 37% to 53% during the project. Participants acknowledged the importance of collecting such data to both evaluate the impact of their work as well as to inform their future plans. Identifying the resources and expertise to collect rigorous data and to interpret these in an effective way was often a challenge.

Having said this, when considering the different types of organisation, Deliverers did report making significant progress with an improvement from 37% to 67% in terms of the percentage of items which were fully in place. It was the Governors who did not make progress with respect to the percentage of items fully in place which remained at 38% throughout the project.

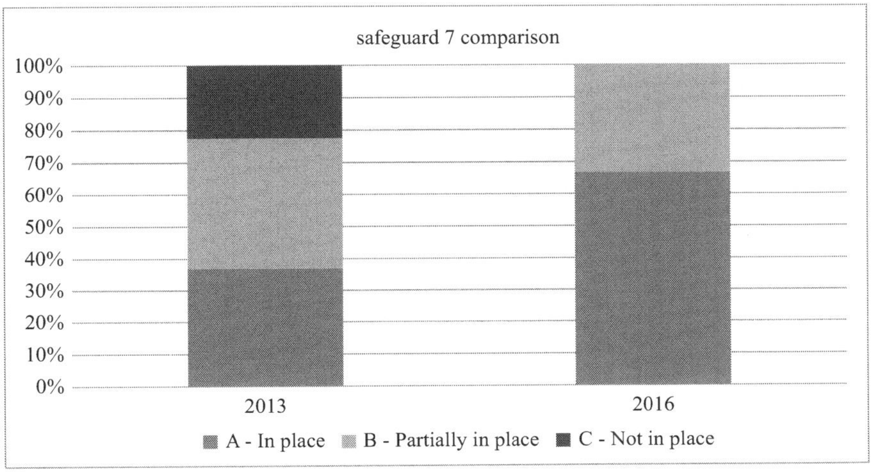

Figure 7.7 Safeguard 7 comparison

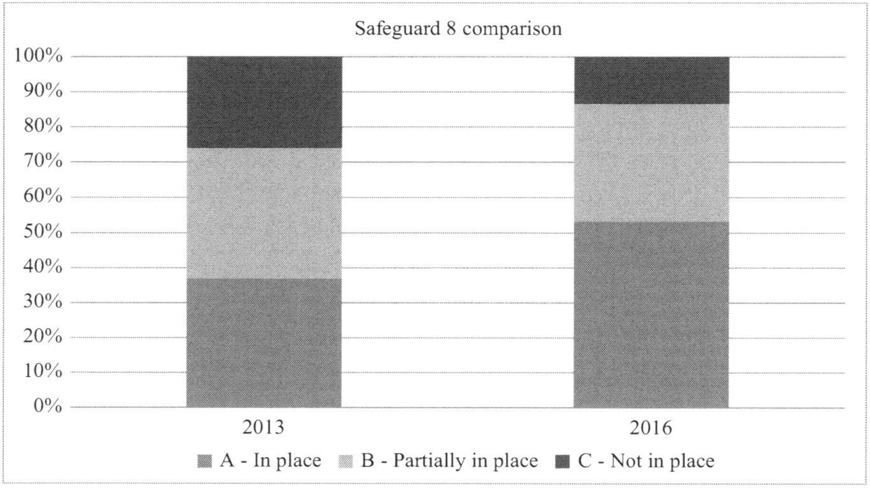

Figure 7.8 Safeguard 8 comparison

This suggests that those organisations who were monitoring and evaluating their safeguarding work already had implemented these mechanisms prior to the project. However, those Governors reporting that they had nothing in place did fall from 63% to 33%. This illustrates that their involvement in the project did help some organisations to make progress in this area. There remains scope in some organisations for monitoring and evaluation to be fully embedded as an integral part of their overall safeguarding system.

7.3 Usefulness of the Self-Audit Tool

Through the interviews, focus groups and online discussions, the participants discussed the benefits of completing the SAT. Participants explained how the SAT provided a framework which helped to identify and clarify the focus for safeguarding children in sport. For example:

> "Safeguarding and child protection can mean 100 things to 100 people. The Safeguards and the Self-Audit Tool help to put everyone on the same page and make sure that they are discussing the same things."
>
> (National Governor)

> "The Safeguards have really helped us in terms of providing a common understanding of safeguarding. It helps to overcome barriers around what the issues are, what terms mean and what needs to be in place."
>
> (National Deliverer)

This discussion can inform the development of a plan which can help organisations to move forward:

> "The Safeguards and the Self-Audit Tool help in terms of showing where someone is at the moment, where they hope to be in the future and this helps them to plan."
>
> (International Governor)

> "The self-audit is an immensely powerful tool. We completed it recently with our management team. We got different groups to complete it and we identified differences. These differences then led to discussions about what is actually in place and where work needs to be focused. I found it so useful that we will now be completing it on an annual basis as part of our monitoring and evaluation."
>
> (Local Deliverer)

The SAT also helps to identify progress and give a sense of achievement:

> "Completing the self-audit again shows us that we have come a really long way in just 2 years. We still have a way to go but it is great to see progress."
>
> (National Governor)

7.4 Summary

This chapter has presented quantitative evidence of the impact of the International Safeguards for those organisations involved in the research project. This evidence has been presented with reference to the SAT. Data from the beginning and the end of the project has been presented, with comparisons made in regard to each individual Safeguard. Throughout this chapter, significant overall developments towards the International Safeguards for both Governors and Deliverers are presented. The ways in which the participants found this process to be beneficial were also considered.

Chapter 8

Assessing impact

Activation States

8.1 Changes in Activation States

In order to assess change through the interview data, the concept of Activation States was utilised (Brackenridge et al., 2005). Activation States offer a heuristic device as opposed to a calibrated measuring tool. The transcripts from the in-depth interviews at the start and end of the research project with the 32 participants were analysed. Each transcript was reviewed with respect to four key dimensions:

- Voices (what people say about the International Safeguards)
- Knowledge (what people know through experience – their awareness, interest or understanding of the International Safeguards)
- Feelings (what people feel – their attitudes and emotions towards the International Safeguards)
- Action (what people do/have done in relation to the International Safeguards)

The inclusion of these dimensions affords an examination of both psychological and social processes (Clandinin & Connelly, 1998; Sparkes, 2002). The 'Activation State' of each response is then identified in relation to each of these four areas. The five states are:

- Opposed (e.g., critical of the need for the International Safeguards).
- Inactive (e.g., demonstrating no awareness or behaviour related to the International Safeguards).
- Reactive (e.g., demonstrating reluctant compliance with the International Safeguards).
- Active (e.g., demonstrating appropriate awareness or behaviour related to the International Safeguards).
- Proactive (e.g., demonstrating full commitment and advocating for the International Safeguards).

During a team meeting, researchers developed and revised the procedures to be used to analyse the data. Following the approach outlined by Brackenridge et al. (2005), all researchers read a sample of transcripts and then independently identified the salient Activation States through completing a grid showing opposed-proactive on the horizontal axis and the four categories on the vertical axis. The researchers assigned the same categorisations on 94% of occasions, which represents an acceptable indication of inter-rater reliability (Brackenridge et al., 2005).

Through the analysis, a clear discrepancy between the individual's state and their perception of the state of the organisation as a whole was identified. As such, each transcript was analysed twice using the Activation State method. The first analysis focused on the individual and the second analysis focused on their perception of the organisation. For instance, an individual may be very proactive, hence this is why they are the lead person for safeguarding within their organisation. However, they may perceive the organisation to be primarily reactive. By including both of these approaches, a more nuanced analysis is revealed.

The identification of Activation States allows us to give a clear visual representation of the state ('profile') of each stakeholder response and to differentiate where these responses are not internally consistent. For example, some people were positive towards the International Safeguards at an emotional level (i.e., Feelings-Proactive) but had not actually done anything related to the project (i.e., Behaviour-Inactive). On the other hand, interviewees could talk critically about the need for safeguarding in sport (i.e., Voice-Opposed) but be aware of the International Safeguards and the relevance to their role (i.e., Knowledge-Active). The modal (most common) Activation State for the group of Deliverers and Governors was identified and these are presented in the following sections.

8.2 Deliverers: individual Activation States

Overall the Deliverers made progress at the individual level to be at least active across all Activation States. The deliverers talked very positively and had a proactive voices profile at the start and throughout the project. Similarly, the profile with respect to feelings progressed from active to proactive. This was perhaps inevitable due to the fact that these participants had voluntarily signed up to trial the International Safeguards and to take part in the research.

Particular progress was made in terms of knowledge (inactive to active) and behaviour (inactive to proactive). This shows that involvement in the International Safeguards project had achieved an important impact through developing these individual's awareness of safeguarding as well as having a clear impact on facilitating an increase in their behaviours related to safeguarding. Table 8.1 presents a summary of the profile of the Activation

Table 8.1 Summary of Activation States for deliverers (individual level)

N = 16	*OPPOSED*	*INACTIVE*	*REACTIVE*	*ACTIVE*	*PROACTIVE*
Voices					Before After
Knowledge		Before		After	
Feelings				Before	After
Actions		Before			After

Table 8.2 Example quotes from deliverer organisations (individual changes)

	Before	*After*
Voices	Proactive – "Our role here is to ensure that enough evidence from the programme is documented such that we can talk about sport for development outside and also to ensure that, conversely, good practice from the sport for development world or conceptual clarity that is required, or good practice from across the world gets fed into the programme. So it is largely about proof of concept and evidence building."	Proactive – Safeguarding is simply fundamental. If our children are not safe then they will not be able to experience all of the other benefits that can be enjoyed through participation. There is a need for everyone to go beyond the minimum to ensure that children, and their safe development, are central to everything we do."
Knowledge	Inactive – "In terms of safeguarding, I did not really know anything."	Active – "Now I have a much clearer understanding of safeguarding and each of the 8 International Safeguards. I understand where we need to go and how we are going to get there"
Feelings	Active – "I like the idea of this project with everyone going to work together and support one another to safeguard children."	Proactive – "Well, I love it, I just love it. You know, because there are different child protection issues and different attitudes to child protection depending on where in the world we are located. It is just very good to understand how it is working out in other places."
Action	Inactive – "I had not done much. We were coming to the end of our sports programme and so changing things at that point was difficult."	Proactive – "I have done so much through this project. I have even volunteered to talk about our safeguarding work at conferences and now advocate the importance of safeguarding in sport to other organisations in our network."

States of the Deliverers before and after the implementation of the International Safeguards.

Table 8.2 presents participant quotes to illustrate the changes that were identified across the group of Deliverers. It is important to highlight that the pairs of quotes come from the same participant and hence they demonstrate the transition made through the project.

8.3 Deliverers: organisational Activation States

The data were also analysed to assess perceptions of the organisation as a whole. At the start of the project, the modal response of the Deliverers for both the voice and feelings categories was opposed. There was a perceived opposition to this project in particular when it was viewed as adopting an autocratic approach with people not feeling a strong need for safeguarding within sport. By the end of the project, the participants reported an active profile in terms of voices and feelings through describing a shared understanding of the importance of safeguarding children.

Furthermore, at the start of the project, the modal response of the Deliverers for both the knowledge and behaviour categories was inactive. Prior to working towards the Safeguards participants reported that there was a lack of knowledge and action regarding safeguarding children in their organisation. By the end of the project, the participants reported an active profile in terms of knowledge and behaviours. Participants perceived that their colleagues now had the knowledge required to fulfil the safeguarding aspects of their role and that people were now enacting the required behaviours regarding safeguarding. This qualitative data suggest that the Safeguards have contributed to changes not only with respect to people's knowledge and behaviours but also in terms of how people feel and talk about safeguarding within the participating organisations.

Table 8.4 presents participant quotes to illustrate the changes that were identified across the group of governors. Again, it is important to highlight that the pairs of quotes come from the same participant, and hence, they demonstrate the transition made through the project.

Table 8.3 Summary of Activation States for deliverers (organisational level)

State ->	*OPPOSED*	*INACTIVE*	*REACTIVE*	*ACTIVE*	*PROACTIVE*
Voices	Before			After	
Knowledge		Before		After	
Feelings	Before			After	
Action		Before		After	

Table 8.4 Example quotes from deliverer organisations (organizational changes)

	Before	*After*
Voices	Opposed – "People are against this kind of work when it is talked about as coming from the attitude of 'we come from the empire and we know what is best for you."	Active – "We get much less resistance. When we get new people there may be some questions as they have just not come across safeguarding before. Everyone else is much more invested and they see how important it is."
Knowledge	Inactive – ". . . the children are not made aware of various rights they are entitled to. Generating awareness is a tough challenge that we face on a regular basis."	Active – "Everyone knows that they need to adhere to the safeguards that are in place and sign the code of conducts for safeguarding children. People now know that there are procedures to be followed regarding safeguarding concerns. parents understand that participants engaged in our programs need consents signed for them to take part in our activities.
Feelings	Opposed – "Scolding children is not seen as abuse. Having a child run around a field five times is not a problem. We are coming from a culture in which these are seen as ok. These are the feelings which we have to engage with."	Active – "Since starting the Safeguards project, we have gone from a position of people saying that they cannot believe you are making me do this to one where they say I would not put my child in a club that did not do this."
Action	Inactive – "Within our organisation, in terms of formal protocols there are very few."	Active – "Before the policy we would finish meetings and girls would be going home, some of them late in the dark. Now we know that at 3pm we have to finish so everyone has enough time to get home before its dark."

8.4 Governors: individual Activation States

Overall, the Governors made progress at the individual level to be at least active across all Activation States. Similar to the Deliverers, the Governors also talked very positively about the International Safeguards and had a proactive voices profile at the start and throughout the project. The profile with respect to feelings was maintained as active.

Significant progress was made in terms of knowledge (inactive to active) and behaviour (inactive to active). This shows that involvement in the International Safeguards project had achieved an important impact through developing these individual's awareness of safeguarding as well as having a clear impact on facilitating an increase in their behaviours related to safeguarding. Table 8.5 presents a summary of the profile of the Activation States of the Governors before and after the implementation of the International Safeguards, and Table 8.6 displays illustrative quotes.

Table 8.5 Summary of Activation States for the Governors (individual level)

N = 16	*OPPOSED*	*INACTIVE*	*REACTIVE*	*ACTIVE*	*PROACTIVE*
Voices					Before After
Knowledge		Before		After	
Feelings				Before After	
Actions		Before		After	

Table 8.6 Example quotes from Governor organisations (individual changes)

	Before	*After*
Voices	Proactive – "To start with, you are not going to have a programme if you cannot protect the child. I mean, it is that core of an issue. It is imperative that we talk about it, and talk about it, and work at it."	Proactive – "The culture of our organisation, the philosophy behind our business, is that we are child centred and all about positive youth development. This means that safeguarding is inevitably at the core of what we do."
Knowledge	Inactive – "We were at the Beyond Sport summit as we were a finalist. As part of this application there was a whole section on safeguarding and this really brought my attention to this. There are ways in which we have been doing this informally but not formally. I attended the session and that was actually my first experience of it."	Active – "The Safeguards are excellent because they are comprehensive but also light. They cover all you need but the document is easy to follow and the self-audit really helped me to review what we do in a systematic way and to know how to plan the next steps with the implementation guide."

(*Continued*)

Table 8.6 (Continued)

	Before	*After*
Feelings	Active – "I really like the fact that everyone is banding together with all of the different stakeholders from grass roots to the highest levels. There really seems to be a drive behind this and everybody agrees that it is important. This may be the most important thing."	Active – "I still feel really positive about this work. It is great to be part of this strong and growing coalition which now has a momentum that will ensure it stays alive beyond the life of this initial phase."
Action	Inactive – "You know the checklist, when I first picked that up, a fairly small NGO working three degrees away from children, using mostly voluntary coaches, I just thought that this is too much. I cannot get my head around this. So I went back to the working group and said that there is no point in us doing this, I can only tick about two boxes and I am about a decade off from ticking the rest."	Active – "I have realised that safeguarding is a journey and something that you are always working towards as opposed to something that you finish and move on. I now complete the self-audit each year and this helps me to highlight a theme on which to focus and plan for the next year. I will continue to do this on an annual basis and it is integral to our other review processes."

8.5 Governors: organisational Activation States

Significant changes were identified across all areas of the Activation States for the Governor's perceptions of their organisations as a whole. At the start of the project, the modal response of the governors for both the voices and feelings categories was opposed. There was opposition to this project in particular when it was viewed as adopting an autocratic approach with people not feeling a strong need for safeguarding within sport. By the end of the project, the participants reported a reactive profile in terms of voices with people discussing the need for safeguarding in relation to other key motivators. Feelings were assessed to be active with members being more engaged in the process after collaborative discussions throughout the project.

At the start of the project, the modal response of the governors for both the knowledge and actions categories was inactive. Prior to working towards the Safeguards participants reported that there was a lack of knowledge and action regarding safeguarding children in their member organisations. By the end of the project, the participants reported an active profile in terms of knowledge with an increased awareness of the nature and importance of safeguarding. Behaviours had progressed from inactive to reactive with organisations now starting to work towards the Safeguards after encouragement and support from the governor organisation. This qualitative data suggests that the Safeguards have contributed to changes not only with respect to people's knowledge and behaviours but also in terms of how people feel and talk about safeguarding for those who support or govern organisations working with children in sport. This impact is shown in Table 8.7 and illustrated with participant quotes in Table 8.8.

Table 8.7 Summary of Activation States for Governors (organisational level)

State ->	*OPPOSED*	*INACTIVE*	*REACTIVE*	*ACTIVE*	*PROACTIVE*
Voices	Before		After		
Knowledge		Before		After	
Feelings	Before			After	
Action		Before	After		

Table 8.8 Example quotes from Governor organisations (organisational changes)

	Before	*After*
Voices	Opposed – "Some people are sceptical, you know, it is those westerners off on another one of their things. We'll just sit it out an in a few years it will be something else."	Reactive – "The argument that we should do it because it is the right thing to do for children does not work. What does work is when we point out that you are growing your game and that there is a potential reputational risk. This gets people to listen."
Knowledge	Inactive – "Our people are experts on the topics and on sport for development but they will not necessarily have the expertise to manage disclosures and maybe they would feel inadequate to help out with those kinds of things."	Active – "In the 3 years of the Safeguards project we have gone from people at the governing body level thinking that this is not our business to now where it is mandated as part of our strategic plans moving forward, this has been a great change. We have also been given time to work through the self-audit with our member organisations in 25–30 countries. In many cases there is nothing yet in place but at least this is a start to the journey. And people agree it is important."

(*Continued*)

Table 8.8 (Continued)

	Before	*After*
Feelings	Opposed – "Even though we try to integrate it, people still see it as extra and as an additional segment. They say here we go again with safeguarding. I have 10,000 other things to do."	Active – "At the beginning people just saw it as hoops that they had to jump through." This was particularly from our coaches, who are mostly volunteers, and they saw it as them having to do this and do that to tick boxes. People have really started to embrace safeguarding. This has come about through us building trust with our coaches and members."
Action	Inactive – "When I go out to our members I get them to see that it is OK if they have got none of this in place because then we are going to put the steps in place to get there. It might take ten years to actually do it."	Reactive – "There is that group of people who are resistant and take time to win over, but that group is getting smaller over time. I think that we will always have people in that group."

8.6 Summary

This chapter has presented qualitative evidence of the impact of the International Safeguards represented using the concept of Activation States. Overall, the self-audit data and this qualitative evidence demonstrate the wide ranging and significant impact of the Safeguards. They help to create an environment which promotes safeguarding. The Safeguards also help to develop individuals' knowledge and skills in safeguarding children which in turn impacted their behaviours. In combination, these changes to the environment, individuals and behaviours are helping to develop and maintain a safeguarding culture within these organisations.

References

Brackenridge, C. H., Pawlaczek, Z., Bringer, J. D., Cockburn, C., Nutt, G., Pitchford, A., & Russell, K. (2005). Measuring the impact of child protection through activation states. *Sport, Education and Society*, *10*(2), 239–256.

Clandinin, D. J., & Connelly, M. (1998). Personal experience methods, in: N. K. Denzin & Y. S. Lincoln (Eds.), *Collecting and interpreting qualitative materials*. London, UK: Sage.

Sparkes, A. C. (2002). *Telling tales in sport and physical activity: A qualitative journey*. Leeds, UK: Human Kinetics.

Chapter 9

CHILDREN pillars

Creating change through policy is clearly aligned with effective policy implementation. Simply publishing documents, such as the International Safeguards, will have limited impact without effective implementation. Fullan has argued that many attempts to facilitate change are unsuccessful because "no distinction is made between theories of change (what causes change) and theories of changing (how to influence those causes)" (2007, p. 14). The present research aimed to understand the factors which influence the causes of change and hence produced a theory of changing, in the form of the CHILDREN Pillars. The following chapter provides an overview of these pillars. The ways in which organisations engaged with children during the project are also described along with the benefits of the International Safeguards, both for children and the organisation more broadly.

9.1 The conceptualisation

The qualitative data collected throughout this project were analysed using thematic content analysis. The data were analysed to identify the factors which influence the causes of change. In other words, the focus was on identifying the factors which facilitated people and organisations to work towards the International Safeguards. Through this analysis, the research team focused on developing a comprehensive yet easily comprehendible conceptualisation of the results. This is based on feedback from the participants, such as:

> "One thing that I would say is simplicity. Looking at it from the outside you could say is this project about this or about that. This whole piece has so many elements. One thing that I have learned through working here is always thinking how to sell this. If you could come up with a phrase, and keep it simple, that captures people. That is the one thing that I would change. No one can remember 11 things. When you are coaching during a time out you can get a maximum of three points across. Once you get beyond this then you lose people."
>
> (International Governor)

Eight key themes emerged from the analytical process. These themes were accompanied by the over-arching message that maltreatment may be more likely to happen to a child when they are given other labels that supersede their status as a child. Examples of such labels included being an elite athlete, from a lower socio-economic class or a girl. There was a consensus that viewing children as children before anything else would be an important initial step to safeguarding their well-being. As a result, the eight themes were labelled using the acronym CHILDREN to reinforce this message in an easily understood and memorable way. These eight pillars are described in Table 9.1.

Each of these pillars is the focus of the following eight chapters. In each chapter, the concept is described and related to relevant literature. Key issues, as well as examples of promising practices, are then outlined. Finally, case studies are presented which show how the given pillar had been used to facilitate progress towards the International Safeguards. These case studies are based on six of the pioneer organisations from whom more in-depth data was collected through visits to their organisation. These case studies include an elite European football club, an International Federation, sport for development organisations in Africa and Asia, an international training

Table 9.1 The CHILDREN pillars of safeguarding

Pillar	*Description*
Cultural sensitivity	There was a clear need for flexibility within the Safeguards such that they can be tailored to the cultural and social norms of the context
Holistic	Safeguarding should be viewed as integrated into all aspects of an organisation as opposed to being an additional element
Incentives	There needs to be a clear reason for individuals and an organisation to work towards the Safeguards
Leadership	The Safeguards need to have strong support from those working in key leadership roles
Dynamic	The safeguarding systems within an organisation need to continually be reviewed and adapted to maintain their relevance and effectiveness
Resources	The implementation of the Safeguards needs to be supported by appropriate resources (e.g., human, time and financial)
Engaging stakeholders	A democratic approach should be adopted which invites and listens to the voices of those in and around the sport (e.g., parents, coaches, community leaders)
Networks	An organisation's progress towards the Safeguards will be strengthened by developing networks with other related organisations

organisation and a governing organisation in the Caribbean. Participants acknowledged the value of including these case studies:

> "That is why your case studies and your actual pictures of people who have actually been there and done it, talking about it and sharing it, is a key way of getting the key messages across. So, it is making it as real to people as possible."
>
> (International Governor)

> "There is always a desire to go back to what can be measured and boxes that can be ticked. The qualitative examples which come from case studies are so powerful because they can illustrate the issues which are faced and the complexities of what we are trying to deal with."
>
> (International Deliverer)

9.2 Genuine engagement with children

A common thread running throughout the pillars was the genuine engagement of children in the efforts to safeguard them. Many of the interviewees reported that the Safeguards have had an impact on the experiences of children. At the start of the project, listening to the voices of children was not common practice, either within the pioneer organisations or in the communities more broadly. For instance, a Founder of a sport for development agency explained:

> "Children come from families where they don't always have a voice. So to be able to voice your opinion at the age of 13 against someone who is older than you, that is not traditionally or culturally, that is not done. So encouraging those kids at 13, 14, 15 to go and speak to the social worker to report inappropriate behaviour by an adult, that has been quite tricky because the cultural practice is that this person is older than me, I have to respect them, I cannot disrespect them. To report against them would be seen as disrespecting an elder."

Organisations now make much more of an effort to give a voice to children and to genuinely listen to what they have to say when developing and evaluating programmes. For example, in reflecting on the implementation of the International Safeguards, the Head of Safeguarding from the European football club said:

> "An important impact is in relation to how we listen to kids across the club. The need to do this was communicated to us from the International Safeguards. Listening to kids effectively is difficult and time-consuming to do well but we now recognise how necessary it is to do

this. Typically on the list of business priorities this is low down the scale. The Safeguards project has really helped to emphasise the importance of listening to kids."

The Head of Safeguarding went on to describe a specific example of how this project had impacted practice:

> "One thing that the Safeguards have made me think about in particular is how we involve young people in the decision-making process. As part of this, when we were writing our disciplinary framework, they were involved and they now own it. They understand it and so when it comes to a time when they are involved in that process, if they have breached our code of conduct, then they understand what will happen to them. They actually have more ownership of that because it is something that they have been involved in. So instead of the organisation forcing rules and activities on them, they are part of the process of development. It is really the Safeguards that have driven this because without this I would not have been able to demonstrate how we involve young people in decision making."

This involvement can also be achieved through more informal engagement, for example:

> "Probably the most interesting part of our work is that the way in which we reach out to children is through volunteers from the communities in which the children live. So the children are reached out to by young people who live and work and share the same space, the same social space, as the children that they are working with. What we are trying to do is to build enough critical mass within the community, through children and through youth, to enable a certain kind of social change to happen and to enable what we call control and choice in their lives."
>
> (International deliverer)

This can also be encouraged through employing modern and innovative methods of communication:

> "In this day and age, notice boards have been replaced with Facebook and Twitter. So, it is about reacting to the best way in which you can communicate with your young people."
>
> (National governor)

The genuine involvement of children was also achieved through the creation of formal roles. These roles were variously called Youth Leaders, Peer Leaders, Peer Liaison Officer or Health and Well-being Officer. For instance, one of the international sport for development organisation supports young people to develop their leadership, conflict management and advocacy skills through appointing "Youth Leaders." The Youth Leaders take part in clubs which work to raise awareness on how to safeguard children amongst parents, schools and the community. These Youth Leaders also sit on event organising committees through which the children were able to make a genuine impact. For example, for one event, Youth leaders were observed making several points about the safety implications of particular decisions. This included points on the potential physicality of some games, the potential time spent standing in the sun and the likelihood of disputes arising from competitiveness. These concerns led to changes in the plans and procedures associated with the event. Speaking on the significance of involving children in safeguarding, a staff member said, "It is a big piece for us and it's very important. For me children's participation is the bread and butter of what we care about in so many ways."

Another organisation employed girls as Peer Leaders to help promote healthy sexual choices. In order to support the girls to fulfil these roles, the organisation hosts an initial training camp to introduce these roles, and provide them with the necessary knowledge and skills to be effective. This is then followed up six months later with an advanced training camp which offers an opportunity for reflection, knowledge consolidation and further development. One girl highlighted the benefit of this approach in saying, "I learned a lot because I have learnt about some rights that I didn't know about."

The girls are also given roles which have welfare responsibilities. For example, during training camps for peer educators, each class has an assigned Peer Welfare Lead. This person is responsible for helping to ensure young girls' rights are not violated during the camp. The Peer Welfare Lead is also a designated person to report any issues or concerns in the instance that they are unable or unwilling to discuss the matter with a member of staff. This approach helps to safeguard children and young people through engaging those children and young people. Participants highlighted the importance of having alternative avenues through which children can disclose concerns, "Once the girl is not ready to share with the field leader she can share with the team captain who can sit with the committee and share the information."

A Senior Executive from the organisation emphasised how these various strategies help to demonstrate the organisational commitment to safeguard children as well as to engage children in this safeguarding, "It really reinforces the message that the care and protection for them is a priority for us, and that it's something we want them to be involved in." A Head of Child Protection emphasised the need for the nature of any participation to be genuine:

> "You see in a lot of organisations it's a tokenistic declaration where children are engaged but they are not active in the decision-making process and they are not actually contributing to the change because they

> are not given that opportunity. So, for us, in any work we do, we want to ensure that if we are asking children something [about the program], then they know where the information is going and what we are doing with it and how they themselves are actively contributing to positive change and decision making."

9.3 Impacts of the International Safeguards

The impact of this project was discussed in terms of the Self-Audit Tool and Activation States in Chapters 7 and 8, respectively. Beyond this, participants identified a range of other impacts of this project and these are summarised in this section. As organisations started working towards the International Safeguards, participants unanimously reported an associated increase in the number of disclosures of safeguarding concerns in their organisation. This may be as a result of the implementation of relevant policy and procedures to manage cases, increased awareness and confidence in the system as well as an increase in the knowledge and skills of the people to whom disclosures were being made. One participant shared a similar experience to that described by many other participants:

> "We have certainly seen behaviour change in terms of disclosures. This has been in two ways. Firstly this has been through survivors coming forward. Before they did not have the language or confidence to speak. The Safeguards empower them and give them a voice. Secondly, other people are reporting concerns much earlier in the process. Before people may have thought, well, no one else is saying anything so I won't but now they have been validated."

Encouraging these disclosures, and critically ensuring that appropriate support is in place for everyone involved, will hopefully result in the safeguarding of more children. Evidence was also found of this project directly impacting the experiences of children. In a focus group, children talked about their experiences at their school, which was not part of the International Safeguards project. They said:

> "I worry about how hard I will be hit."
>
> "I worry about if the teacher will be bored of me and hit me."
>
> "I am worried that the teacher might hit me where I already have a wound."

However, when talking about their participation in a programme which was delivered by an organisation working towards the International Safeguards, all of the children said that they felt safe. The children all said that they felt confident in talking to any members of staff on the programme if they ever did have any concerns.

Through the project, participants discussed how they had observed changes in the ways in which people interacted with children. Helping people to develop and maintain healthy relationships with children should in turn contribute to the safeguarding of those children. In one sport for development agency, a significant reduction in incidents of corporal punishment was observed. This was perceived to be associated with an increase in the use of questioning techniques by teachers during interactions with children. One member of staff at the agency observed:

> "They tell us that they have changed the way they respond to children. So for example if there's a naughty child they are not so quick to punish, they try to understand their behaviour and cover all angles."

This represented a significant change in attitude and behaviour. Further reflecting on their work in detention centres through their programme, a member of staff from the agency explained:

> "If you go to the centres you will see some of it, the interaction level, particularly with youth in conflict . . . you are worthless, you are nothing, you are the trouble and you are a problem with society. The interaction was showing when we first saw them. It was so negative. But then when we worked with them with the coaching practices we see that has changed. The interaction level. There's an emotional safety for youth and now they feel they are someone they feel like they are something and they can be someone after they get out of this."

Another participant described how the training of coaches had helped to safeguard children both within and outside of the organisation:

> "One way in which our involvement with the Safeguards has impacted children is through our provision of first aid. As part of the self-audit, we reviewed our injury log. We identified that the kinds of injuries being suffered were not really being addressed by our training for coaches. We adapted the curriculum to include foot and spinal injuries, which are both prevalent in our society. The coaches really liked this as they could transfer these skills back into the community, such as dealing with road traffic accident injuries. This may appear tangential to the Safeguards but it came about as a result of our involvement in this project and has helped to better safeguard the children in our organisation."

Working towards the International Safeguards also helped to safeguard children through raising awareness amongst parents:

> "Since starting the project we are now trying to create a more friendly atmosphere for the children. We are communicating with parents much

better on what the children are going to be doing. Parents did not really have any concept of child protection before this project."

(National Deliverer)

This was then believed to have a broader impact:

"The more they get into the culture that, you know, my child is receiving this level of protection, the more it begins to leak into their personal lives."

This impact also had an unexpected benefit for the organisation:

"It has actually proved a good marketing tool. Parents now look to see if the safeguards are in place before letting their children join."

This illustrates the argument that effective safeguarding is not just about preventing negative outcomes, but it also has the potential to have significant positive outcomes for an organisation, such as in relation to increased participation rates. The impact was also perceived to go beyond sport to impact other areas of the organisation. For example:

"What has been interesting is that the impact has gone beyond sport. It has also impacted our work on participation, the use of the media and our other clubs for children."

The impact also extended to key figures within the community. For instance, one participant described the following case:

"We had an issue in one community where a young girl had been sexually abused by her brother. Usually in those situations, if you have engaged sexually with someone, you have to marry them, otherwise it angers the gods. The elder in the community had been involved in the safeguarding work for some time and he decided that they would do something different, sacrifice something else to the rain god and they would get the girl some support. So she wasn't forced to marry her brother. She was provided support, she was given counselling and connected with other people and she kept being involved in the programme for social support."

9.4 Summary

This chapter has provided an overview of the CHILDREN Pillars, which were developed based on the findings of the research project. The CHILDREN Pillars represent a comprehensive yet easily comprehendible conceptualisation of the factors which facilitate progress towards the International Safeguards. Having presented the CHILDREN Pillars, this chapter discussed the significance of genuine engagement with children, the impact that these factors had on the amount of disclosures received, children's perceptions of safety and interactions with key stakeholders, such as parents and children.

References

Braun, V., & Clarke, V. (2006). Using thematic analysis in psychology. *Qualitative Research in Psychology*, *3*, 77–101.

Fullan, N. (2007). *The new meaning of educational change*. New York: Teachers College Press.

Chapter 10

Cultural sensitivity

The first pillar that underpinned the implementation of the International Safeguards was Cultural Sensitivity. This relates to an awareness that there are cultural similarities and differences which need to be taken into account at all times when working towards the International Safeguards. It is important to emphasise here that these similarities and differences are not assigned a value in terms of being right or wrong, good or bad, better or worse.

The implementation of global intervention measures face a clear tension between fidelity and adaptation (Castro, Barrera, & Martinez, 2004). Fidelity concerns the implementation of a programme as designed by the developer, whereas adaptation relates to how the programme may be revised to meet the needs of the given group (Castro et al., 2004). Interventions that are culturally blind are likely to have a limited impact (Kumpfer, Alvarado, Smith, & Bellam, 2002). The programme adaptation approach has particularly been developed in the context of community-based health promotion interventions which advocate user participation of all stages of the programme from development, through implementation to evaluation (Minkler & Wallerstein, 2003). Cultural adaptation is therefore a key consideration when considering the implementation of an intervention in different contexts (Marsiglia & Booth, 2015).

Successful policy implementation depends on a range of political, social, economic and organisational factors which interact to create a unique context (McLaughlin, 1987). As a result, a focus on developing generic solutions can lead to ineffective and incoherent policy implementation (Marsiglia & Booth, 2015). Cultural sensitivity thus emphasises that these contextual factors merit consideration. An Educational Strategist of an international organisation who deliver sport for development programmes highlighted how a lack of policy and attitudinal coherence creates circumstances in which cultural sensitivity plays a critical role:

> "Many of the contexts are not either legally or attitudinally in line with many of the taken for granted principles or the agreed rhetoric in the developed world. So therefore we have laws that are not aligned and we have cultural and engrained attitudes that are not aligned with them."

This was supported by a national representative of a partner child rights organisation who highlighted that cultural sensitivity is important, irrespective of the developmental stage of the given country:

> "To ensure that protection is part of or the pillar of sport you need to make sure you actually understand the environment that you are in, and it doesn't matter if it's a developed country or a developing country."

A similar view was expressed by local coaches in Zanzibar, who stated that the philosophies and cultural views of people who live in the developed world are often extremely different to the views of people in countries like theirs. Consequently, coaches admitted feeling some anxiety about the application of the International Safeguards on the grounds that it may engender western ideological superiority and be implemented aggressively, with little considerations for their beliefs on such matters. A national representative of a partner child rights organisation gave one explanation of this apprehension with the following quote,

> "Child rights and child participation is recognised as a very new and a very western concept . . . this idea is a western idea or is for mzungus [white people] who don't know the realities of the world."

The International Safeguards were developed to provide a guiding framework which retained an appropriate level of flexibility such that implementation could be tailored to the characteristics of the given context. Such tailoring was observed to enhance a sense of ownership amongst the key stakeholders which in turn contributed to a more meaningful and impactful adoption of the International Safeguards.

10.1 Key issues

At the fundamental level, most countries have signed up to the UNCRC. The UNCRC is the most ratified human rights treaty in the world. By signing the treaty, nations indicate their commitment to recognize children's dignity and healthy development as a fundamental right, as well as to incorporate the provisions into national law. Signees also agree to provide institutions and mechanisms to ensure children's rights are met and protected. There are three general categories of rights under the UNCRC: 1. Rights of provision, 2. Rights of protection and 3. Rights of participation. Each of these have relevance to the sports context. The UNCRC is the only legally binding framework with the aim of protecting children in sport.

- Article 19 states that everyone has the responsibility to protect all children from all forms of harm, abuse, neglect and exploitation;
- Article 31 expresses every child's right to participate in play and recreational activities.

Despite this global standard, there remains significant variance in the social norms relevant to children. It is important that such norms are understood and recognised as the International Safeguards are developed, implemented and evaluated within specific organisations and the contexts in which that organisation operates. Examples of the dimensions along which different contexts can vary are outlined in the following sections and illustrated with participant quotes.

10.1.1 Recognition of child maltreatment

When one is working to safeguard children in sport, an important first step is a shared understanding as to what constitutes child maltreatment. The conceptualisation of child maltreatment differed throughout the organisations and contexts involved in this research. As a result, child maltreatment may not be recognised in some contexts. The following examples illustrate different conceptualisations of what is meant by 'child' and 'childhood' as well as what is perceived to be normal and appropriate in terms of how people interact with children.

> "With the International Safeguards there's a baseline assumption that everyone agrees that child protection is a good thing, so the International Safeguards has itself a solid foundation where those things are in place . . . but we are working in places where those things are not in place. There's FGM, it's legal to hit kids amongst other things."
>
> (International Deliverer)

> "In some countries, some forms of abuse are just accepted. A colleague was telling me that a 14-year-old girl was raped by her uncle. Her mother had said that next time he needs to make sure he wears a condom. Actually, no, there should not be a next time. There needs to be a complete attitude change."
>
> (International Governor)

> "I think that the main thing is the way in which we understand issues of child protection in the country. So, while everybody seems to agree in principle that children are vulnerable and should not be abused in any kind of drastic way, no sexual abuse or anything like that. Here, for example, scolding children is not necessarily seen as abuse. Or, having a child run around a field five times is not seen as a problem, you know, or stand in the sun. I mean, these are all things that have been done to us while we were in school."
>
> (National Deliverer)

In such contexts, children may come to view abusive practices as normal:

> "It is about the normalisation of child abuse. Lots of children are hit by their parents in this country. Now some of this would be a brutal beating but some of it would be perceived as the norm. It is also perceived by the children as the norm, especially if their peers are suffering the same. We may perceive it as abuse, but they probably do not, that child would probably not feel abused. It is very complicated, a lot of these things are relative."
>
> (International Governor)

Specific challenges around cultural norms were identified regarding the experiences of girls:

> "There is a lot to do with gender because how a lot of the cultures that we are working in treat women is very different, particularly in relation to young people. So, for example, our regional manager went to deliver some training to girls in youth centres. Normally those girls are looking after their siblings so that their parents can go out to work."
>
> (International Governor)

Other challenges regarding the safeguarding of girls were identified:

> "We are working in parts of (country name omitted) where 100% of the girls are subject to female genital mutilation. So we are having to be sensitive to cultural issues whilst still holding true to Article 19 of the United Nations' Convention on the Rights of the Child."
>
> (International Deliverer)

> "In this community we have a lot of sexual abuse, girls that are dropping out of school because they are pregnant, or the school does not allow them to come back because they are a bad example. Sometimes it is the parents who do not allow the girls to go to school because they are ashamed or they decide that the girl should marry. So there are those things which are happening within the organisation but there are also things which are happening outside of the organisation. Sometimes these things overlap a lot and this is another challenge because we sometimes forget on what we are focusing."
>
> (Local Deliverer)

This point is also relevant to governor organisations working with members in a range of cultural contexts. What is considered to be safeguarding can vary across personnel and member organisations, as explained by a senior member of staff for an international federation:

> "When I first mention safeguarding, people asked what does safeguarding actually mean. Some people link it in with anti-doping. This is a high priority for some of our members. For others this is considered as a low risk and so that is not a major issue. Then in terms of health and safety. We went to one of our members recently and there was a concrete court. There were not the run-off areas [that we recommend] if you had presented that to someone in the UK then they would have said, no way, we are not playing; whereas this was a really good [facility] for that region."

It is therefore important to have an open discussion to develop a shared understanding as to what constitutes maltreatment, abuse, violence and exploitation. Once this is recognised, it is then necessary to consider how people should respond.

10.1.2 Responding to child maltreatment

In working towards the International Safeguards, there is a need to consider how to respond to concerns about child maltreatment. Participants identified that even when people are able to recognise child maltreatment, they may not take any action. This was discussed with respect to a general denial that maltreatment and abuse in particular did actually take place in their sport or the broader community. For example, during a workshop on safeguarding in the Caribbean, staff members stated that child protection and abuse are taboo topics. One deliverer said:

> "Child protection is taboo in the Caribbean in general, things like religion play a big factor and people don't want to acknowledge these things."

Another staff member at another event said, "people do not like discussing such things" and went on to explain that the failure to discuss such issues has encouraged the belief that they simply do not occur in the region. Indeed, three sports deliverers argued that child protection is not a particular concern for the Caribbean.

Coaches in some rural areas of Africa also argued that another reason for the hesitance to report cases is the fear of being gossiped about within the community. Coaches explained that in their small society everyone knows everyone, therefore people tend to keep their issues within their family unit to ensure that they do not become the talk of the neighbourhood. A government official spoke of this, suggesting that this is an issue for prosecuting offenders, though is typical for such rural African communities.

> "We live in this kind of African society. We know each other and everyone speaks a lot. Unlike (British society) where everyone has his own business, so if it's yours, it's yours and your neighbours are not aware. Here we live in a community where anything that happens everybody knows. So, people are hesitating in sharing information."

Another local coach said:

> "It's because of culture, we feel shy to say it . . . there's a huge embarrassment because all people in the community will be looking at me and saying . . . oh you have had this done to you. That is one of the reasons."

10.1.3 The culture of the sport

As well as considering the context at the political and social levels, participants described how the culture within their sport represented an important factor to consider. This concerned the nature of the relationships which are developed as well as the practices which are viewed as normal and acceptable. A National Governor illustrated this point as follows:

> "I think that there is the general resistance to change. A lot of the things that we have done have asked our membership to change, not significantly but it is so much embedded in the culture of sport that things are familial and familiar and so to bring on a bunch of rules and background checks and hiring practices and all of these things that feel a lot more desk-jobby, for want of a better phrase, or that we are all skeptical of each other or that we are going to tell on each other, I think that people did not like that because it felt inconsistent with the reasons that they love and connect with sport."

The priorities of an organisation may also create a culture which may be resistant to working towards the International Safeguards. An International Governor cited the recent example of a high-profile case:

> "I keep referring back to Penn State [sex abuse case] but it seems as though they had a culture which prioritized protecting the organisation over the children."

There are also challenges in terms of working with coaches who are perceived to be very effective but were also viewed to be acting inappropriately:

> "I'll give you an example. We have been working with a coach for years who is very dynamic. He is very good at motivating people and is a very

good football coach and was very good at getting over the HIV messages. We realized though that he made very sexist remarks about the older girls in his team such as once people are not virgins anymore then they will never do what you say. He also made a pass at another NGO worker. Which is pretty much par for the course, he was not a particularly nasty piece of work. It just opens your eyes because if he is doing this that I know about, what is he doing with the older girls?"

It is fundamental to develop a good understanding of the complex safeguarding context which arises from the interaction of different cultures at the national, community, sport and organisational level. The recognition of child maltreatment, as well as the challenges with respect to responding appropriately and changing the culture of the sport all merit consideration. Without such understanding, the prospects for making sustainable impacts through the International Safeguards are likely to be limited.

10.2 Promising practice

Through the research, strategies which can help to facilitate cultural sensitivity were identified. These strategies helped to promote the tailoring of the International Safeguards to the given context as well as a pragmatic approach. This helped to ensure that the International Safeguards were implemented in a culturally sensitive way.

10.2.1 Tailoring to the context

The need to allow flexibility within the International Safeguards to enable people to shape implementation to their context was found to be a really effective approach which helped to overcome some initial resistance to change. The following quotes from the start of the project illustrate concerns around this initial resistance:

> "My main concern is that we could come out of this process with a beautifully written document but is it any more useful on the ground? Are we actually any better off than we were before? I think that the people in the countries we work in will be even more cynical than I am and this does not help when you are trying to facilitate change."
>
> (International Governor)

> "We did not want what I call a filing cabinet system. Something which on paper looks perfect but it did not necessarily address the real issues for the people with whom you are working. We wanted to develop something which had real impact in the communities in which we are working."
>
> (International Deliverer)

Participants highlighted that the success of this project is based on the ability to localise the International Safeguards in order to make a real impact. This was highlighted by participants working at both the international and national level:

> "Localisation is key: you really have to try and adapt things to suit the context where you are working."
>
> (National Governor)

> "You have to really understand and embrace the local context. What is the age of consent? Can you speak to local people in local communities? What is the local infrastructure to train up people to talk to local communities?. . . as they will relate much more than a foreigner coming in and doing that."
>
> (International Governor)

Whilst the importance of localisation was acknowledged, significant challenges were highlighted when trying to implement this effectively:

> "I have three challenges globally: translation, translation, translation. We make way too many things in English. This leads to resistance when you put something in English in front of a coach from another country, in a way it is a slight, an insult. There would be pushback there if it is not translated."
>
> (International Governor)

> "There is a tension that I deal with every day. We have our general rules which we apply locally. They are so general that they have no meaning. To do something for all of the different cultures, that is a lot of work. If you offer best practice then everyone understands those examples."
>
> (International Governor)

Cultural sensitivity can therefore be promoted through striking a balance between the standardised information which is provided and the flexibility which is afforded for the International Safeguards to be adapted to a given context. This is encapsulated in the following quote:

> "In terms of the Safeguards, it is really comprehensive but, speaking from the field, is that Standard contextualized appropriately to the field context? Every country is different and it is very difficult to have one Standard that can cover all because you have to consider the unique contexts of each country. What is useful is that you create this structure for us in terms of safeguarding children in sport, but in terms of the details, is there any flexibility? Is there a minimum standard that if you

> are in this context then you need to meet this minimum standard. Then there should be the flexibility, I hope, to contextualize the Safeguards."
>
> (International Deliverer)

Cultural sensitivity can also be manifested in a practical sense in terms of how people work on the ground:

> "Coaches should create a safe space and recognize that cultural norms influence both practice and expectations but consider them carefully to ensure that children's rights are protected. If something happens which would be culturally normal for that setting, we have to balance up whether you actually create more problems by addressing it in the way in which you would address it in the west. That is a judgment call which does not have the precision that many people may want from policies but it is the only way we can find to address complexity."
>
> (International Deliverer)

10.2.2 Pragmatism

The use of cultural sensitivity also extended to adopting a pragmatic approach to safeguarding. Participants described how taking safeguarding to the extreme may mean that no sport would actually take place. A balance therefore needs to be found such that children are safeguarded as far as possible, given the constraints of the context. One participant who was a director in an international sport for development organisation explained:

> "I think it's important to establish safety . . . I think if you went by the rules, 90% of the programmes around the world couldn't run . . . a lot of the fields wouldn't pass British or American standards of safety. For example, children having no shoes and playing on fields that have no grass, in my logical world when I am sitting in England those children should not be allowed to play. We would class it as not being safe. However, in the locally owned programmes some play with shoes and the majority don't play with shoes. So, we have to be very much aware of local issues when we determine what this word safe means."

The general consensus was that safeguarding should be culturally sensitive and involve a strong degree of cultural realism, taking into account the challenges of the given context. For example, sports delivery staff in the Caribbean discussed the inevitability of facilities being somewhat dangerous due to the terrain, or a lack of safety equipment such as helmets. One Senior Official from the Sports Division said, "The terrain is often a lower image of the mountains; there are a lot of rocks on it and a lot of wear and tear." Ministers argued that this is a natural challenge of safeguarding within the Caribbean. It was also discussed as a catalyst to the speed at which equipment can deteriorate. In conjunction with a lack of resources to continuously update facilities and equipment, officials believed having the resources, equipment and the facilities to safely deliver sports provision is a substantial challenge. As such deliverers were wary of foreigners who come in to offer safety based advice without acknowledging such constraints.

10.3 Case study: Coaches Across Continents

Coaches Across Continents (CAC) is an international sport for development organisation that trains and educates local coaches in developing countries. CAC achieves this through year-round support for partner organisations and one-week long training events. The approach adopted by CAC is fundamentally based on cultural sensitivity.

CAC utilises a self-directed learning approach which is about asking critical questions and facilitating conversations that allow participants to gain their own ideas and solutions. Speaking on this approach, the CAC Executive Strategist said:

> "For us it's not about coming in and saying well you must do this, instead we are working in partnership so we view and question their cultures and traditions. They have to buy in and say, yes this is important and is a good way to go forward, not just . . . well my dad hit me and I turned out fine."

CAC's Education Strategist explained:

> "Our learning model is not one of pouring information into people's heads. We consciously seek to encourage participatory learning. That leads to value judgements about a safe learning environment."

The Global Strategist said:

> "Our biggest thing is that we create self-directed learners and we have the ability to look at situations and learners and create various solutions. They identify their social issues and where they would like to be in the coming years, they then use our games and resources to help them to get there."

CAC believes that when it comes to child rights and child protection training, organisations typically focus on classroom workshops to the neglect of how it may be applied on the field of play. One founder said:

> "I think one of the issues with sport for development is that people don't invest enough time on the field. They think that is the easy part and it's not, that's actually the hardest part and it has the most impact."

This view is also accompanied with the suggestion that, "Some just haven't had the skills to work with children in ways which don't involve violence." Therefore, CACs child protection training seeks to combine the lessons learnt in classroom workshops with practical development given to coaches on the field of play. This allows participants to apply the lessons learnt in child protection training. CAC's Global Strategist argued that:

> "It's not just about organisational structure it's about people. So many western organisations have to sign things and it goes into a cabinet, but it's still not happening on the field. So it's the personal buy in, but also having the skills to conduct those programmes without abuse. Many people don't have the skills."

CAC recognises that in the environments that they deliver, formally written policies are not always valued and appreciated as much as personal pledges, which are viewed as a sign of honour. As such each child protection workshop involves the communal formulation of a list of pledges and each coach is asked to agree to them. Agreement is indicated by signing their name on the paper that the pledges were initially written on, but more importantly shaking the hand of a CAC member of staff as they look them in the eyes and verbally agree to the pledge. CAC is aware that violating this pledge does not bear any legal consequence as it is not a legally binding document. Nonetheless, throughout the training event, and, before the programme ends, coaches are reminded of the pledge they have made and are asked to bear that pledge in mind as they deliver sport to children in their community. Through combining these different strategies, CAC promotes change at the cognitive, emotional and behavioural levels. This facilitates more sustainable change which is more likely to impact the experiences of the children with whom the staff of the partner organisations interact.

10.4 Summary

This chapter presents the first of the CHILDREN Pillars, cultural sensitivity. It has presented evidence of the significance of cultural sensitivity and cultural realism when implementing the International Safeguards. Some of the key issues are discussed. This includes variances in the definition and recognition of child maltreatment, responses to child maltreatment and the culture of the sport itself. Also included in this chapter are examples of strategies which can help to facilitate cultural sensitivity. These strategies focus on tailoring the International Safeguards to the contexts, and being pragmatic. More specific evidence of the significance, of cultural sensitivity, and how it may be it may be achieved in practice is discussed through the case study of the international sport for the development organisation Coaches Across Continents.

References

Castro, F. G., Barrera, M., Jr., & Martinez, C. R. (2004). The cultural adaptation of preventive interventions: Resolving tensions between fidelity and fit. *Prevention Science*, *5*, 41–45.

Kumpfer, K. L., Alvarado, R., Smith, P., & Bellamy, N. (2002). Cultural sensitivity and adaptation in family-based prevention interventions. *Prevention Science*, *3*, 241–246.

Marsiglia, F. F., & Booth, J. M. (2015). Cultural adaptation of interventions in real practice settings. *Reaching in Social Work Practice*, *25*(4), 423–432.

McLaughlin, M. (1987). Learning from experience: Lessons from policy implementation. *Educational Evaluation and Policy Analysis*, *0*(2), 171–178.

Minkler, M., & Wallerstein, N. (2003a). *Community-based participatory research for health*. San Francisco, CA: Jossey-Bass.

Chapter 11

Holistic

The second CHILDREN pillar was labelled Holistic. It suggests that safeguarding should be viewed as integrated into all aspects of an organisation as opposed to being an additional element. Many influential organisations have advocated for a systematic approach to protecting children. UNICEF, UNHRC, Save the Children, and World Vision (2013) have defined safeguarding systems as "certain formal and informal structures, functions and capacities that have been assembled to prevent and respond to violence, abuse, neglect, and exploitation of children" (p. 3). Based on the Convention on the Rights of the Child, the systems approach moves away from a focus on single issues (e.g., sexual exploitation or child labor) in order to facilitate a holistic rather than a fragmented approach. It aims to safeguard children through promoting supportive mechanisms as well as preventing abuse, exploitation and violence. The essence of a holistic approach is encapsulated in the following quote from the Head of Safeguarding for a local deliverer in Europe:

> "My mantra has always been that safeguarding is a thread and not a blanket. In some organisations that you go to you end up seeing a blanket that is shrouded over everything and covered by reams of paper and policies. That is not to say that we do not have policies or paperwork, they are threaded through the business. Safeguarding is not something that you should physically see in your face, it is something that is subtly positioned throughout the organisation, whether it is people, whether it is posters, people know that it is there."

Adopting a holistic approach should help to avoid a reliance on specific people and vulnerability when people leave the organisation:

> "When you have good structures in place, you can have turnover, you can have people come and go because there's a fall back. There's something that exists for them to either learn from or to use or to reference. I mean, ideally you have really good structures and really good people,

but if you have really good people and no structures you're not going to be in any position to impact things."

11.1 Key issues

As emphasised throughout this book, safeguarding is a multi-faceted issue with a range of complex interacting factors. This research found that progress was more readily observed when a holistic approach was adopted. Examples of this are now considered to illustrate the influence of external factors (i.e., those outside of the organisation), interacting factors (i.e., those at the intersection between the work of the organisation and the broader context) and internal factors (i.e., those concerning the operationalisation of safeguarding within the organisation).

11.1.1 External factors

Governments clearly play an important role in shaping the context within which safeguarding takes place in a country. This context is created, for example, through the legislative landscape, the conditions attached to government funding and the systems which are implemented to conduct criminal background checks or manage safeguarding concerns. Participants who worked in a variety of countries described how operating within different legislative landscapes creates challenges. For example:

> "This is another challenge that we have, we can have rules but they are not strictly followed in all parts of the world. Every country has different laws and requirements for coaches."
>
> (International Governor)

> "In some countries, everything is much legalised. You have to do certain things or you do not get funding. From this through to where there is nothing in place and the fact that this represents a whole new way of thinking."
>
> (International Governor)

For some participants, the complete lack of a national policy with respect to safeguarding children in general created difficulties when trying to work in a holistic way. For example, government officials in the Caribbean acknowledged that the absence of a policy of safeguarding greatly limits the work that can be done. A senior member of staff suggested that in the absence of safeguarding policy, arbitration occurs with great difficulty, and there is little to convince organisations that safeguarding is to be taken seriously. Government officials also argued that it is difficult to encourage the public to take safeguarding seriously without policies and procedures from above. They also expressed an understanding that organisations and deliverers have little basis upon which to develop their policies and practices on without this broader guiding framework. One government official explained:

> "Policy is really a challenge because without the policy you are acting on your own and you are at the mercies of consumers of sport. People can either accept what you are doing or not, but if there's policy that guides what you should do then it becomes a lot easier."

When national policies are in place, it can be of a generic nature rather than being specifically focused on the context of sport. For instance, a Government official in Africa explained:

> "In terms of written policy in sports, we don't have any that demonstrate clearly but we are promoting the rights of children generally."

The absence of a national policy means that deliverers of sport are given very limited domain specific knowledge or guidance on safeguarding children in sport. During a workshop with coaches in Africa, the coaches expressed that they are motivated to do more in regard to safeguarding, but feel they don't always have the support to do so. The coaches explained that Government support is necessary to validate and enhance their child protection work and ensure people do not merely dismiss them as going beyond their role. With reference to the role of Governments, the coaches said:

> "We need action, talking is not enough" and "These things might help people to wake up."

When broader policies or legislation is in place, challenges were reported when there was a lack of coherence between these frameworks and those of the organisation. In other words, certain behaviours may be legal according to the laws in a country but not adhere to the policies of an organisation. For example, one International Deliverer said: "I was shocked a few years ago in one of the countries in which we work because the law makers had just passed a rule that it was ok to hit children with a stick." This Executive Strategist when on to explained:

> "When you start dealing with coaches . . . whose laws are different to ours in terms of when people can marry, or where corporal punishment is still allowed . . . you wonder how the International Safeguards are implemented."

The following scenario serves to highlight the complexities of trying to adopt a holistic approach:

> "We had one situation which illustrates the difficulties we are facing. One of our coaches also worked as a Physical Education teacher in a local school. The school policy permitted this teacher to use corporal punishment. However, this was against our organisation's safeguarding policy. So, you have the same adult and the same child interacting on the same day. Corporal punishment is permitted before 3pm in the school context but is against our policy when they are interacting throughout our sporting activities in the evening."

Any efforts to safeguard children therefore need to acknowledge and adapt to the constraints and opportunities offered by the given context. They need to, as far as possible, be coherent with the legislative and policy context to ensure that a coherent approach is implemented.

11.1.2 Interactional factors

Issues were identified in terms of the definition and scope of safeguarding in sport. A lack of consistency in this area created challenges for organisations trying to work in a holistic way. For example, in one context, officials from the Department of Health discussed safeguarding in relation to the physiological appropriateness of individuals for physical activities. In contrast, the official from the Ministry of Sport discussed safeguarding in relation to having appropriate boundaries in the coach athlete relationship. The Department of Youth Services Official viewed safeguarding as ensuring that there are appropriate numbers of male and female coaches. This diverse conceptualisation of safeguarding can result in confusion and incoherence when these organisations try to work together. An important first step when such collaborations are established is to ensure that a consensus is reached in terms of the definition and scope of safeguarding for the given context.

A second identified issue was the management of safeguarding concerns when interacting with other organisations. While the International Safeguards recommend that organisations should have reporting systems in place, challenges were often experienced in ascertaining to whom to report concerns outside of the organisation. Participants argued that without recognised structures and systems within the community or country the effectiveness of safeguarding initiatives are somewhat limited. This can leave organisations in a very challenging situation when safeguarding concerns are identified.

Associated with the concerns around case management was the perception of the Police. For example:

> "There is a disconnect between local and government processes – often projects are well founded at community level but where there is a lack of structure at government level, it's difficult to know what to do when issues extend from a community capacity. At community level there is often a lack of trust in the Police."

Participants often discussed a lack of trust in the Police along with a lack of confidence that reporting any concerns would actually lead to action. Participants stated that often cases are not dealt with properly, particularly when the abuser has powerful associates or when the officer charged with investigating the issue is familiar with the alleged abuser. One local coach said:

> "They will say . . . oh you said it's him that did it? No, No, I know him he wouldn't do that! Or when he comes they will just talk to him and say . . . Don't do that again ok? Don't worry you go. That kind of thing."

11.1.3 Internal factors

Challenges when working with a holistic approach were also discussed within the organisation. Safeguarding measures were less impactful when they were seen as additional element of the work of the organisation as opposed to being central to the work being done. One Director of safeguarding for an International Deliverer explained:

> "Do not make people feel that this is extra. This does happen for us, even though we try to integrate it, people still see it as a segment. You know, they say here we go again with safeguarding. I have 10,000 other things to do. I have to develop curriculum and so on, but it is not new, you are already doing some of it. So you have to make them see that it is integrated and it is not extra work. We show them during training and we share experiences. It is on-going stuff for staff and it takes a long time."

Organisations therefore reported resistance when safeguarding measures such as a policy, procedures or training were separate from the reality of an individual's role. A lack of pragmatism was perceived to contribute to a lack of engagement with safeguarding. This section has shown that the holistic pillar calls for salient external, interacting and internal factors to be considered in an approach which encourages coherence where possible to ensure that safeguarding measures are complementary, as opposed to conflicting. The following section outlines some ways in which this was achieved by the pioneer organisations.

11.2 Promising practice

Some of the challenges discussed in the previous section are often perceived to be beyond the control of an organisation working in sport. However, progress can be made through advocating the need for change with key Government departments and other organisations in the community or country. Improved relationships with these organisations can also be facilitated through establishing working groups which can meet periodically to discuss safeguarding issues. These groups can include representatives from the sports organisation, the Police, local schools and other child protection agencies, for example, to share experiences, resources and good practice. Participants were able to observe particular progress when adopting a holistic approach within their organisation through implementing an integrated and embedded system.

11.2.1 Integrated

Participants reported that one important strategy was to work with the philosophy that safeguarding is integrated into every aspect of the organisation as opposed to being an additional component. This helped people to see the relevance of the safeguarding measures and to ensure a pragmatic approach which was more likely to impact behaviour. A local deliverer described their experience of using this approach:

> "We used to tag it on with different things. I have been here for three and a half years. When I came in it was very much this is coaching, this is welfare, this is safeguarding. By having these mixed up sessions it is getting people to understand that this is working with young people. You do not divide the categories. When you are working with young people you need to be aware of safeguarding. They are not separate entities. We get that message out from day one."

Another local deliverer described a similar experience:

> "We have had a really big shift. My work over the last three months has been working with the Board to show how things tie up with the coaches, the physios, the youth workers, so I can happily say now that I think we have got a good balance throughout the club."

This experience was also reported by governors. Through working with organisations, they observed how people started to see the ways in which safeguarding is integrated in all areas of operation:

> "What has been interesting is that when we have worked with organisations to develop their codes of conduct, they have themselves identified a need for clear policies regarding issues such as hiring and the specific action which will take place if the codes are not followed. When they see the initial success they can see the benefits of this kind of work in other areas. In truth, many of these areas are integrated with each other."
>
> (National Governor)

Achieving a fully integrated approach to safeguarding was viewed as the ultimate goal of one Director of Safeguarding:

> "What I would consider to be a really big win, is that the Safe Sport items are just woven in with everything else we are doing. It is not ringing an alarm, or it is not such a drag to say do not forget to think about safeguarding."

An integrated approach should therefore help to mitigate the risk that people view safeguarding as being simply an additional component and as core to the operations of the organisation.

11.2.2 Embedded

Another effective strategy to promote a holistic approach was to focus on embedding safeguarding strategies once these had been introduced. This ensures that safeguarding is evident at each stage from an individual's induction into the organisation, through the training and support which is offered to on-going measures to regularly reinforce the importance of safeguarding via messages tailored to that individual's role in the organisation (e.g., child, coach or parent).

By thinking holistically, people can go beyond viewing safeguarding as a series of independent measures to embed safeguarding as part of the culture of the organisation. A safeguarding culture of the organisation can be developed through specific activities, such as that described by an International Deliverer:

> "Everything that we do centres around team. So we have specific coach-child ratios and training around team-building. These are games which make everyone feel comfortable and that everyone has a voice. A team can present a negative place for things like hazing but it can also be positive. So everyone has a voice and access to an adult both formally and informally, such as during water breaks. We also ensure that there are at least two adults around. The very first training that we do with people is around team-building and having a positive culture. I guess that this is preventative, although it is not directly about safeguarding."

Once a strong safeguarding culture has been developed, it can be maintained and strengthened through reinforcing key messages. A powerful way of embedding the safeguarding culture was reported by participants working at all levels whose organisation's focused on retaining and developing children within the organisation such that they ultimately take on youth leader roles or work as a coach or member of staff in the future. An International Deliverer explained:

> "Having a clear culture and consistency with the same coaches, mentors and peers over time creates a really safe environment and so we

think that this is a way to keep the children emotionally and physically safe."

(International Deliverer)

Another participant working at the national level reported a similar experience:

> "A majority of the coaches in our organisation are participants who have graduated from the program through the years. We put them through various training modules and thus when they take up a coaching role, the importance and need for safeguarding children is embedded in them. This works to our advantage as we can completely trust our coaches who are the ones working with our participants at the grassroots levels on a daily basis."
>
> (National Deliverer)

This was also viewed as an effective strategy at the local level:

> "It is about building support structures around the programme so you have that a formal pathway from when you have a participant who comes in and you train them and then they become a young leader who mentors new participants. The young leader can then be trained to be a coach and so you have that pathway."
>
> (Local Deliverer)

Staff can then play an important role in terms of maintaining the safeguarding culture through, for example, challenging any behavior which is not in line with the safeguarding policies, procedures or practices of the organisation:

> "Once a clear culture is in place, new kids coming into it can sense it right away. We have had children come in who try to change the culture but we train our coaches on how to bring them into the fold to maintain the culture. This is an important piece."
>
> (International Deliverer)

This embedding can be facilitated through including safeguarding responsibilities in everyone's contract across the organisation. One International Deliverer is starting to use this strategy:

> "It's a new requirement to have at least 15% explicitly in the job description. It supports them to access different opportunities, shows they will be evaluated and allows us to ensure that we have the time to do it. Prior to this, in a lot of places 15% of the job time means that their job becomes 115%."

This helps to communicate that safeguarding is a part of everyone's job, rather than something that stops people from doing their job. One Head of Welfare at one of the clubs explained:

> "We are all of one mind-set, which is that it is our job to care, and to take most of the worries away."

The holistic approach can retain an element of flexibility to ensure that people expect the unexpected:

> "It's not perfect and I don't think it ever will be, but I'm always striving to embed systems into whatever we do . . . although the majority of your work is proactive, you recognise that sometimes things will go wrong and you have to be reactive."

11.3 Case study: the Caribbean Sport and Development Agency

The CSDA is a leading advocate and activist for sport for development (Sfd) in the Caribbean region. The CSDA works in collaboration with a plethora of local, national and international organisations in 13 member states under the umbrella organisations of the Caribbean Community (CARICOM) and the Organisation of Eastern Caribbean States (OECS). The CSDA positions themselves as a regional hub. They work with partners to support organisations and governments in the Caribbean region to advance their delivery and organisation of sport and recreation. This help is provided through policy development, capacity building, building safeguarding systems and by conducting research. The CSDA was selected as a case study for their work in facilitating a holistic approach across the region. Senior members of staff, implementers, affiliated governors, relevant government officials and both direct and indirect beneficiaries were all interviewed and the key findings are outlined below.

11.3.1 Developing a national policy

One of the most significant solutions was the CSDA's effort to bridge the policy and systems gap that hinders safeguarding in the Caribbean. Having lobbied and led discussions on Safeguarding in the Caribbean in the OECS and CARICOM, the CSDA encouraged Governments to develop national safeguarding policy. This is potentially a very significant step forward if this is achieved across the member states. This will provide the foundation for the advancement of safeguarding in the region and promote general awareness of safeguarding and the under-pinning principles. The CSDA also provides policy support to several non-governmental sport for development organisations within the Caribbean, while also working with Health, Education and Sport government departments to influence their policy creation and development. This co-ordinated effort can help to promote synergies as well as coherent policies which are well aligned.

11.3.2 SafeStamp

In a bid to ensure that organisations are taking steps to appoint suitable sports coaches that are appropriately trained without a criminal record, CSDA have developed a new system named SafeStamp. SafeStamp provides organisations with a registry containing information about implementers who have met the minimum standard of safeguarding. This makes them appropriate to work with children. This information includes whether individuals have attended safeguarding training, the results of their background checks and any self-declarations they have made. SafeStamp is supported by the Trinidad Directors of Sport as well as several regional sporting organisations marking a significant step in safeguarding children in sport and sport for development in the Caribbean. This regional approach may provide a solution to the issue of individuals, about whom there are safeguarding concerns, moving to a neighbouring island to continue working with children. This innovation was well received by stakeholders. For example, the owner of a sports club said:

> "SafeStamp is brilliant and it will feed into how we work with coaches in the future, it's an awesome plan."

11.3.3 Conference: Re-Defining Normal

A milestone on the journey towards the International Safeguards was the organising of a conference to bring all key stakeholders together to discuss safeguarding in sport. The CSDA called this conference 'Re-defining Normal.' This was a very apt title which highlighted the need for a fundamental cultural change. This event was attended by government officials, sports coaches and implementers of programmes across the region. The conference included presentations and workshops from various researchers and delivery staff in the region. Condensed versions of the safeguarding workshops which the CSDA provide were also delivered. Although it was initially intended to be a regional conference, it was attended by a total of 62 international delegates from a total of 15 countries worldwide. This demonstrated a significant step towards increased awareness, acknowledgement and pro-activity around safeguarding children in sport in the Caribbean and beyond.

The CSDAs safeguarding workshops provide evidence of a ground-breaking campaign to build the capacity of those involved in sport regionally and increase their awareness of safeguarding. This is open to all organisations in the region and the only criterion is that the organisation is working with children, using sport directly or indirectly. The introduction to safeguarding workshop in particular has been delivered in a total of six member states with over 130 deliverers, co-ordinators and ministers taking part. This also includes five attendees from Nevis who worked exclusively with children with special needs and received tailored workshops.

The holistic approach to safeguarding was illustrated through the use of workshops to build capacity. Individuals who received training from the CSDA are responsible for disseminating the information back to their own organisation. Dominica provides a perfect example of this as the delivery staff that have received safeguarding training have been working on Engage 360 for four years and have contributed to its integration into their schools Physical Education programme. A Senior Officer from the Ministry of Sport in Dominica discussed the success of this training, stating that more than ever coaches are reporting things that they would have failed to report previously. Similarly, in the focus groups with deliverers in Trinidad and Tobago, it was said that "[w]e didn't really think about safeguarding, but now we are so much more aware and that's important."

11.3.4 Building capacity in partner organisations

Through its various avenues of work, CSDA has effectively encouraged growth in its partner organisations by working in partnership to ensure that collaborations are in line with the International Safeguards. For example, when speaking about how CSDA have helped their organisation to develop and implement a safeguarding policy, one sports coach said:

> "They helped us to set up a child protection policy and generally helped to build our organisation, I'm not sure what we would have done without them."

Similarly, when speaking about gaining funding, and facilitating effective partnerships that may ensure organisations can grow by engaging with other experts in the field, another sports coach said:

> "They have encouraged us, and help us with funding or forums like this and we get a lot of exposure through them so they have really helped us."

Additionally, in a focus group with various stakeholders, the owner of a sports club said:

> "They are doing such good work with child protection, it feels like they are one step ahead of some of the other organisations."

11.4 Summary

The present chapter has discussed the second pillar, the need for sporting organisations to approach safeguarding in a holistic manner. The key issues of this pillar are discussed. This includes external factors, such as national or regional policy and legislation. This is coupled with discrepancies which may occur as organisations work in collaboration or when organisations work outside of their ordinary nation or region. These issues can create great difficulty, although some solutions which are discussed include integrating and embedding safeguarding throughout the organisation. Another potential solution is for organisations to take a leading role in ensuring that the elements which hinder holistic implementation of safeguarding are removed or their impact is lessened. Examples of this are offered with the illustrative example of the CSDA, which helped build the capacity of partner organisations, took a leading role in the development of a national policy on safeguarding, developed the SafeStamp registry for deliverers to be used throughout their region, hosted a regional conference and took a leading role in developing the capacity of various partner organisations.

Reference

UNICEF, UNHRC, Save the Children & World Vision. (2013). *A better way to protect all children: The theory and practice of child protection.* New Delhi, India: UNICEF.

Chapter 12

Incentives

The third CHILDREN pillar concerns incentives. There needs to be a clear reason for individuals and an organisation to work towards the Safeguards. This pillar therefore relates to the strategies which are used to motivate people to safeguard children within the organisation. As discussed in Chapter 1, there are a range of different rationales for the importance of safeguarding. The characteristics of the context, organisation and individual will shape the extent to which a given rationale has a significant influence on attitudes and behaviours towards safeguarding.

Incentives are required to initiate action and then to maintain momentum. Without such an incentive, progress can be challenging, as identified by a local deliverer:

> "This does not add money, it does not add impact. It can often create more work and more trouble because you are aware of things and how you ought to be doing something about it and the organisation may have to adapt."

This sentiment was echoed by a National governor:

> "If I am a national governing body, why would I want to operate with such standards? Why would I want to have a policy in place?' Especially if I am still getting funding without it . . ."

The importance of incentives when trying to promote safer practices has been highlighted by previous research. This has been shown in a range of industries, including healthcare (Parker, Lawrie & Hudson, 2006), oil manufacturing (Mearns, Whitaker & Flin, 2003; Filho, Andrade, & Marinho, 2010) and construction (Choudhry, Fang & Mohamed, 2007). In the present research, effective implementation was found to be associated with the facilitation of one of the two fundamental forms of motivation, intrinsic or extrinsic (Ryan & Deci, 2000). Participants often referred to these reasons as using either a 'carrot' (i.e., to foster intrinsic motivation) or a 'stick' (i.e., to foster extrinsic motivation) to encourage engagement in the process. With this label, a preference for a 'carrot' approach was evident:

> "It is a carrot versus stick thing. I like to use encouragement first and then if they are really not doing it then you can consider a stick or incentive, and an incentive is usually better than a punishment."
>
> (International Governor)

12.1 Key issues

Throughout this research project, important considerations were identified which are likely to be faced by other organisations working towards the International Safeguards. The following section provides a summary of the most pertinent and common issues discussed around the key topics of generating initial engagement and then sustaining this engagement.

12.1.1 Generating initial engagement

As with many organisations in sport, the majority of the participating organisations rely on volunteers to operate. These volunteers bring a wide variety of skills, knowledge and experience to their role. However, these volunteers will have limitations in terms of how much time they can contribute, as explained by the Chief Executive of an International Federation:

> "One of our key challenges is that outside of our small core team, we do not have any paid staff, they are all volunteers. They are all doing it on top of their day jobs."

As a result, the time that volunteers have to offer an organisation is inevitably limited, both in general terms and specific to safeguarding. This challenge is compounded by the fact that there is a myriad of demands being placed on this limited amount of time (e.g., helping with training sessions, organising events and club administration etc.). This can make it difficult to generate initial engagement with the International Safeguards.

Another consideration was the way in which safeguarding was perceived by these volunteers. Participants reported that safeguarding can be viewed as bureaucratic, time consuming and challenging. As a result, there were issues with respect to volunteers being resistant to safeguarding, and in taking on a safeguarding related role, due to the perceived amount of work that would be involved. The Chief Executive went on to explain:

> "The name is also important because there has been some jumpiness around calling the person the Safeguarding Lead. They are already busy volunteers and this makes it sound like a lot of work."

In taking on a safeguarding role, an individual can quickly become the perceived safeguarding expert without the necessary skills, knowledge or expertise. The volunteer nature of the participation of many people thus needs to be considered, specifically in terms of how motivation towards the International Safeguards is to be promoted. As volunteers will have a wide range of reasons for participation, a single strategy to motivate everyone may not be universally effective. As volunteers are more likely to be intrinsically motivated, as opposed to extrinsically motivated, the 'carrot' strategies, which tend to be more aligned to intrinsic motivation, may be more impactful. This is relevant given the preference for the 'carrot' strategies expressed by the participants in this research.

12.1.2 Sustainability

Once initial engagement with the International Safeguards has been achieved, it is important that measures to sustain this interest are implemented and maintained. This was supported by an International Governor:

> "There are so many priorities for an organisation that unless you have something to keep reminding you and explaining why it is important then it can slip down the priority list."

Creating this on-going engagement can be challenging, particularly for organisations working internationally in a variety of contexts. Identifying effective channels of communicating the safeguarding message was viewed as a key consideration. For example, an international federation working with members around the world using limited resources can find it difficult to facilitate regular face-to-face communication. This is even the case with regional staff, who may conduct visits to member organisations, but will only do so for limited periods of time. This can result in a reliance on online forms of communication, which can have different levels of impact in different contexts. Speaking on this issue, a staff member at one of the International Federations explained:

> "What you tend to find is that when you send out communications, we have certain countries that we can always rely on to respond immediately. We know there are certain countries where you have to do a lot of follow up."

Safeguarding initiatives are tasked with not being viewed as competing values that inhibit progress towards enhancing and maintaining success from a performance and financial perspective. A Head of Safeguarding acknowledges that:

> "Sometimes people may feel I can be a pain when they try to push the club forward and I have an objection, but it is about keeping people's mind-sets on, 'yes you have to do your job, but don't forget safety.'"

The strategies used to generate and sustain engagement therefore need to be tailored to the given individuals, organisations and contexts to enable optimal impact. The following section considers different ways in which the participating organisations were able to effectively incentivise their key stakeholders to engage and work with the International Safeguards.

12.2 Promising practice

Through the research, a range of strategies were identified which helped to incentivise individuals and organisations. This section provides an overview of the areas of promising practice which were reported. These are outlined with respect to those strategies which use internal drivers (e.g., those which stem from strategies primarily initiated within the organisation) and external drivers (e.g., those which stem from strategies primarily initiated beyond the organisation).

12.2.1 Internal drivers

Resistance to the introduction of safeguarding measures was experienced when it was viewed as being additional or not aligned to the priorities of an individual or organisation. Through challenging these underlying assumptions, participants reported that people became incentivised when the links between safeguarding and the priorities were highlighted and explained. Such links were often not obvious to people who may have preconceptions about what safeguarding involves (e.g., a mountain of paperwork or an inhibitive influence with respect to achieving other goals). For example, some organisations were focused on increasing participation rates. Therefore, rather than being a barrier to this goal, it was possible to utilise this motivation through highlighting the potential for effective safeguarding to actually facilitating the achievement of this goal. This strategy was discussed by an International Governor:

> "We have to influence members through finding out what is their motivation, what is their passion. Normally they are passionate about the sport and about growing their sport. So this is what we tend to focus on. It is about making sport a positive experience so that they want to come, when they come they want to stay and when they go home they want to come back. Word of mouth is the best marketing tool."

"I think that the core thing is that everyone we talk to is passionate about their sport. So the way we presented it was doing what was right for our sport so that people have a positive experience and want to keep coming back again and again. It is not just about the children, it is everyone. It is about the whole sport and not just the children."

Working to highlight such links was viewed as being a preferable approach, as explained by a Director of Safeguarding:

"Everyone wants to grow their sport and this is a positive way of doing this rather than having a club to hit them around the head to get them to do it."

Another influential driver within the organisation was the disclosure of safeguarding cases. Such cases served to highlight the reality of abuse not only in sport but within the given organisation. It also served to challenge individuals who may feel that safeguarding is addressing a non-existent or extremely unlikely risk. Cases within the organisation were observed to be a powerful initiator of change. When talking about a high-profile case within their sport, a Director of Safeguarding explained how this can contribute to a reactive approach:

"I would love to tell you that we were visionary and that we had recognised this as a responsibility but we definitely came to this effort out of a crisis. Negative media attention, law suits, concern of abuse. One of our initial and on-going challenges is that sense of urgency so we did not have the opportunity to roll it out in a more deliberate way that told a story and made sense. So, whatever we had ready and whenever it was ready we put it out."

(National Governor)

Another Senior Manager within a National Government described a similar experience in the aftermath of a high-profile case of abuse within their organisation:

"I'll tell you what has been easy, and it is a sad thing to say, there has been an acceptance that it needs to be done. We have a legacy that nobody wants to revisit. Even as I am sitting here I have a chill down my spine."

For governing organisations, criteria related to the International Safeguards may be specified as a condition of membership. One National Governor explained:

"If you are in direct and frequent contact with athletes as a regular part of your duties then you must be a member. So that includes coaches, other athletes, officials and then for volunteers who do not necessarily have a named role. For these people, you have to be a member. In order to be a member you have to pass a background check and complete our athlete protection training. Once you are a member you are required to abide by the code of conduct. We can take action against you if you have violated this code of conduct."

Speaking on this, a staff member from an International Federation highlighted the importance of effective governance once such measures are in place:

> "We expect our members to continue their membership and they don't just pay a membership fee. We expect them to keep up to date with constitutional documents and updates and things, and historically they have not been so good at that so we have looked at putting a database together that will enable them to update that information immediately."

12.2.2 External drivers

Work towards the International Safeguards was further encouraged by actions primarily focused outside of the organisation. Whilst participants acknowledged that the 'carrot' approach and change created by intrinsic motivation may be preferable, they also explained that it was the 'stick' which bought about real change. One influential mechanism was the linking of safeguarding to funding which was the most significant incentive. An employee of a key funder for sport for development programmes explained:

> "One way is to tie it to funding. To say that you need to have a policy, or at least commit to having one in place by a certain time, to get the funding."

Participants from delivery organisations also acknowledged that linking this work to funding was a key incentive and that it was this that initiated change:

> "For the funders there is a definite requirement. They want to see an organisational document to demonstrate that you have safeguarding or child protection policy in place. If the project is focused on children or vulnerable people then they do want to see what measures have been taken. The trouble is that money talks. If it is a requirement of the funding then people will do it."
>
> (Local deliverer)

> "We were, sort of, encouraged to participate by our funders."
>
> (Local deliverer)

> "In terms of child protection, I think that it is always a bit imposed from the top. Of course we discussed our policy with the staff and the girls but if it had not been for our donors pushing for it then it probably would not have happened."
>
> (National Deliverer)

Participants also suggested that having their work to safeguard children recognised, such as through an accreditation process, would provide a clear incentive. This would be an important motivator for some organisations, as explained by the Head of Safeguarding for a Local Deliverer:

> "From our point of view, as an organisation, we are very keen to have a badge. When there is an accreditation or an evaluation process, or a set of criteria to be measured against, and at the end of the process someone says that you have met the criteria and here is your badge, that is actually important to our business."

Participants discussed the possibilities around accreditation in terms of who may be the awarding body. For example:

> "We are looking at accreditation for National Olympic Committees. If they ask for accreditation then that would just be the ultimate win. In many countries the NOC is very powerful and this is where the funding comes from."
>
> (National Governor)

Whilst there was strong support for accreditation, the practicalities as to how this would be funded and governed represent very important questions which would need to be thought through. One National Governor said:

> "If a WADA (World Anti-Doping Association) -type organisation is set up then there is a need to consider who would lead that and how it would be funded."

The specific details of what exactly would be accredited is also important to clarify. The most pragmatic first step would be to establish a symbol which indicates an organisation's pledge to work towards the International Safeguards. It would be a signifier of commitment rather than providing any indication of quality. The introduction of assessments of quality would require a substantial investment in an organisation to development, implement and govern such processes.

As discussed in the previous section, another key instigator of change was the disclosure of high profile cases. However, in this section it concerns cases happening outside of the organisation (e.g., in other sports or in other organisations outside of sport such as churches, schools or care homes). For example, a participant working in North America said:

> "This is such a rampant topic in the United States now after what happened at Penn State and there is a major push to formalize and enact policies and procedures. We are under a lot more scrutiny around background checks."
>
> (International Deliverer)

The potential for safeguarding to be an inhibitor to the performance of the organisation was also expressed by Community Coaches. Coaches expressed the view that due to popular cases of abuse and external training that tends to focus on protecting coaches from allegations, Coaches can perform their jobs in a rigid and limited manner because of the fear of an allegation. For example, one Community Coach said:

> "Some of it is the media and some of these courses putting the fear into you . . . sometimes this creates a culture where people don't want to even help a child through fear . . . for us sometimes it is the fear factor of getting into trouble."

Overall, people felt that once safeguarding measures were enacted, people could then see the potential benefits in action and then it became normalised. For instance, one National Governor reported that through enforcing behavioural change this can then lead to a broader acceptance of the need for safeguarding once it has been seen in practice:

> "Like anything, if you put it to be compulsory then it will only be achieved through that way and then, through time, people will accept that it is something that needs to be done. That is the cultural acceptance."

12.3 Case study: International Netball Federation

The International Netball Federation (INF) is the recognised world-governing body for netball. The INF's mission is to support high performance and growth in participation in order to make netball one of the world's most popular team sports. The INF is managed by its congress, which meets every two years to review and update the organisation's strategy and operations. Between these bi-annual meetings, the INF Board of Directors also meets three times a year to make key decisions on conditions and communication of INF membership, along with the regulations, rules and policies of international netball. This is operationalised and communicated through the CEO and the INF Secretariat, who are based in England. The INF has over 70 affiliated National Netball Associations in five regions around the world: Africa, Asia, the Americas, Europe and Oceania. Within each of its global regions, the INF has a Regional Federation which is responsible for governing netball in their specific region.

The INF staff does not typically work directly with children and hence this is a good example of an International Governor. Nonetheless, the organisation recognises its important role in ensuring the safety of children who experience netball through its members. A board member of the INF said, "I think we are there to provide the leadership on this and provide the tools to monitor how that is going." For this reason, the INF has been working with UNICEF to develop the International Safeguards for Children in Sport since 2012. The INF also contributes to an international learning set to learn from other experienced organisations and share experiences. The INF's Guidelines for Safeguarding Children provides a detailed guidance to help members to develop their own policy and procedures. This is influenced by the International Safeguards, taking elements from the content of the safeguards, and explicitly stating that practices should comply with the International Safeguards for Children in Sport. Key strategies which have helped the INF move towards the International Safeguards were identified. These strategies were expressed as more than simply changing behaviour, but involved changing attitudes and values towards safeguarding. Indeed, one member of staff said, "For some of these people we are actually changing the way in which they think, winning their hearts and minds." This was achieved using the following useful strategies.

12.3.1 Raising awareness

An important first step in incentivising people to safeguard children is to raise awareness. The INF identifies one of its key roles as raising awareness to all members. As staff at HQ have engaged with the International Safeguards, and the Virtual Learning Sets in particular, they have been purposeful in seeking to raise the awareness of safeguarding amongst members. A staff member of The INF spoke of the various ways in which they communicate with members:

> "The way that we communicate with our members is a combination of newsletters and emails that we send out to our members on a regular basis. We also have our congress every two years. I presented a section on safeguarding and talked about the international safeguards and that's all about raising direct awareness."

The INF recognises the opportunities offered by international tournaments which are large events in which staff have a rare opportunity to meet groups of members in the same place at the same time. The INF has recognised that this provides a unique opportunity to promote safeguarding and the International Safeguards. For example, in 2013 alongside the World Youth Netball Championships, the INF delivered a 'Safeguarding Netball' Seminar for members. A staff member at the INF said:

> "Next year, 2017 is our World Youth Cup in Botswana and we will have sessions on safeguarding and helping our members there to develop."

Another change encouraged by the International Safeguards was the consideration of safeguarding for those young people in attendance at these events. Speaking on this, another staff member said:

> "Since we have been involved in this (the International Safeguards project) we have put in a requirement for there to be a safeguarding officer at each international event, we are working on job descriptions now."

12.3.2 Using members as safeguarding champions

The INF recognises that members can be used as champions and examples of good practice for three main benefits. Firstly, it serves to acknowledge and encourage those making progress in terms of safeguarding. Secondly, it encourages other members by demonstrating how it can be done which can represent a role model for other member organisations. Finally, this approach may also encourage some friendly competition between members who also seek to be recognised for positive contributions. Speaking on this, a staff member said:

> "One of the most effective ways I have found to get our members to do things is to show where members have good practice. What I find is that people come and say . . . oh we have done that too! By their very nature member federations compete with each other, they like to do better than the other so in some respects it's useful to have that comparison."

Similarly, another member of staff said:

> "When we first went to the congress, one of our members came out saying, no, it is too far, we are not there yet. It is not something that we need to look at. Within a few weeks of being involved with this process they turned around completely and are now on-board whole-heartedly. This is why we got them to come and talk at the conference. It is far better coming from them to say, well, when we first looked at it, this did not seem relevant and that we had got a long way to go to even develop basic provisions and so therefore safeguarding is something down the line. They did change their mind and realised that it runs through everything that they do. If you integrate it from the start, then you are going to develop good practice."

12.3.3 Support members requesting guidance

The INF recognises that many of the changes that they have experienced are attitudinal, and are reflected in shifts towards proactive approaches to safeguarding. It is important to ensure that guidance is provided when requests are made and that people are encouraged to access this guidance. Speaking on this matter, a senior member of staff acknowledged that not only are staff now more forthright in admitting that they have experienced things that cause concern, but also that they need help to know what to do. For example:

> "I think the immediate impact following the presentations of congress when I met with the individual federations, they were all asking me for help and I think that's a starting point, it's the recognition that something can be done. They are saying we have seen behaviours that are not appropriate. For example, coaches shouting during junior competitions and they don't know how to deal with that."

The INF presents an example of a pioneering International Governor that is proactive in its approach to organisational growth and stimulating the growth of its members. The INF's work is made especially challenging by the variety of nations and cultures that its work cuts across. This creates a necessity for the INF to appreciate the different stages that its members may be at. Nonetheless, by using various practical means to influence its members, and by engaging in various means of organisational learning, the INF demonstrates a manner in which safeguarding and the International Safeguards can be gradually integrated to members in ways that are meaningful to individual organisations in a variety of countries. Other international organisations can learn from the promising practices successfully employed by the INF through this project.

12.4 Summary

The present chapter presents the third of the CHILDREN pillars, incentives. This chapter outlines the importance of incentives, which have been grouped as those which are intrinsic, or 'carrots,' and those which are extrinsic, or 'sticks.' Key issues have been discussed. This includes the difficulty of generating initial engagement and sustainability. This chapter then goes on to provide examples of strategies which may be used to incentivise individuals and organisations. A representative case study is provided in the form of the INF, which has incentivised organisations and individuals by raising awareness, using members as safeguarding champions and supporting members to request guidance.

References

Choudhry, R. M., Fang, D., & Mohamed, S. (2007a). Developing a model of construction safety culture. *Journal of Management in Engineering*, *23*, 205–212.

Filho, A. P. G., Andrade, J. C. S., & Marinho, M. M. D. (2010). A safety culture maturity model for petrochemical companies in brazil. *Safety Science*, *48*, 615–624.

Mearns, K., Whitaker, S. M., & Flin, R. (2003). Safety climate, safety management practice and safety performance in offshore environments. *Safety Science*, *41*, 641–680.

Parker, D., Lawrie, M., & Hudson, P. (2006). A framework for understanding the development of organisational safety culture. *Safety Science*, *44*, 551–562.

Ryan, R., & Deci, E. L. (2000). Intrinsic and extrinsic motivations: Classic definitions and new directions. *Contemporary Educational Psychology*, *25*, 54–67.

Chapter 13

Leadership

The fourth pillar was labelled Leadership, and it highlights the need for strong support from those working in key leadership roles at the top and throughout an organisation. Overall, the research identified the influential role played by leadership in enabling an organisation to progress towards the International Safeguards. The leadership of organisational change is a topic which has been the focus of a considerable body of literature. The leadership of change can take a top-down or a bottom-up approach. Top-down advocates view designers as the key influencers and hence focus efforts on factors that can be manipulated at the central level (Matland, 1995; Sabatier, 1986). It is argued that this leads to consistent strategies (Matland, 1995). However, it has been criticised as overly focusing on administrative aspects of change and not valuing the role played by local change agents. In contrast, the bottom-up approach argues that policies are more effectively developed at the local level by those stakeholders who are actually going to work with the policy (Matland, 1995). Key stakeholders identify goals and strategies and these inform discussions with those in charge of implementing a policy (Hanf & Fritz, 1978). This helps to facilitate local ownership and that contextual factors are taken into account. This approach can be undermined by an over-estimation of the level of accountability and autonomy at the local level (Matland, 1995).

The present research found that these approaches needed to be effectively combined to gain the most impact. Strong leadership from the top of an organisation helps to drive the implementation of the International Safeguards (e.g., prioritisation and resources). Bottom-up strategies need to be employed to support the top-down approach to promote the engagement of those people working on the ground such that they have ownership regarding the operationalisation of the International Safeguards. Through the use of top-down and bottom-up approaches, organisations can enjoy the benefits of each approach whilst overcoming the possible limitations (Fullan, 2007). Leaders could also influence change through promoting peer learning within and across organisations. There appears to be less resistance when support is provided from the 'side' (e.g., another department within an organisation or from a similar organisation) as opposed to being from the 'top' (e.g., either from the internal leadership of the organisation or an external organisation). This is an important message for leaders in that this 'sideways' approach can be adopted in a philosophy that promotes *facilitation* as opposed to *dictation*. The use of all of these strategies are discussed in this chapter.

13.1 Key issues

Throughout this research, participants highlighted issues related to the broad scope of salient aspects of safeguarding for which issues of leadership merited discussion. The need to gain genuine buy-in from leaders is also a key consideration.

13.1.1 Scope of leadership

The biggest challenge discussed by participants was the sheer scope of the issues relevant to safeguarding and hence the variety of areas in which leadership was required. This scope firstly concerned the actual locations of the operation. Some organisations worked in many countries and hence having leadership on safeguarding not only at the top of an organisation but throughout all areas was a key issue. This scope also concerned the different areas of the work of the organisation. For example, staff of a football club in Europe explained that this includes sports delivery, both in the community and as part of the academy, along with its international programmes. Furthermore, the club is tasked with ensuring the safety of children who visit the extensive range and large scaled facilities as competitors or spectators.

Considering this, the workforce as a whole are routinely exposed to a wide variety of children in hugely varied contexts. This continuously brings about unexpected safeguarding challenges ranging from children being separated from their parents on match days, to gang based bullying and hazing in local communities. This is reflected in the following quote from the Head of Safeguarding who said:

> "The sheer scale of the things that we are doing throws up new challenges that the world is not so familiar with."

13.1.2 Senior leadership buy-in

The most senior figures in an organisation have the power to influence the development of a safeguarding culture within an organisation. An example of this was provided by a National Deliverer:

> "I think that a lot of the credit will go to the Chief Executive Officer. It is the same person who founded the organisation and because, from

> the outset, the people who developed the programme, from the very beginning one of the pillars of the programme was ensuring a safe environment. So even before we were using the words child protection, we were working on issues of safety, you know, and this built a culture through the organisation of child protection which has just held us in good stead. It has been very easy then for the new Chief Executive Officer to say that we have made this commitment as an organisation and we hold to it both in policy and in practice. So that culture of safety and inclusion has been built in from the beginning. It is not possible to think about our programmes without those things. So that is nice and it is nice to be working on child protection in an organisation like this."

This was supported by a Safeguarding Officer in a National Deliverer organisation:

> "The Chief Executive Officer is the person with terminal responsibility for that surface and he is accountable to the Board on child protection issues. I have never had to go into somebody and remind them that something needs to be sent out or that we need to have a meeting on something, you know. There has been support and commitment right from the outset."

Having strong support from senior management within the organisation was a key pillar towards building the safeguarding system. Broad support from the board was also identified as important by a local deliverer:

> "I was involved in the Equity Standards and there was a lot of resistance to that at the beginning. The key thing was to get the Board to take a level of responsibility for it. It is the same thing here and we have had support from the Board."

Thus, clarifying the scope of safeguarding in an organisation and demonstrating genuine buy-in from senior leadership are central considerations when building the safeguarding system. These issues can be addressed through utilising the promising practices reported by the participants in the following section.

13.2 Promising practice

Along with the important issues to be considered, the participants also identified some examples of what were perceived to be promising practice. This section provides an overview of these examples, illustrated with quotes from participants.

13.2.1 Effective delegation and support

An important point to note is that the support of senior figures for the International Safeguards does not necessarily mean that they personally need to develop, implement and evaluate safeguarding efforts. Promising practices were described which constituted the senior leaders effectively delegating responsibility for the operationalisation of safeguarding and then fully supporting the person or people in that role. The senior leader still retains the ultimate responsibility and should continue to ensure the effective governance of safeguarding.

A local deliverer highlighted that having this support, through two-way communication, was important:

> "In terms of the Board, they let me get on with it but if I do have an issue then I have an open door to them. For example, last night the Chief Operating Officer phoned me up and so he is not afraid to call me and I am not afraid to call him. He knows who I am and what I do and I know what he is there for. So I do not go to him with mundane things but if it is a key thing then we do have a good two-way communication."

Interestingly, a senior manager acknowledged this point through describing their role as one of facilitation in terms of their organisation working towards the Standards:

> "Trying to teach someone this kind of thing, I would say from our experience, is seen as very Euro-centric and so it is like, well, just because it makes sense to them, they are just these foreigners telling us what we have to do again. So I did not participate at all. I am the one foreigner in my organisation. Very conscious of this I took no part in elaborating the child protection policy and that is a recommendation that I would also make. So you can lead but you need a local leader who actually says I am going to do this and who actually makes sure that the process is done within their organisation."
>
> (Local Deliverer)

13.2.2 Building your workforce

Participants reported that effective leadership of the safeguarding work was facilitated by clearly identifying people with a safeguarding role throughout the organisation. Evidence of this approach was found at the international level, as exemplified by one of the sport for development organisations. For this organisation, there was a safeguarding expert based at the HQ. There are also regional Co-ordinators who work with the HQ and partners to deliver safeguarding workshops. They are supported by country-level managers and officers. Communication between these personnel is enabled through regular group phone calls. This was also highlighted by a National Governor who identified personnel to lead the work at the national level:

> "We had never had a full time dedicated person and now we have two people whose only job is to think about this all of the time. It is our job to oversee all aspects of the Safe Sport programme. This is both the proactive educational side as well as the case management, adjudication and taking reports side."

The same National Governor then explained how safeguarding leads were then identified at the regional level before being rolled out to the local level:

> "Another success is that each of our regions in the last year have identified a Safe Sport contact. Our ultimate goal would be for each of our clubs to have a Safe Sport person. Just having a person at the regional level, building your army, has been really exciting and is a big win in general, just showing how our membership has embraced something that at first they were not that psyched about. Also just having these people thinking about the issues and coming up with new ideas, extending the reach, has been a good win."

The same principle is reflected in the following quote from a local deliverer:

> "It really is about identifying your key staff in key areas and up-skilling them. I could work seven days a week, I really could. So it is about finding key people in different areas to deputize for that area of work. So if I am not here for whatever reason, or someone does not feel comfortable coming to me, then there are avenues within the club that they can go down."

Whilst having leadership at the top of an organisation is important, this needs to be driven forward and embedded by those working at the local level, as explained by a National Deliverer:

> "I am working with other members in various operational areas. I am sitting at the top here at the national level. If you look at our structure we have a number of operational areas in various parts of the country so those people are helping me to drive this."

13.2.3 Safeguarding champions

As well as identifying people with a safeguarding role, the importance of having safeguarding champions was also highlighted. These people do not necessarily have a safeguarding role but they help to lead work in this area through championing the cause throughout the organisation. A National Governor explained:

> "Champions are also important, you need to have people throughout the organisation who are supporting whatever it is you are trying to do."

One club identified Safeguarding Officers who champion the International Safeguards within their area of the organisation. This network of personnel helps to ensure on-going communication about safeguarding and that all employees have regular contact with additional safeguarding responsibilities.

The group of Safeguarding Officers meets regularly to share updates on their respective departments. This provides an important opportunity for peer support and the sharing of experiences. The group is led by the Club's Head of Safeguarding, who has the jurisdiction to make changes to various aspects of the organisation. This facilitates changes in a broad array of areas ranging from coaching delivery through to building development and maintenance.

Another National Governor supported this point and highlighted that high-profile figures could potentially be important champions:

> "We have identified that our elite athletes or our high profile coaches could do that but we have not had anyone call us up to do that and to be honest we have not done a great job to reach out. I do not think that we know the methods yet to get out there and do that so this is maybe in the second phase."

If managed sensitively, young people who have also benefited from the International Safeguards could also be important safeguarding champions:

> "We can also involve some of the girls, those girls who have been propelled to a visible level, so we show some of the beneficiaries and some of the people who have succeeded I think that we can be able to have that impact and have these people on board."
>
> (National Deliverer)

13.3 Case study: the Club

This case study focuses on a top European football club. The identity of this club will remain confidential and the organisation will be referred to as 'the Club.'

The Club engages with children from a wide variety of backgrounds, ages and capabilities in a range of contexts. One of those contexts is the Club's Academy, which is a training scheme delivered by elite youth football coaches with the main purpose of developing the footballing ability of children aged nine to 16 and providing them with a pathway into professional football. The Academy primarily engages with children and young adults in the form of weekly football coaching sessions. This takes place at the Club's training complex, a large, world-class facility with multiple football pitches and security patrol. The facility also has indoor facilities, including pitches, gyms and fully equipped changing rooms. The Club's pathway into professional football is further extended beyond the age of 16. Graduates of the Club's Academy programme become part of the Under 18 setup. This progression allows young people over the age of compulsory schooling to become full-time scholars of the Club.

The Club works closely with partner football clubs to support their delivery of football coaching and sports provision, providing a wide range of international football programmes. The Club's international work also includes regular trips abroad for the academy players for the developmental experience of international competition. The Club also delivers an array of health, coaching and education programmes in their local community. Examples of this work include multi-sports coaching in local schools, community cohesion programmes and health and activity workshops. Through these programmes, staff engage with an extremely diverse demographic of children and young adults within the community.

Amongst this work, the Club is acutely aware of the significance of safeguarding children and young adults. The Club's Safeguarding Policy outlines that it is their legal and moral obligation to do so. The Club is also aware that the failure to do so may also have grave repercussions considering their status as a reputable professional football club. As such, the Club have developed a comprehensive yet concise Safeguarding Policy that is both reviewed and signed off by senior management. This policy sets out their core values, vision, aims, expectations and safeguarding practices.

The Club has invested significant funds into its safeguarding programme, appointing a highly experienced Head of Safeguarding (HoS), supplementing this with the commitment of funds for a team of Safeguarding Officers (SgOs). This team is comprised of full-time staff who are situated in a wide variety of departments throughout the club. These staff members are remunerated for taking up the additional role of SgO and are provided supplementary training to support them in their roles as the face of safeguarding in their respective departments. This team ensures there is a safeguarding presence at training, matches and events. Furthermore, the team is advantaged by gaining additional expertise from their close work with the welfare and education team. This can be viewed as the strategic operationalisation of the Club's Safeguarding Policy, which sets out the desire to "Have a safeguarding presence in all areas of the club." The Club demonstrated strong leadership at the top and throughout with respect to working towards the

International Safeguards. A number of key strategies were identified and are outlined below.

13.3.1 *Evidenced commitment through leadership*

The most significant positive contribution to the Club's safeguarding initiatives come from the support received from those in the highest positions of power at the Club. It is clear that the management recognises that safeguarding is not only a legal obligation, but a moral obligation, too. As such, their commitment to ensuring the club has a world-class safeguarding programme is not only evident in policy documentation, but also in practice. When providing an overview of the Club's approach to safeguarding, the HoS spoke on this, saying:

> "Everyone is on board and that filters down to everyone else and allows us to be very conscious."

This was echoed by one of the Coaches, who said:

> "The club is really hot on these things, from the top downwards."

One of the methods employed by the senior management to ensure the Safeguarding Policy is operationalised is to provide the HoS with the power and flexibility to have an impact on all areas of the Club. Providing the HoS with this jurisdiction sends a strong message to staff that safeguarding is something that should reach all areas of the operation. Furthermore, it sends the message that it should be considered a part of the work of all employees. The HoS explained:

> "You need the right resources, people . . . and to give someone like me the opportunity to help and look from a different perspective. Often people do a job and what they have to do is that job with safeguarding in the back of their head. It's about having the understanding that you have protocol but if you have a concern speak to your safeguarding team."

In addition to this, the commitment of senior management is demonstrated by the allocation of a significant amount of funds to develop a safeguarding team that can reinforce the work of the HoS. This team includes match day, events, HR and coaching staff. This is viewed as a significant positive contribution to the work of the HoS, who said:

> "I am helped by the fact that it's not just me. At many clubs there are people that are head of safeguarding but it's just them, so sometimes

I think it can be a bit of lip service. Here I pay people to help and be the eyes, ears and the face of safeguarding. They spread the message and they are out there."

This strong leadership goes a long way towards developing and maintaining a safety culture at the Club, in which safeguarding is perceived to be a fundamental aspect of what is done and the way things are done at the Club. This leadership is not just about saying that safeguarding is important. It is about also showing that it is important through, for example, the ways in which a leader behaves, allocates resources and highlights priorities for the organisation. This is driven by the Head of Safeguarding who concedes:

> "I am in most situations very determined to see a conclusion . . . sometimes to the annoyance of other staff!"

This is further evidenced by the way safeguarding is perceived in general by staff in various distinct departments. For example:

> "That's what we are there for really"
>
> (Academy Coach)

> "We have a very protective culture"
>
> (Match Day Steward)

> "It is a safety culture because we are able to go up to people and have a conversation about safety issues and not always be frightened."
>
> (Match Day Staff)

13.3.2 Visible and approachable leadership

In line with the aim to ensure that there is a presence of safeguarding in all areas of operation, SgOs and the HoS are strategically placed to maximise visibility and their influence within the organisation. For example, Welfare and SgOs are on site at most times of the week until 9pm and later on match days. The HoS moves freely across the site and the open plan arrangement of offices lends its self to this culture of visibility and approachability. The HoS also has an online presence to offer advice, guidance and clarity on issues such as reporting concerns.

Having a presence in all aspects of the operation makes a significant contribution towards the dispersal of the attitudes, values and beliefs that would constitute a genuine safety culture. Furthermore, staff discussed it as being advantageous in providing all employees the opportunity to have less formalised and therefore less intimidating interactions about safeguarding. The HoS highlighted the significance of this, saying:

> "People know where I am, so it helps because people come by and say . . . oh yeah . . . I was meant to tell you . . . or what do you think about this? This is important, you want people to come and speak to you."

The broad presence of safeguarding has also been coupled with the insistence that safeguarding should not be something to fear. In light of this, the Safeguarding Team have made the effort to remain approachable, this is expressed by several members of staff, as demonstrated below.

> "Our HoS is very approachable, you know that if you have a problem you can take it to them or pick up the phone."
>
> (Community Coach)

> "This is very important because it helps to remove some of that fear factor. You can just go and say to HoS and they will say the policy isn't there to scare you they are there to help you."
>
> (Community Coach)

> "Our HoS takes things to management if there's a need for things like training."
>
> (Safety and Security Training Manager)

> "If you don't know what to do you can always go to our HoS and they will sort it out for you effectively."
>
> (Community Coach)

For staff members, this support supplements and reinforces teaching on internal and external training. Though they are also offered other, less formalised methods of support and guidance as SgOs openly and regularly offer advice and reassurance to staff. This was discussed by Coaches, who felt that the on-going verbal support offered is invaluable. One Coach said:

> "If there are issues I have all sorts of avenues and people I can go to . . . I'm not (an expert) in those things so it's good to know that I can go to this person."

13.3.3 Empowering staff

What has been essential to staff is the tendency for the Safeguarding Team and the HoS in particular to empower staff members to use the knowledge they have and be confident in their abilities to safeguard children. A member of the Match Day staff said:

> "Our head of safeguarding is good, he is proactive, he empowers people when the opportunity is right and he takes the lead when he needs to, he is always a phone call away, despite the fact that he isn't here 24/7."

The approach to leadership therefore serves to create a supportive culture which encourages people to engage with safeguarding as opposed to a culture of fear where people are afraid to do the wrong thing. This is evidenced by the following quote from a Community Coach, who said:

> "Sometimes it's just about assessing each situation, and they are great at that, sometimes you can just ask, well what about this? and they say, yes, this is fine."

It can be said that there is a degree of risk in this approach as it is important to ensure that staff do not become overconfident and stray from the organisation's official policies and procedures. However, given the broad scope of safeguarding, it is understandable that some unexpected situations may arise in which staff will be required to use their initiatives. Furthermore, the Club is confident that staff are adequately knowledgeable, qualified and of the necessary mind-set to be able to assess the appropriateness of their response to certain situations. This is summarised by the following quote by the Safety and Security Manager referring to issues emanating from the hosting of a pop music concert:

> "It's very important that you can use your initiative to make a decision. I was getting called over from all over the place for separated parents and children. By the time I get there they have been reunited. I have trained people to use their own judgement on things like that now because some things are not quite incidents yet, within two minutes they have been united. It's just a case of training stewards to trust their own judgement so I don't get called out for everything, so now they know which ones to call me out for."

11.4 Summary

This chapter is based on the fourth pillar, Leadership. It outlines the importance of strong support from those in key leadership positions. This may be in the leadership of significant change or in order to ensure momentum towards the complete implementation of the Safeguards is maintained. This chapter discusses findings of the importance of top-down and bottom-up approaches being used in tandem to foster philosophies rooted in facilitation, rather than dictation. The challenges to achieving this are discussed in relation to the scope of leadership required, the potential requirement for buy-in from those in the most senior position at the organisation (i.e. owners and board members). Though examples of promising practice include; the effective delegation and support of staff and volunteers, the development of the workforce for leadership roles and the use of safeguarding champions throughout the organisation. The Club is discussed as a representative case study, particularly the commitment evidenced by leadership, the ability of leadership to remain visible and approachable, along with the tendency for leadership to sufficiently empower staff.

References

Fullan, N. (2007). *The new meaning of educational change*. New York: Teachers College Press.

Hanf, K., & Fritz, S. (1978). *Intra-organisational policy making: Limits to co-ordination and central control*. London: Sage.

Matland, R. (1995). Synthesizing the implementation literature: The ambiguity-conflict model of policy implementation. *Journal of Public Administration Research and Theory*, *5*, 145–174.

Sabatier, P. (1986). Top-down and bottom-up models of implementation research. *Journal of Public Policy*, 6, 21–48.

Chapter 14

Dynamic

The fifth pillar was labelled Dynamic, and it argues that the safeguarding systems within an organisation need to continually be reviewed and adapted to maintain their relevance and effectiveness. Effective policy implementation will inevitably take time. It will require key stakeholders to work together to facilitate policy implementation and impact (Fullan, 2009). Beyond successful implementation, on-going efforts are required to reinforce and sustain any change. This process can be informed by periodic monitoring and reviews. This, in turn, informs the development of future plans. Organisations thus need to build on implementation and adoption to achieve institutionalisation (Fullan, 2009).

Working towards the International Safeguards should therefore be viewed as a dynamic journey along which one never actually reaches the destination. Many key influencing factors (e.g., cultural/social norms, political landscape, and different forms of abuse, increased understanding through research) will change over time, ensuring that one needs to continually review policy and practice. Through adopting a temporal approach, the Standards can help to ensure that organisations have a realistic goal to work towards, no matter where they are on their safeguarding journey. This sentiment was supported by the Head of Child Protection for an International Deliverer, who explained:

> "I think the main challenge is the rollout process. With anything you do it takes time. Particularly when working in global contexts. We have 20 countries around the world with staff and volunteer teachers and children and community members and how that gets effectively integrated into the work that you do and how its transferred into being meaningful for that specific contexts."

14.1 Key issues

Participants identified the importance of understanding the current status of the organisation with respect to safeguarding prior to making any progress.

The need to recognise the salient limitations and constraints being faced was also highlighted as a key consideration. Each of these issues is now discussed with examples from the research.

14.1.1 Understanding where you are

Participants found it difficult to establish a baseline in terms of where the organisation was with respect to safeguarding. This was challenging particularly for organisations where there was a lack of any safeguarding measures in place. There was a risk that people may become disheartened. One Director of Safeguarding for an International Governor explained:

> "I was concerned that an organisation that is very early on in this process may end up filling in the questionnaire where the answer to everything may be no. I thought it might be rather demotivating if they haven't got the policy, they haven't involved children etc. I mean if they do the questionnaire and everything is 'no' they might just close the book and say . . . this isn't for me."

Associated with this issue, there was a concern that people may attempt to manage impressions through over-representing what was in place. This may be a particular risk when there are links to membership, performance reviews or funding allocations. Speaking on this matter, a senior member of an international government suggested that differences in this regard may have a cultural element:

> "Another challenge is people admitting that they do not know or do not understand or that they have got quite a way to go. Some of our cultures are hierarchical. Admitting that you do not know is seen as a weakness."

Similarly, another staff member said:

> "The challenge when I go out to our members with the self-audit is to get them to see that it is ok if currently they have got none of this in place because then we are going to put the steps in place to get there."

14.1.2 Adaptability

Governing organisations will inevitably find that the current status of safeguarding will vary across the organisations which they are supporting. Similarly, the status of safeguarding will differ within delivery organisations (e.g., between different departments or areas of the operation). For these reasons, the participants discussed the issues around using a dynamic approach which has the adaptability necessitated by the context. One International Governor said:

> "One of the challenges we have is that our members are at different stages of their safeguarding journeys, so we have some very developed countries, who would have had very . . . strong and well documented safeguarding policies. And they are well down in the process of enacting, perfecting them. Whereas we have other countries that are perhaps at a lesser stage of development as a member federation. They may be an associate member They may be at the stage of grassroots development. For those it is initially about awareness building and setting them up on their safeguarding journey."

Another International Governor of member organisations described a similar experience:

> "This is one of the strengths and weaknesses of our membership because it is so diverse! We have some members that are at the very beginning . . . to other countries which are almost run like full blown businesses. They have many more staff than we do and a much wider reach."

This issue was also raised by the Head of Child Protection for an International Deliverer working in sport for development contexts:

> "Whenever you are looking at a development agency you have to understand that every country will have its strengths and weaknesses. E.g., some countries will be excellent at gender work, others will be awful. You go to some countries and there are already systems in place, whereas you go to others and there is nothing in place."

14.1.3 Working within constraints

The dynamic approach needs to take into consideration the constraints and work within them such that progress can be made. These constraints can relate to the broader culture of the given context. The Chief Executive of a National Deliverer said:

> "It has been important to take small steps. We have started by working in areas where we felt that we could have success. Issues such as homophobia are more challenging at this time because it is still illegal in some areas. This is something that we will move onto in the future but it is important to build on initial success towards these more challenging issues."

These constraints can also relate to the actual culture of the sport. Whilst these factors do not represent a permanent barrier, change may be more likely to be achieved through a longer-term strategy. A National Governor explained how the culture of their sport would take time to change:

> "I think that to really change the culture we have to get way down into the heroism around sport and the thought that we need to make kids tough for them to succeed. It is really deeply embedded in there, including the parents. We need a more holistic approach that it is not just this abuse piece that we are dealing with but we are really changing these big issues around masculinity and so on but this would be a really big cultural change."

Another International Deliverer shared a similar view when talking about the diversity observed across the organisations with which they collaborate. Employees within these partner organisations may need time for knowledge acquisition, attitude and behaviour shifts to feel confident in the approach of this sport for development organisation. This may be based on differing perspectives on matters such as what safety is, the best way to achieve it and the best way to evidence it. A staff member explained:

> "You are dealing with a lot of perceptions, beliefs and a sensitive matter. People are formed to see one thing but you are telling them to see something different that they are not trained to see."

A number of promising practices were identified by the participants which could help to address these identified issues. These are outlined in the following section.

14.2 Promising practice

The promotion of a dynamic approach was enabled through viewing safeguarding as a journey. This involved setting appropriate goals, monitoring progress and celebrating success. In combination, these strategies help people to make on-going progress towards the International Safeguards.

14.2.1 Safeguarding journey

As discussed in Chapter 5, the approach used in this project moved away from the language of meeting standards to one of moving towards the International Safeguards. This was facilitated through using the analogy of a safeguarding journey. Safeguarding is something that you should always be trying to improve as opposed to something which can be met, ticked off the list and forgotten about as other areas take priority.

The analogy of a safeguarding journey was found to be helpful to show that it does take time to develop adequate safeguarding initiatives and that support is given, irrespective of the current state of safeguarding. In other words, it is understood that organisations are working towards the same standard rather than at the same standard. This is expressed in the following quote from a senior member of staff of an International Governor:

> "We would like all of our member federations to have a policy in place and to be moving faster along the journey but we have to respect the capacity that those member federations have in order to first of all develop their own policy or even just build the awareness that they need these policies in place."

This approach was expressed as being made possible by the promotion and valuing of self-awareness which is focused on progression, rather than results alone. This is illustrated in the following quote from a Director of Safeguarding:

> "We turn this around in terms of self-awareness and knowing where you are at, knowing where you want to go, this is key to progressing in that direction."

This gradual approach may help to avoid people becoming over-whelmed and disheartened by the nature and scope of safeguarding in their organisation. For example:

> "If you go ahead with every Safeguard it is going to overwhelm the people and then you already fail before you even begin because it is too much to do. Especially if you are working with a group of people who are not aware of safeguarding at all and then you give them all of these standards, you are not going to earn their buy-in. So you have to do it bit by bit, one at a time. Then you can start to build on this. I am sure that it will take time but at the end we will have consistency of implementation and it will be sustainable as well."
>
> (International Deliverer)

14.2.2 Setting goals

Aligned with the approach of viewing safeguarding as a journey is the need to agree goals which help organisations move towards the International Safeguards. These goals can be set using the SMART principles, such as those outlined by Yemm (2013), i.e., Specific, Measurable, Achievable, Relevant and Time-Bound. A local deliverer discussed how such goals can be tailored to the given context:

> "People are at different stages of the journey and organisations have very different scope. Everyone involved in the process needs to have an achievable goal, whether they are right at the start or at the end of that journey."

This can help to guide progress, as explained by a National Governor:

> "The detail of the International Safeguards has been helpful in making you think that you can make incremental steps towards something."

14.2.3 Monitoring and reviewing progress

The dynamic approach was also enhanced through periodic monitoring and reviewing of safeguarding. An illustrative example of this was described by an International Deliverer:

> "I think that what I do here is to really consider the work and the context and where they are at. Even though I have all these pages of the Safeguards it does not mean that my staff can see them all or they will feel overwhelmed and I could not do anything at all. So at the beginning I had to think about our programme and see how we could use some of it, not all of it. We can start from a tiny bit, do the easy one first and then start to link it to another step. So this year we integrated some of the standards concepts into our training so we could build the capacity of the coaches, the leaders and the teachers. We used components of the standards in there so we can create awareness and now they know the importance of safeguarding. Then, during the on-going support when we follow up with them, we also start to mention these other aspects as well. So it is an on-going process. You build awareness, then you make sure that you really see them doing it and you make sure that children are protected during your observations. When you see the progress you can review and evaluate again, maybe after six months or a year in terms of what else do they need and what capacity do they need more of?"

The International Safeguards, and the associated Self-Audit Tool, can provide a framework which facilitates the review process. For example, when monitoring and reviewing, one of the International Deliverers referenced the International Safeguards to benchmark their work, ensuring that when they audit their work, it aligns with the International Safeguards. Such reviews can inform plans for future safeguarding efforts. For this organisation, the review highlighted the need to more effectively listen to the voices of children when developing, implementing and evaluating their safeguarding measures.

Another local deliverer regularly monitors the performance of the organisation in regards to safeguarding. The Head of Safeguarding keeps records of matters relating to safeguarding projects, criminal record checks, reports of abuse and how they were dealt with. This feeds into reflective evaluations which outline the lessons learnt and feed into the on-going development of the Safeguarding Policy and accompanied procedures. This work is supplemented by mandatory evaluations by the National Association of the sport, who also report on how the Club is performing in line with its legal requirements.

14.2.4 Celebrate success

As well as highlighting gaps on which to focus future efforts, the monitoring discussed above can also help to identify progress which can then be celebrated. Within a dynamic approach, it is also important to celebrate successes when key milestones have been reached. This can serve to reward people's achievements and sustain motivation related to safeguarding. One National Governor emphasised the importance of celebrating success:

> "We have built the foundation and we have done a lot of work. I feel really good about what we have done, but there is still a long way to go. I think that if we did not take a breath now and celebrate that we have reached a certain level, in that we are far beyond where we were three years ago, we would lose our people, thinking that we have already done so much, how much more do you want us to do?"

Celebrating successes is also aligned with the dynamic approach through acknowledging that it is a longer-term project:

> "It is about saying that it can take up to ten years and that here are the key staging posts along the way. The self-audit is useful for this to say, right, here is the baseline, here is where I came in, and two years down the line here is where we are now. So you actually feel as though you are progressing somewhere. Even if you have just targeted a couple of areas and you have a couple of things in place, you have actually shown progress and someone is acknowledging that."

14.3 Case study: Right to Play

Right to Play (RTP) is a global SfD organisation that delivers community programmes that train community leaders and teachers to become coaches and facilitators of specifically designed games. In doing so, RTP builds the capacity of local people to use play to empower and educate children facing adversity. This enhances the ability of community leaders and teachers to facilitate social change by providing quality education, building peaceful communities, ensuring gender equality and teaching positive health practices.

Since its inception in 2000, RTP has grown exponentially with HQ in Canada, and delivery of programmes in 20 countries. RTP has country bases in Asia, Africa and the Middle East, where its programmes are delivered. The organisation also has national offices throughout Europe and North America which raise funds, build awareness and advocate for key agendas in the area of sport for development.

RTP has had a Child Safeguarding Policy since 2005. This policy is reviewed annually and is accompanied by extensive safeguarding training for staff and an implementation guide. All staff must sign this policy, training is mandatory for all staff and extra workshops are available depending on the issues in a particular country. RTP also has various staff globally whose responsibility is to ensure the safety of children, including the RTP Child Protection Specialist, who oversees this work.

The present case study was conducted within one of the programmes in Asia. In this context, RTP engages in a wide range of activities from work with refugees in camps, to integrated play-based learning into the education curriculum. The present case study focussed on the correctional facility and the Life Skills programme, which looks at integrating play-based learning into their education curriculum.

RTP's approach is built on the dynamic pillar through recognising that sustainable change takes time. One staff member explained, "It's difficult to step in and tell the teachers what to do because they have been teaching for such a long time using their methods." When change is achieved, it is important to consider how this change can be maintained. Another member of staff acknowledged this as a challenge:

> "It is a challenge to ensure that teachers don't just go back to the status quo. These teachers are in an environment in which they have the power and they are not being questioned. All of a sudden, they are using methodologies where questioning becomes very much part of the activity. In a way that becomes a paradigm shift as far as teachers are concerned."

RTP have developed the following strategies which can help to facilitate the dynamic approach.

14.3.1 Adaptable implementation of the International Safeguards

RTP have taken the approach that the organisation's Child Safeguarding Policy should be dynamic in its application from country to country. Therefore, throughout RTPs policy, there are instances in which implementers are given a choice of how they may operationalise the policy. For example, in the case of police checks, the Safeguarding Policy makes explicit mention that "[i]n some countries police checks may not be credible sources."

This is based on the findings of RTP's compliance audit, which found that within some countries, criminal record checks can be purchased and have no validity. Therefore, RTP's Child Safeguarding Policy suggests that "[i]n these circumstances, all other child safeguarding recruitment procedures will be adhered to." Furthermore, RTP also use all other applicable means to safeguarding children in recruitment practices (e.g., reference checks, asking safeguarding questions during interviews).

On the one hand, it is essential that safeguarding initiatives are firmly applied so as to leave no grey areas for potential harm to children or injustice following harm. However, within the global contexts, a degree of flexibility for the implementation of safeguarding policy may be an advantage. It allows country bases to use vital local knowledge to assess the most appropriate course of action in a manner that demonstrates an appreciation for practical and cultural discrepancies. A member of staff from RTP HQ spoke about the necessity to contextualise safeguarding as an inevitability:

> "How we wish that there was a standard formula but unfortunately contextualising means dealing with cases one step at a time. So you deal with the issue as they come up because not all lessons learned will be consistent across the board."

Another staff member from RTP HQ spoke positively about the organisation's recognition of national and cultural differences saying:

> "We have made a lot of significant changes so that our policy can be a better overarching piece and then the more context specific aspects are designed at a country level. And that's where you will see differences, and we want those differences."

As a result of this, RTP HQ does not rigidly prescribe standardised processes. This means that the organisation must be adaptable and country bases need to rely upon their own contextual knowledge, as well as country-level formal and non-formal processes to effectively implement safeguarding initiatives.

Another important area of promising practice for RTP is the on-going monitoring and evaluation of the Child Safeguarding Policy and the accompanying procedures. RTP continuously reviews the applicability of the policy. RTP conducts a formal comprehensive global review every three years. This allows the organisation to keep itself up to date with global trends, while regularly evaluating the policy's effectiveness. Part of this effectiveness is the extent to which the policy is being successfully contextualised in differing country bases. A member of staff at RTP HQ said:

> "We have our child safeguarding policy and in each year we conduct reviews, look at complaints and acknowledge and make changes based

> on them but we also do interviews and ask questions like Are there parts of this policy that aren't realistic in your contexts?"

This approach is particularly significant given the variances in perspectives of safeguarding children across the contexts in which RTP operates. These variances can come from failed understandings of the relevance and applicability of established policies, principles, documents or international agreements. Although with the ongoing engagement of local people, RTP is able to continue to make steps that ensure their policies, procedures and documents are communicated in a community friendly way and deemed comprehendible, relevant and applicable to local people.

14.3.2 Valuing feedback and reflective practice

Following RTP training events, it is customary to reflect and give feedback. This commonly occurs within large groups and involves conversations about successes, the challenges and the next steps emanating from the training. A member of staff from RTP HQ described this as a crucial aspect of RTPs organisational culture:

> "What is good with RTP is that we have a culture that is really into feedback. So at the end of any learning event, we have action learning. We try to look back and see 'ok what went well, what didn't go well?' So it becomes a conscious learning on our part."

Throughout the case study this was described as a great way to reinforce learning, while also ensuring that the individual can reflect on how the issues discussed may impact upon them. A member of staff from RTP HQ said:

> "This includes a reflection on who they are, their experiences of abuse, how that may inform their views of abuse and how they interact with others."

A member of staff from RTP Thailand described the feedback and reflections process as also being important for managers and supervisors who can learn about their staff. The staff member said:

> "I think this is an important feature in which the supervisor can say things like Ok, I noticed you were saying this . . . or you know. It allows the supervisor to reflect on the staff and for the staff to also reflect on themselves so I think the debrief is a very useful process."

A further example of this reflective approach is seen with Programme Managers and Focal Point staff who are required to partake in quarterly meetings with the Child Protection Specialist at HQ and other Child Protection

Focal Points from around the world. These meetings act as opportunities to share experiences and learn from colleagues, while also presenting a platform for staff to offload any issues. Furthermore, these discussions may contribute to the organisation's annual review of its policy. A member of staff from RTP HQ said:

> "When we have the quarterly calls we share our experiences and challenges. Then others bring different ideas . . . from sharing experiences we can see some things differently."

14.3.3 Mentoring and social support

In order to ensure that staff are consistently applying the learning from training events, feeling supported and consistently being given new and effective approaches to solving issues, RTP ensures that staff are continually mentored and provided with social support. A senior member of staff at the programme encapsulated this philosophy with the phrase "Watering the seeds you have already laid." This support is made available for staff at all levels of country bases as well as for the delivery staff. A member of staff at the programme in Asia spoke positively about the support offered from management and senior staff saying:

> "Lucky for us every time we deliver activities there will be someone there coaching us . . . We may forget and act improperly with the students and you know . . . play jokes with students that may affect them. My manager would come and . . . a bit like coaching . . . would say, What would happen if we do that and how can we do it again so the student doesn't feel that way?"

This approach was experienced as empowering, with one member of staff saying, "I would say training isn't as important as the coaching we receive."

14.4 Summary

This chapter presents the fifth pillar, Dynamic. It discusses the importance of safeguarding procedures and systems being continuously reviewed and adapted to maintain their relevance and effectiveness. The key issues which are discussed are the need for organisations to understand where they are in relation to their ultimate goals, ensuring that the system is adaptable, particularly when working with varied contexts and organisations. The difficulties that this may present when working with particular constraints are also discussed. Examples of promising practice are presented, including; the necessity of viewing safeguarding as an ongoing journey, setting, updating and reviewing the progress towards SMART goals and celebrating success.

An illustrative case study is offered in the form of a global sport for development organisation, RTP. This organisation offered adaptable implementation of the International Safeguards, valued feedback and reflective practices and a strong sense of mentoring and social support for deliverers.

References

Fullan, M. (2009). Large-scale change comes of age. *Journal of Educational Change*, *10*, 101–113.

Yemm, G. (2013). *Essential guide to leading your team: How to set goals, manage performance and reward talent*. London, UK: Pearson Education.

Chapter 15

Resources

The sixth pillar was labelled Resources. This is in recognition that implementation of the International Safeguards needs to be supported by appropriate resources (e.g., human, time and financial). Building and resourcing the International Safeguards was found to be a significant factor in shaping the nature, and crucially, the quality of safeguarding within an organisation. This is consistent with previous research which identifies resources, including those which may be used for training or ongoing development of the workforce, as crucial for the development of a strong and positive culture that is rooted the protection of children from harm (Glendon & Santon, 2000; Frazier, Ludwig, Whitaker, & Roberts, 2013; Bottani, Monica, & Vignali, 2009).

15.1 Key issues

Issues were identified by the participants which are relevant to the resourcing of safeguarding. This resourcing was not limited to the financial resources but also included issues related to having the right personnel in place as well as the limitations salient within the physical environment.

15.1.1 Financial resources

Participants highlighted that there is a perception that safeguarding fundamentally costs money. The progress made by the pioneer organisations described in this book demonstrates that not all effective strategies require significant funding. Despite this, the perception remains and hence represented a key issue. The Head of Child Protection for an International Deliverer explained:

> "We all know that funding effects the amount of time that we can spend on some of these really critical pieces so it's important that you recognise the pieces that are critical and the pieces that you are going to continually grow on."

In a minority of cases, participants reported that safeguarding was well funded within their organisation. For example, one Local Deliverer said:

> "I count myself lucky that we have a lot of resourcing from my company. They give me enough money to do what we need to do and to go beyond what we are required to do by our governing body."

In some organisations, the funding comes from the participants. Creating funds through increasing the cost of participation may actually result in some of the more vulnerable children not being able to attend. This may then actually leave them in a more vulnerable situation. One local deliverer said:

> "Most of the kids that we are working with are coming from poor backgrounds. We cannot ask for more money otherwise we would be leaving out the children who need us the most. The poorer children would not be able to raise the money."

15.1.2 Human resources

Linked to the previous section was the issue of ensuring that sufficient human resources are in place to enable effective safeguarding. This concerned an overall lack of people working in the area of safeguarding:

> "I am working on my own here and I do not have the human resources."
> (Local Deliverer)

> "I am a department of one person. It is just a resource issue."
> (National Governor)

In other cases, the lack of human resources was with respect to situations in which safeguarding was just one part of an individual's role. Safeguarding therefore had to compete with all of the other demands being placed on a person's time:

> "The other challenge is that this is only a small part of my job. We are very eager to do it but it is just finding the time to try to do everything, especially for a developing federation."
> (International Governor)

This lack of resourcing was perceived to contribute to a negative perception of safeguarding as it is viewed as being additional workload for already over-worked people. For example:

> "One of our key challenges is that outside of our small core team, we do not have any paid staff. They are all volunteers. They are all doing

it on top of their day jobs. They tend to see safeguarding as a bit of a noose sometimes."

(International Governor)

Where possible, having a dedicated individual can be of real benefit:

"Having the resource for a person to be able to support clubs to achieve the International Safeguards helps. Sometimes they need someone to drive this."

(National Governor)

15.1.3 Physical resources

Resources also concerned the physical environment and extended to issues around the equipment, sports pitches and the broader landscape. For example, Government officials in the Caribbean said:

"The terrain is often a lower image of the mountains; there are a lot of rocks on it and a lot of wear and tear."

Ministers argued that this is a natural challenge of safeguarding within the Caribbean. It was also discussed as a catalyst to the speed at which equipment can deteriorate. Children in this setting also discussed their biggest worry in sport as being the potential to fall over and break bones, particularly given the hard ground on which they were playing.

15.2 Promising practice

Participants identified a variety of areas in which they had seen promising practice in terms of resources. These are now discussed with reference to the development and dissemination of resources.

15.2.1 Developing resources

The research highlighted the need for resources to be tailored and practical in order to have a genuine impact. In terms of tailoring resources, the importance of providing flexible resources was highlighted such that these can be adapted to suit the context rather than simply 'copied and pasted.' This was applicable at the national level:

"Keeping it flexible and having templates helps."

(National Governor)

It was also found to be particularly important for those working in international contexts. One International Governor began working towards the

International Safeguards by developing resources that are flexible, while still ensuring key elements of safeguarding are present in each member organisation. Staff recognise that:

> "One of our roles is to establish guidelines that member federations can use to establish policies that they would use when they are running activities."

The Chief Executive of this organisation recognises the importance of ensuring that the guidance offered is not rigid, but instead allows members to adapt the guidelines to their specific context. The Chief Executive explained:

> "The approach that I have adopted is around frameworks. To say these are the core competencies, these are the things that you are trying to get to. How you get there may differ because the circumstances that they are working in and the resources that they have will vary significantly."

This tailoring also includes the use of appropriate language. For international organisations, communicating with people across the world does inevitably have a range of logistical and practical challenges. These challenges can relate to not just the language being spoken, but culturally specific understanding of words and phrases in that language. A senior member of staff at an International Governor explained:

> "One thing that's helpful is that in our sport English is the first or adopted language. We are very active in Africa, the Caribbean and Oceania. In all of those territories, English is the first Language or is the adopted language. We have a challenge in Asia where we have a lot of new members and English is not their first language."

As resources are developed, the importance of cultural sensitivity (as discussed in Chapter 10) is particularly relevant. The absence of culturally specific and regionally recognised training can inhibit the impact of the International Safeguards. For example, in the Caribbean, staff recognised that the absence of culturally relevant training often creates resistance and offers limited applicable guidance. As a result, the given cultural norms merit consideration as training and resources are developed. For example, one trainer said:

> "The children are very loving and we are a small community. When they see you they want to hug you, but what are we to do, should we push them away? So any safeguarding initiatives should take our culture into account."

Many participants were wary of people with a lack of understanding of their culture offering safeguarding resources and advice without demonstrating cultural sensitivity. The resources also need to be developed with a focus on pragmatism.

> "I think it's more important that the coaches, and teachers and administrators know what's good practice, what's poor practice, what's abuse, and what's your responsibility . . . what do you do? Both in terms of your role and responsibility, but also critically, what do you do if there's an incident of poor practice or of abuse."

This pragmatic approach was specifically discussed with respect to what people should do when they either have a safeguarding concern or are approached by an adult or a child who has a safeguarding concern. At the local level, the European football club has safeguarding resources which offer pragmatic advice on the approach one should take in obtaining information after a report, stating staff should stay calm, reassure the child, take everything seriously and make no promises. Furthermore, The Club has established Referral Management groups which deal with and provide guidance on referrals. Indeed, a recent report from their National Football Association praised the Club for having:

> "A clear referral process for children, adults, staff, parents or others to report concerns on the understanding that they will be dealt with swiftly, carefully and with empathy."

This clear and practical advice for managing concerns was also recommended by organisations working at the international level. One such organisation makes an effort to ensure that reporting incidents is as simple and inviting as possible for all stakeholders (e.g., children, parents, coaches, volunteers and managers). As a result, there are three streams for reporting incidents. The organisation has an email address which incident report forms can be emailed to, an international phone line to which anonymous reports can be made and an online whistleblower website for confidential reporting of concerns.

15.2.2 Disseminating resources

Once resources have been developed, it is important that there is on-going and effective communication to ensure that these resources impact practice. This can be achieved through embedding the resources into policies and procedures. For example, one approach was the introduction of a roll call before sessions. This provided a simple solution to combat the vulnerability experienced by coaches in checking whether any children had gone missing from the session. One coach described how this had already come in useful when the attendance of a missing young pupil had been questioned.

Having formal training sessions also helps to develop and maintain engagement with the International Safeguards:

> "It is important to not just have the International Safeguards but you need to support organisations to achieve them through training. There needs to be something tangible that can be seen otherwise it ends up as just another booklet that gets sent around. Some kind of method needs to be in place to ensure that they are implemented."
>
> (Local Deliverer)

As such, one International Governor has developed two workshops with an explicit focus on safeguarding within the Caribbean, Safeguarding Awareness and Safeguarding Foundations. These workshops seek to increase awareness of safeguarding and child protection issues, discussing its necessity in sport. Furthermore, the workshops provide an open forum to discuss the obstacles that may inhibit delivery staff from safeguarding children.

Training was typically discussed in the form of one-day workshops with topics such as; identifying, defining and characterising maltreatment, familiarising participants with the organisation's safeguarding policy, considering the implications of a failure to safeguard children, discussing the appropriate means of responding to safeguarding cases and, in some instances, role-playing responses to allegations or concerns using scenarios.

The available resources can be highlighted through training delivered at critical stages of a person's interaction with an organisation. A good example of this was provided by one of the International Deliverers. Initially, the safeguarding policy is given to staff as part of the orientation package, and new staff are mandated to sign it. Staff are also given the opportunity to ask questions about the policy and procedures in a presentation from the Country Manager. Reflecting on their experience in this process a staff member from one of the programmes in Asia said:

> "I feel like there is an emphasis on safeguarding and that was made known to me quite early on in my work."

Following the initial orientation, staff are given annual training on safeguarding to highlight any updated resources. This provides a reminder of responsibilities, while allowing country managers to discuss topical issues that may have become apparent. This training is then integrated into the work that Training Officers do with Teachers and Community leaders. Another member of staff at the programme in Asia said:

> "I think the organisation does what it can to provide broad but deep training for staff who are working with children on any level. All staff take training, including the finance person, who is never really going to be around a child, but needs to know. I think because of the training we

do our staff are really on board, not just with the theoretical side but the practical implications."

People are then given additional training and resources relevant to their role. The Head of Child Protection explained:

> "We go above and beyond so depending on the country, they engage in other workshops, whether that's positive discipline or child protection mapping'. This includes the Country managers and CP Focal points who are trained bi-annually by an external organisation."

This organisation views safeguarding as a central element of their work. Therefore, at all periods of an individual's time within the organisation their knowledge and skills are developed in this regard. This process begins at recruitment, continues with training, feedback and personal reflections and the ongoing mentoring and social support of staff. The Head of Child Protection emphasised the importance of taking this approach:

> "The fact that we build in child protection as a core component of our work demonstrates its importance to us. And when I say build it in I don't just mean that we talk about it, we develop resources, we secure resources and then we develop technical resources, provide training, we provide the oversight and evaluation of that work. Doing so we are able to certainly impact improvements in child protection and safeguarding."

Participants perceived regular face-to-face training regarding resources to be the most effective. However, this was not always possible. This can particularly be the case for International Governors whereby the distant nature of the relationship creates challenges in facilitating direct contact. Speaking on this, a member of staff for an International Governor said:

> "Ideally we would go and do regional training but a lot of it is to do with resources. Having recently run this seminar there is clearly backing for it as everyone wants people to have a positive experience of our sport. It is how we do this in the regions."

As well as more formalised communication, resources can also be highlighted on an on-going basis through more informal means. For instance, the European football club have developed a Safeguarding Code which presents the clubs philosophy and key messages related to safeguarding. The Code has been communicated via colourful and succinct posters that are situated in various points around the training ground and stadium. It is also used in the form of a large banner on remote course locations. The posters provide a means to educate members of staff and stakeholders with key information about the clubs approach to safeguarding. They include a promise to all children and parents, what the club does to keep people safe and information on the training and qualifications of staff.

15.3 Case study

During this project, the need for a guide to support organisations working towards the International Safeguards was emphasised by many participants. The Chief Executive of an international government said:

> "I didn't want to give the self-audit and not have the implementation tools because for the countries just thinking about this, I don't want them to say . . . oh my gosh where do we even start and how."

These resources need to bridge the gap between written materials and practice. Providing examples and training materials for each International Safeguard was supported by an International Deliverer:

> "I do struggle in terms of the jump from the written policy to how can this really guide your day to day safety for children. I think that each Safeguard should have a list of examples of how you can actually comply. You know, here are five suggestions and here are the tools that go with it. That would be really helpful."

There was also strong support for this resource amongst deliverer organisations working at a local level:

> "I think that one of the things that this working group needs to do is to build up a library of policies from around the world from small organisations, not big organisations, because organisations which work in sport tend to be small and therefore they need not to be these 50-page manuals but rather a few pages long with a few forms from which people can get ideas. The kinds of forms that they need people to sign off on and the kinds of topics that they need to cover."
>
> (Local deliverer)

As a result, the Implementation Guide was produced. This resource helps organisations on their safeguarding journey from the initial discussions around safeguarding through to a fully embedded safeguarding system. It includes explanations of what each Safeguard means, questions to prompt people to consider safeguarding in their context as well as examples from organisations that have already started putting the International Safeguards into practice.

The guide breaks the safeguarding journey into five steps:

- Step1: Foundation level (e.g., understanding the need for safeguarding)
- Step 2: The Self-Audit Tool (e.g., understanding the current status of safeguarding)

Each of the eight International Safeguards then has their own section that takes you through Steps 3–5, as follows:

- Step 3: Developing your Safeguard (e.g., creating an action plan)
- Step 4: Implementing your Safeguard (e.g., promoting engagement with the policy or procedure)
- Step 5: Embedding your Safeguard (e.g., monitoring and reviewing practice)

Versions of the Implementation Guide which are specifically designed for deliverer and governor organisations have been produced. The Implementation Guides are also available in the following languages: Arabic, Bengali, Chinese, English, French, Hindi, Japanese, Portuguese, Russian, Spanish and Swahili. Examples are given in the following sections which illustrate how this resource could be used in practice by an organisation to help them move towards the International Safeguards.

Step1: Foundation level

This section of the Implementation Guide introduces people to the International Safeguards. It helps people to understand key terms and why there is a need for safeguarding children in their organisation. It includes tasks which facilitate discussion and reflection around what it is like to be a child in the given context. Ultimately, it helps to raise awareness and prepares the ground for the audit to be conducted in the next step.

Step 2: The Self-Audit Tool

This instrument was discussed in Chapter 6, as it was utilised to collect data in order to assess the progress made by the pioneer organisations towards the International Safeguards throughout this project. This tool gives an indication as to where an organisation is on the safeguarding journey, and it helps to identify the areas to be prioritised when deciding the next steps. It will identify areas of strength and areas in which an organisation may need to improve. It is emphasised that the Self-Audit Tool (SAT) is not a test and that it is important for people to be honest through their self-reflections. The key point is that people know where they are on their safeguarding journey.

Each of the eight International Safeguards is presented along with the related criteria. People indicate whether each area is in place, partially in place or not in place. Many participants made suggestions along the lines of the following:

> "I think that it would be very useful for organisations to have some visual map which is also a temporal map. This would facilitate an understanding that it is on-going and it is not something that you come to the end of."
>
> (Local deliverer)

As a result, people complete a simple table at the end of the SAT to summarise where the organisation currently is in terms of each of the International Safeguards.

Step 3: Developing your safeguard

This section of the Implementation Guide focuses on the important task of action planning. People are encouraged to review the results of their self-audit. If a Safeguard is not in place, then people are guided to the ways in which it could be developed. If it is partially in place, then examples of effective implementation are outlined. If the Safeguard is already fully in place, then people are encouraged to continue the safeguarding journey through periodically reviewing the Safeguard to ensure that it is maintained and embedded throughout the organisation.

Irrespective of the results, people are guided to develop a realistic action plan. The following table gives examples of the actions that could be taken for organisations thinking about Safeguard 2 (Developing Procedures to Respond to Safeguarding Concerns) for whom this is not in place (c), partially in place (B) or in place (A). Safeguard 2 has been used for illustrative purposes because resources appeared to be particularly important in this area. People are able to complete their own action plan with respect to each of the International Safeguards.

Deliverers gave examples of what had been done as a result of their own action plan:

> "We needed to take a look at all of these things and make sure that everything is OK and that we have a response ready should anything happen. As part of this we talked to our kids to get their views."
>
> (Local Deliverer)

> "We looked into the various resources and organisations that were available in our local community. We discussed how the gaps in our procedures may be filled through building local partnerships."
>
> (Local Deliverer)

Table 15.1 An example action plan

Current Status	*Action*	*Who will do this*	*By When*	*Indicator of success*
C	Create draft procedures	Identify an external expert to work with	1 month	Draft is shared for feedback
B	Explore awareness of the procedures amongst stakeholders	Safeguarding Officer	2 months	Gaps in awareness are identified
A	Review the cases managed over the past year from a range of perspectives	Director of Safeguarding	3 months	Revise procedures as required and communicate these to all stakeholders

Further examples were also given by governing organisations, such as:

> "One area where we were not strong on is the channels of reporting. I imagine that I am not alone in not understanding how this works in each state or in different countries. I would hate to enact a policy without knowing what to do if something happens."
>
> (International Governor)

Step 4: Implementing your safeguard

This section helps organisations to actually implement the strategies associated with a Safeguard once they had been developed. An example given by a deliverer organisation related to Safeguard 2 was:

> "We give a printed copy to every kid who signs onto a course so that makes them aware of their rights and the expectations that we have of the coaches. If the kids feel that this has been breached then we encourage them to speak to me, social worker, or the centre of the NGO. They then start to share this with other new kids and so it becomes institutionalised."
>
> (Local deliverer)

Another example for Safeguard 2 given by a governor was:

> "To implement these procedures, there was a requirement that every club had to have a welfare officer. This helped to ensure that there is at

least one person in each club and organisation who can help manage disclosures."

(National Governor)

Step 5: Embedding your safeguard

This area of the Implementation Guide supports organisations to embed the strategies associated with a Safeguard once they were in place. An example given by a deliverer organisation related to Safeguard 2 was:

"We now think about it at the planning stage of a new project. We work to ensure that there are clear procedures and support in place."

(Local Deliverer)

Another example for Safeguard 2 given by a governor was:

"Initially this can become a tick-box exercise and you have to go beyond this to embed the procedures and create a real impact."

(National Governor)

15.4 Summary

The present chapter discusses resources, which is identified as the sixth pillar. It expresses the significance of a variety of resources (e.g. financial, human and material), which can support the adoption and successful implementation of the international safeguards. Difficulties with attaining such resources are discussed considering limitations in time, finances and/or personnel. Nonetheless, pragmatic examples of promising practice are offered in order to guide organisations to developing and developing such as developing resources. This is discussed with reference to the International Safeguards Implementation Guide.

References

Bottani, E., Monica, L., & Vignali, G. (2009). Safety management systems: Performance differences between adopters and non-adopters. *Safety Science*, *47*, 155–162.

Frazier, C. B., Ludwig, T. D., Whitaker, B., & Roberts, D. S. (2013). A hierarchical factor analysis of a safety culture survey. *Journal of Safety Research*, *45*, 15–28.

Glendon, A. I., & Santon, N. A. (2000). Perspectives on safety culture. *Safety Science*, *24*, 193–214.

Chapter 16

Engaging Stakeholders

The seventh pillar was labelled Engaging Stakeholders. It advocates for a democratic approach to be adopted which invites and listens to the voices of those in and around the sport (e.g., parents, coaches, community leaders) when working towards the International Safeguards. Stakeholders play a key part in the development, implementation and embedding of the International Safeguards. These stakeholders range from the children themselves (discussed in Chapter 9), those around the children within the organisation (e.g., peers, coaches), and those around the children outside of the organisation (e.g., parents) as well as the broader community (discussed in Chapter 17).

A lack of engagement can strip stakeholders of the power to use their initiative and solve issues in ways they deem appropriate (Lund, 2004; Nichols & Tucker, 2000). This may rid stakeholders of a sense of achievement that can be attained from successful self-motivated engagement (Cox & Vassie, 1998), instead promoting the more extrinsically motivated and limited form of stakeholder involvement, compliance (Christian, Bradley, Wallace, & Burke, 2009). Makin and Winder (2008) have argued that highly prescriptive safeguarding systems may struggle to be effective in environments that are more difficult to regulate and control. It is arguable that sport represents one of those environments due to the unpredictability and range of risk factors (the child, perpetrators, facilitators, the physical environment and the sport). Therefore, this research suggests that sport organisations need to adhere to the recommendation of Tharaldsen, Mearns, and Knudsen (2010) to develop systems which enable stakeholders to engage with organisational changes. Such engagement can in turn promote ownership which can further contribute to an effective safeguarding system (Hale, Guldenmund, & van Leenhout, 2010).

Previous research has identified consistent, honest and bi-directional communication with stakeholders is one of the hallmarks of safe organisations (Frazier, Ludwig, Whitaker, & Roberts, 2013). Participants also supported previous research through identifying that engagement can be achieved through the use of a variety of communicating channels (Christian et al., 2009; O'Toole, 2002). Though the findings of this research also identified the need to recognise that engaging stakeholders is a long-term project and that it will take time. Changing attitudes, values and behaviour is unlikely to happen very quickly and will require reinforcement to maintain any change over time:

> "You are dealing with changing perceptions and changing values. Sometimes you have to reduce your expectations. You need to really give some time for people to understand this."
>
> (Local deliverer)

> "We need time to build awareness, to bring people on board so that they understand. We have to prepare the ground before we implement the policy."
>
> (Local deliverer)

16.1 Key issues

Before thinking about how best to engage with stakeholders, the participants highlighted the importance of considering the social constraints which may represent a barrier to engagement. A range of influencing factors were identified, including:

Poverty – Members of staff highlighted that many of the families within the community in which they run programmes are struggling to afford basic provisions, let alone appropriate footwear for playing sport. This creates a high degree of social pressure for young girls to work rather than attend the programme in order to support their parents financially. A member of from a local, delivery-based organisation in Africa explained:

> "Sometimes we will ask . . . why they are selling firewood and they say it's because they don't have money to buy flour to eat so they have to help their family. It's really an issue of poverty at home sometimes."

Staff were forthright about the difficulty of addressing these issues, as in many cases the extra finances of the child may be crucial to the maintenance of the family. Therefore, they can often be faced with strong resistance from not only their families, but also their friends who believe it is the girl's role to support her family, rather than attend the programme. During focus groups, the young girls themselves discussed the pressure from various sources, stating:

> "We are often told, what are you doing there your wasting your time! Stay home and help make money or do housework!"
>
> "In my village they always say things like . . . I am just playing, I am not going to do anything, I am just wasting my time."

Poverty also contributed to the low likelihood of parents pursuing criminal prosecutions where their children had been the victims of abuse. This even applied in cases in which the abuser was one of the caregivers of the girl as demonstrated in the following quote from a divisional co-ordinator:

> "Another example is a case where the father used to have a sexual relationship with the girl. The girl reported the issue to the mother and the mother refused to take action because the mother felt if the case was reported, maybe the father is jailed there will be no support in the family because the father is the bread winner of the family."

Parents were also described as resistant to going to court because of the price of travel. One coach said:

> "Sometimes when the parents are called to give evidence they say they don't have money to go to court so we should just leave her alone at home."

Awareness of children's rights – Another significant social constraint was thought to be the lack of understanding of child rights amongst the community. A staff member highlighted this as a key challenge:

> "Most of the parents don't understand their own rights, let alone the rights of the child . . . some people think that, you know . . . when a child starts going to school they are no longer a child, so if people have that idea, where do we start talking about children's rights?"

Similarly, discussing the awareness of children's rights, an executive member of staff said:

> "Issues like child labour which are settled issues in some parts of the world are not so settled here, so when you start to say children must leave the field at 3. . . the mother is looking at you thinking . . . I send her off to pick firewood at 6pm . . . what do you mean!? . . . So sometimes we have issues getting parents to understand why we do what we do . . . as with anything that's new there's some resistance simply because its new."

High Levels of Illiteracy – For a multitude of reasons, including the price of education after the mandatory primary school, many in this community are illiterate. As such there is a high level of illiteracy. This presents a challenge in regards to presenting information such as the child protection policy or key forms such as incident report forms. Furthermore, with a general dislike for paper-based information sharing, reporting cases becomes a challenge. An executive member of staff said,

"There isn't a culture of paper based information or reporting . . . it's important you add that verbal layer because people don't want to be filling out forms because they can't write, or they can write, but they can't write in English. It's also difficult to ensure processes are standardised and the information is correct or correctly remembered."

Denial of Child Abuse – Resistance was experienced from stakeholders in some settings, and this was often based on a denial that child abuse was actually a problem in that community. In a focus group with session deliverers and affiliated child protection agencies, it was said that:

"On the field of sport it's something we haven't heard of, we have never heard of something like that, this is not a problem for us."

Current Behavioural Norms – It is also important to understand the social norms in terms of what behaviour would be acceptable in the given context. For example, when attempting to challenge a physical educator tightly embracing a student following a tournament victory, one official said that the implementer asked:

"What's the big deal!?"

This also extends to the accepted behaviours relevant to safeguarding in the setting. One Coach gave the example of coaches being able to ask a friend to deliver their session for them as they had other responsibilities. In lamenting such actions, the Coach said:

"We don't even know who this friend is, you may think you know him, but do you really know him?"

Participants described how it was important to try to understand the thoughts and feelings underlying such attitudes through a genuine engagement if one is to achieve real change. This principle was also observed by those working as a governor organisation. For instance, one of the pioneer organisations works as an International Governor in a variety of countries. Therefore, the organisation encounters a great variety of perspectives on matters relating to safeguarding. These views may differ along the lines of location, culture, demographic, or social status. Indeed, when questioned on the degree of consistency between views on the prevention of harm to children during sport and recreation. A staff member said:

"I wouldn't say with confidence that everyone shares the same views. There is a big diversity of views if you speak to the different countries and the people from our Head Quarters."

Where fundamental disagreements do occur, established policies, principles, documents, or international agreements are not necessarily influential to local people. Particularly as understandings of their significance may be lost on local people who fail to see its relevance to them. Discussing this matter, a staff member said:

> "When you are using international documents, you are talking about the United Nations' Convention on the Rights of the Child . . . in schools . . . In the middle of nowhere. I mean, what does it mean to them!? We come in with a set of views that . . . this is what we will do, this is what we think you need but what do they think? Do they have other needs that we haven't identified? Or you know . . . we haven't paid attention specifically to."

These factors illustrate how challenging and complex a situation can be when trying to implement safeguarding in a sports programme. Clearly, the salient issues within any given context need to be well considered such that the risk of them becoming a barrier to engagement can be mitigated.

16.2 Promising practices

Participants perceived that a democratic approach should, as far as possible, be adopted to earn the buy-in of all key stakeholders and to facilitate a sense of ownership amongst these groups. Key stakeholders should be considered at all levels. This can ensure that the Safeguards are developed for a community, by that community and implemented through the community. One Programme Manager explained:

> "Those who make the policy are not the ones implementing the policy, that's why I think the most important thing is that those who are using it should be part of the drafting, so it becomes realistic."

Areas of promising practice were identified which can facilitate this approach.

16.2.1 Self-awareness

Before working to engage with stakeholders, one has to explore one's own assumptions and beliefs related to safeguarding. These have the potential to unwittingly create barriers to engagement. The importance of this approach was emphasised by a senior member of staff for an International Deliverer with particular reference to how this shapes their approach:

> "We are very passionate about not being 1st-world experts going in to fix people. We want everything we do to be about growing people within their community, acknowledging their reality and helping them

to identify their next steps. Our concept of education is not about an empty vessel which needs to be filled, whether they want it or not. We move people from learned helplessness, through self-organised learning through to self-directed learning."

An autocratic approach with a perceived air of superiority may lead to resistance. The same senior member of staff for this International Deliverer gave a powerful example of the kinds of experiences which have contributed to this approach being used:

"I have a memory of a young girl who was very bright, around 21 years old, who had been abducted as a child soldier and had obviously been raped etc. She was now learning to be a welder and came to participate in our programme. She was as quick as can be in her thinking. She wore a t-shirt that said, 'Every 10 seconds in America, someone is diagnosed with AIDS,' and this was a tremendous message to me as she was saying do not come over here and tell me what to do, you have got your own problems in your own country. By all means work with me, do not impose on me. She would not know how much she has influenced me but that particular t-shirt influenced us greatly."

16.2.2 Engaging parents

Participants highlighted the importance of engaging with parents (including guardians and carers) to help to safeguard children within and beyond the organisation. Parents have been highlighted as playing a key role in youth sport, and hence their active engagement should be encouraged (Knight, Little, Harwood & Goodger, 2016). A member of staff from a sport for development organisation said that the need to engage with parents had been identified throughout a periodic review of their safeguarding practices:

"I think one area that we should look a little bit more into is the engagement of parents, so what is the parent's role in the safeguarding of children? This was also one of the recommendations of the evaluation that we need to look more into it and foster that awareness of rights and how children develop."

Another Programme Manager supported this view in saying:

"We are trying to influence the parents now because we realise that effective behaviour change can happen when we include parents."

The use of the term "include" is particularly apt as it points to the need for this engagement to be one of collaboration and partnership. This inclusion was also advocated to be throughout all stages of Safeguarding from development through to evaluation as opposed to just involving parents as passive recipients at the implementation stage. Communication with parents can take a variety of forms, such as leaflets, digital communications, traditional community meetings, parent training days and community days. These can help to improve people's awareness of safeguarding as well as how to report concerns.

16.2.3 Engaging coaches

Another key stakeholder is the delivery staff who are working with the children, such as coaches. It is important to earn their buy-in, and this may be achieved by using culturally sensitive strategies. This technique has been employed by an International Deliverer who employs an innovative technique to facilitate a powerful and symbolic pledge from coaches:

> "With our local coaches we try to get a commitment from them by them shaking hands and making a verbal commitment. To our policy as a pre-requisite to getting a certificate from our training. This is based on the fact that we know that a personal commitment is a hand shake or a 'look you in the eyes' and agreeing to it when you have understood that you are both talking about the same thing. That actually has far more weight than a piece of paper."

The European football club found that a multi-faceted and comprehensive rationale for safeguarding helped to promote the engagement of coaches. The Head of Safeguarding explained:

> "I talk about three prongs; protecting them (children), protecting you and protecting the [organisation's] reputation . . . in that order."

16.2.4 Starting from a clear baseline

Having talked about the importance of a democratic approach in this section, it is also important to highlight that participants felt that there was a limit to this approach. In some areas, there needed to be a clear message sent out to stakeholders by the organisation. For example, the safeguarding policy can be an important way of communicating clarity to stakeholders. A member of staff described the impact of their policy:

> "Before the policy we would finish peer leader meetings and girls would be going home. Some of them late in the dark and that's a child protection issue in itself, but now with the policy we know that at 3pm we have to finish so everyone has enough time to get home before its dark."

Not only is the policy assisting staff and volunteers to constantly consider their actions in the context of child protection, but it also assists in addressing one of the key challenges of the organisation, winning parental support. An executive member of staff said:

> "It really helps because it says to parents that we are not just saying things, but there is a policy and rules and guidelines that are behind this. This helps the organisation to qualify things like the curfew."

The executive was also able to identify how this may contribute to a culture shift that impacts parents at a personal level. The executive said:

> "The more they get into the culture that, my child is receiving this level of protection, the more it begins to leak into their personal lives."

This Executive has also enforced the philosophy that:

> "The child protection policy always wins."

This means that where stakeholders are faced with a conflict, the direct instructions or general principles of the policy must always be more important than other considerations. For example, staff will not be hired if they do not sign the child protection policy upon arrival, and any ideas for a project that contradicts the policy will not be accepted. This is irrespective of how good they may be. An executive member of staff said:

> "This can be quite frustrating for staff sometimes because they think they just came up with this great idea and you're going to say no . . . but at the end of the day the child protection policy always wins . . . it has to!"

16.3 Case study: Moving the goalposts

This case study was with Moving the Goalposts (MTG) who are a sport for development organisation with programmes in East Africa. Since 2002, they have worked with young women and girls between the ages of nine and 25 to address gender-based imbalances and empower women and girls. The organisation hosts youth football leagues and tournaments, while delivering educational and developmental schemes that address broader social issues. With over 27 members of staff and an extensive team of youth volunteers, they serve over 5,000 beneficiaries in six divisions across the region.

This organisation faced many of the issues outlined earlier in this chapter. Indeed, the members of staff, players and volunteers discussed attaining the co-operation and wholehearted support of the community and parents as the biggest challenge they face. The children themselves were forthright about the need for more parents to take heed of the messages coming from MTG in ensuring that the rights of girls and young women are not routinely violated.

Issues such as rape, child trafficking, child labour and the potential risks during travel were a constant feature throughout the interviews and focus groups. The following MTG coach expressed their frustration at failed attempts to communicate with parents by saying:

> "Let's say we call a meeting with parents, you may find that parents ignore the invitation so they don't get the information, that's a big challenge."

A former player and peer educator discussed a similarly difficult alternative:

> "Sometimes they listen but they don't implement, that is also quite frustrating."

Similarly, in a focus group with district co-ordinators, one member of staff discussed a lack of parental co-operation, even in cases in which children had been raped. The district co-ordinator described the following example:

> "There was a case in which one of our girls was raped and when she went to the hospital they told her she was pregnant. The case went to court but when the court date came the family did not attend. I followed up and went to the mother to ask why, I tried to convince her to go to the court so action can be taken and it will not be repeated again. She totally refused to turn up."

16.3.1 Getting to know each other

This organisation recognises that engaging with stakeholders is vital to achieving their mission to empower young girls in the region. They employ a "grassroots mobilisation" process which brings together various direct and indirect stakeholders of MTG projects (e.g. participants, parents, volunteers and staff) in what is referred to as an intergenerational dialogue or 'Tumanyana' (let's get to know each other). There was a shared understanding that these meetings offer a fantastic opportunity for dialogue between the community and the organisation. The divisional co-ordinator, who described themselves as the link between the community and the organisation, explained:

> "It gives us a chance to discuss the problems and come up with a solution."

Furthermore, these meetings can be viewed as opportunities to advocate for safeguarding, as demonstrated in the following quote from the divisional co-ordinator:

> "This is where we advocate for the implementation of the child protection policy."

The efforts of the organisation to engage with all stakeholders are not only appreciated by the staff, volunteers and parents but by the children taking part in the projects. The children were full of praise for the Tumanyana meetings, believing that is helped their parents to get a better understanding of the organisation and their rights, allowing them to engage further with the organisation.

16.3.2 Protecting children's rights

Another example of the impact of this work is the increased positive intervention of staff on behalf of children. Interviews, focus groups and observations uncovered several manifestations of the child-centred culture, within which staff were happy to take the extra effort to ensure the safety and protection of children. Indeed, focus groups with children suggested that their trust in the organisation was based on the belief that it fights for the rights of children. This was highlighted a significant factor in children wanting to both join and remain part of the organisation. This demonstrates how effective safeguarding can have benefits, such as through increased participation and commitment to the organisation from children.

Children were of the belief that the organisation was able to connect with parents and carers in ways that ensure an amicable solution is found to matters that violate the rights of children and young people. Furthermore, staff and volunteers offered examples of when they had taken practical steps to protect children from harm. An example is offered in the following quote from a divisional co-ordinator:

> "I contacted a parent to discuss the benefits of her child going to school and after she understood, she allowed her to go to school. We even approached the employer and he doubled her wages which allowed her to pay for school fees and continue to support her family, she completed class 8 this year."

A further impact of this work was an increase in the level of safeguarding concerns being reported. Though increased reporting may be seen by some as a negative outcome, it can actually be viewed in a positive light. It represents increased levels of awareness of the safeguarding procedures as well as in people's confidence to use them. Various staff members throughout the organisation observed a gradual increase in the likelihood of reports from not only children and young people, but their parents and carers, too. A key member of the events team said:

> "We have really tried to educate the parents so that they can be aware, and we have seen some of the parents are now really doing a good job of how they follow up cases of child abuse and rape . . . we have tried our best to provide information to the parents, even the teachers . . . and through their support we have really helped a lot of children."

16.4 Summary

This chapter discusses the seventh pillar, Engaging Stakeholders. It outlines the benefits of a democratic approach that invites and listens to the voices of those in and around the sport (e.g., parents, coaches, community leaders) when working towards the International Safeguards. It also recognises that this is a long-term project, and contextual issues such as high levels of poverty and illiteracy may make this more difficult. However, solutions such as adopting a high level of self-awareness, targeting key gatekeepers and starting from a clear baseline. A representative case study is offered with Moving the Goalposts, an SfD organisation with programmes in East Africa. Examples of strategies which underpinned their successful engagement of stakeholders include employ a "grassroots mobilisation" process and their development of a child-centred culture which also facilitates more profound engagement with children and their parents.

References

Christian, M. S., Bradley, J. C., Wallace, J. C., & Burke, M. J. (2009). Workplace safety: A meta-analysis of the roles of person and situation factors. *Journal of Applied Psychology*, *94*(5), 1103–1127.

Cox, S. J., & Vassie, L. H. (1998). Small and Medium Size Enterprises (SME) interest in voluntary certification schemes for health and safety management: Preliminary results. *Safety Science*, *29*, 67–73.

Frazier, C. B., Ludwig, T. D., Whitaker, B., & Roberts, D. S. (2013). A hierarchical factor analysis of a safety culture survey. *Journal of Safety Research*, *45*, 15–28.

Hale, A. R., Guldenmund, F. W., van Leenhout, P. L. C. H., & Oh, J. I. H. (2010). Evaluating safety management and culture interventions to improve safety: Effective intervention strategies. *Safety Science*, *48*(8), 1026–1035.

Knight, C. J., Little, G. C. D., Harwood, C. G., & Goodger, K. (2016). Parental involvement in elite junior slalom canoeing. *Journal of Applied Sport Psychology*, *28*(2), 234–256.

Lund, H. L. (2004). Strategies for sustainable business and the handling of workers' interests: Integrated management systems and worker participation. *Economic and Industrial Democracy*, *25*(1), 41–74.

Makin, A. M., & Winder, C. (2008). A new conceptual framework to improve the application of occupational health and safety management systems. *Safety Science*, *46*(6), 935–948.

Nichols, T., & Tucker, E. (2000). OHS management systems in the UK and Ontario, Canada: A political economy perspective. In K. Frick, P. L. Jensen, M. Quinlan, & T. Wilthagen (Eds.), *Systematic occupational health and safety management: Perspectives*. Oxford: Pergamon Press.

O'Toole, M. (2002). The relationship between employees' perceptions of safety and organizational culture. *Journal of Safety Research*, *33*, 231–243.

Tharaldsen, J. E., Mearns, K. J., & Knudsen, K. (2010). Perspectives on safety: The impact of group membership, work factors and trust on safety performance in UK and Norwegian drilling company employees. *Safety Science*, *48*(8), 1062–1072.

Chapter 17

Networks

The eighth and final pillar was labelled Networks. It argues that an organisation's progress towards the Safeguards will be strengthened by developing networks with other related organisations. It was found that more effective safeguarding systems were perceived to be developed when people and organisations worked together. These networks can be developed within the organisation (as discussed in Chapters 11 and 13) and through engaging with stakeholders (see Chapter 16). This chapter focuses on collaborations with organisations locally, nationally and internationally. Many key publications have advocated for multi-agency working based on the argument that this would facilitate improved safeguarding outcomes for children (Home Office, 2014; H. M. Government, 2013). This concerns inter-profession and inter-organisational collaborations (Frost & Lloyd, 2006; Frost & Robinson, 2007). Existing literature has primarily focused on how multi-agency working can help to specifically protect children at risk. The present research identified that such practices can also be beneficial at a more generic level through helping organisations to put the International Safeguards in place.

Through working towards the International Safeguards, the participants highlighted the importance of building these networks. This is illustrated by the following quote from a member of staff working for a sport for development organisation:

> "Over the last three years, as we have grown, we have also realised that if you want to engage in social change, you not only have to engage the children but also their families and the systems in the communities which should be accountable to children and their families. So we now also engage in conversations with parents every month and also work with institutions, schools and health organisations and services that people should be getting such that they reach them."

17.1 Key issues

In discussing the need for building such networks, the participants highlighted a range of salient issues which merited consideration. These related to both the challenges being addressed through the networks as well as the factors which represented significant barriers to building these networks.

17.1.1 Challenges addressed through building networks

Participants described a real sense of isolation prior to their involvement in this project. This can be isolation within their own organisation as well as a broader sense of isolation with respect to the local, national or international community. This was perceived to be particularly important for smaller organisations for whom isolation can be a significant challenge:

> "I think that it is very important because the tendency is a lack of, a feeling of isolation by small organisations. So this is actually a way in which people can actually talk about it. There is a challenge in the day to day work. There is a conscious need but, again, it is isolation. I mean, I don't know what it is like in other countries but here and child protection policies, it is like what planet did you come from?"
>
> (Local deliverer)

Another frequently discussed challenge was the poor integration of government services and lack of information sharing. This meant that if one department or organisation possessed crucial information about a child that may affect their safety and well-being, there were difficulties in ensuring that such information was appropriately shared with other key stakeholders whilst working within any relevant data protection legislation. Participants from both deliverer and governor organisations suggested that a more integrated working relationship with relevant personnel and organisations would benefit all stakeholders and ensure that knowledge could be shared more efficiently.

17.1.2 Barriers to building networks

Participants highlighted a range of factors which they had experienced as possible barriers when trying to build networks. The first of these concerned the ways in which children and safeguarding were generally perceived in their community. Participants identified a need for education across the community about safeguarding children in sport and sport for development. The present study found evidence to suggest that the wider public would also benefit from education about the purpose and nature of safeguarding. For instance, in a focus group, when referring to attitudes towards child protection and safeguarding in the community as a whole, one Officer from the Children's agency argued:

> "We need a cultural education about the whole child protection thing."

Participants suggested that this may take the form of a public campaign which directly addressed some of the popular beliefs and myths regarding abuse in society and in sport in particular. A second factor was the availability and effectiveness of broader social systems within the given context which are focused on safeguarding children. This was evident in a range of areas. For example, one participant from a local deliverer discussed the impact of the local transport infrastructure:

> "It's great to have these sports facilities . . . but if a child has to walk a number of kilometres just to get there than that begins to be a security factor in itself."

As participants worked towards the International Safeguards one of the initial areas of focus was typically around recruitment. Specifically, participants wanted to put measures in place to check that an applicant was suitable to work with children. However, the lack of social systems to facilitate this often made it challenging to build a network to support the recruitment process. For example, one sport for development organisation working in Africa explained the difficulty of gaining a background check in the country in which they operated. The Police were able to provide a "Certificate of Good Conduct", but this was only valid for three months and often took a significant amount of time to obtain. As a result, this organisation often used more informal checks, which rely on the honesty of members of the local community.

A Head of Safeguarding for an organisation working with partners to deliver sports programmes around the world shared a similar experience. Difficulties were reported in obtaining criminal checks for the staff of international partners who work in places where criminal record checks are less formalised, are an entirely different practice or take a radically different form. These challenges were ones that are not always possible to identify prior to the trip, and it was difficult to build networks to help to overcome this possible barrier to safeguarding.

The final challenge concerned allegations of corruptive practices within some justice systems. When people do not trust these social systems, participants reported that encouraging people to disclose safeguarding concerns and to follow the case through to a conclusion was challenging. This was perceived to contribute to the normalisation of abuse. This was identified in a range of settings as illustrated by the following quotes:

> "The richer cannot be jailed because they pay off the judges."
>
> (Coach, Local Deliverer)

> "It is very easy to have cases thrown out when you pay money."
>
> (Divisional Co-Ordinator, National Deliverer)

> "Families with a big reputation know they can pay off smaller families and make abuse issues go away."
>
> (Volunteer, Local Deliverer)

> "When a chief is ready to take it up, they can influence and give up things to make sure the chief is no longer active in this case."
>
> (Coach, National Deliverer)

Whilst these challenges were significant and on-going, a range of promising practices were discussed which did help participants to build networks. These strategies are outlined in the following section.

17.2 Promising practice

Progress was reported when people used the following strategies. These approaches are discussed with respect to community mapping, peer learning and engaging with external networks.

17.2.1 Community mapping

When first thinking about the International Safeguards, participants often perceived that there was a lack of organisations who could support their safeguarding. However, through completing a community mapping task, people often identified a range of people, resources and organisations with whom they could collaborate of which they had not previously been aware. The mapping task, which was completed as part of one of the Virtual Learning Sets, asked participants to think about the following questions:

1. Are there local or national organisations who are also working to safeguard children in sport? (e.g., another local sports club)
2. Are there local or national organisations who are also working to safeguard children in areas other than sport? (e.g., a local school)
3. Are there community resources that may support safeguarding children? (e.g., advocacy or faith groups, charities, social services, the Police)
4. Are there resources which may help your work? (e.g., Government guidance, professional networks, conferences, websites)

An example of how this community mapping helped organisations was provided by a local deliverer:

> "We looked into the various resources and organisations that were available in our local community. We discussed how the gaps in our procedures may be filled through building local partnerships."
>
> (Local deliverer)

17.2.2 Peer learning

Throughout the research the participants highlighted examples of how they had benefited from the relationships developed during this project. This peer learning was found to be effective as it was not associated with any of the resistance which was reported when support was perceived to come from a top-down perspective with a tone of dictation rather than facilitation. Sharing experiences with other organisations who were facing similar challenges was viewed as being helpful:

> "It has been really useful listening to the experiences of other organisations who are in our virtual learning set. Mainly this is in terms of communities where it is difficult to come across background checks when you are working with informal coaches or you are working in communities where there are not formal structures so how do you make sure that you are not recruiting people who have a criminal record or who have been involved in inappropriate behaviour in the past? So just listening to other people and how they have gone about that has been really useful. They just give us a bit more faith in what we are doing."
>
> (Local deliverer)

A National Deliverer was also reassured that this was an issue which was being faced by all organisations in all parts of the world:

> "It is also very good to know, for example, that in even what we think of as the first world, there are challenges with understanding and things like that. So often it gets cast as a third world issue and some of us can get a bit defensive about that. You know, so it is just really good, I love it. I loved the idea and I like that it is organisational representations and it is not just about individuals. It is just something that we are very excited to be part of."

This sharing of experiences helped to identify and spread the use of promising practices. This was identified by the Head of Child Protection for an International Deliverer:

> "The cross country sharing that comes out is a big piece for us. It's all about how one country can share with another country a best practice, something that has worked, what's not working, what are huge challenges etc., it's instrumental."

Participants also valued the way in which people were willing to share resources. This was identified by International Governors:

> "This is a good thing about the networking. I think the sport for development network is probably one of the most generous networks with the sharing of knowledge and resources. So, we used that to develop our own policy, and then identified issues and areas for development."
>
> (International Governor)

"This is why I am excited about this project because it is creating networks that we can tap into and share resources. This should open up some opportunities that just would not exist if we were trying to do this on our own. There is real potential for cross-sport working on this issue."

(International Governor)

It was also valued by deliverers:

"It is nice that everyone can share tools to help each other implement the Safeguards in different contexts. I am sure that we can learn from each other."

(International Deliverer)

One local deliverer described how these resources had actually made their progress towards the International Safeguards possible:

"I have been learning a lot of things. I have been happily getting a lot of stuff and downloading resources from the workspace. These are very useful for us to start working on and adapting for us. Without these we would not have been able to do anything."

Some participants also used this peer learning, through the Virtual Learning Sets, to seek feedback on their resources as these were developed.

"We have started to develop a number of training guides for the various levels of programme that we deliver. These will be reviewed by my learning set on an on-going basis."

(International Governor)

17.2.3 Engaging with external networks

Through the community mapping process, participants were able to identify external networks with which they then collaborated. This worked at the individual level through working with a relevant expert. One example was provided by an International Governor. This organisation, which does have a number of experienced staff, recognised the benefits of periodically utilising external experts. Speaking on this, a member of staff explained:

"We were working with a lawyer to develop our own guidelines. We took some standard guidelines and compared them with the International Safeguards to make sure we were completely aligned with those safeguards as they were developed. So it's really working with technical experts to make sure that we had covered off all the areas."

Participants also reported progress through working with local schools. Such organisations often have experience of issues related to safeguarding children with well-developed policies and procedures. An example of this was provided in the Caribbean where teachers from the local school were invited to attend sessions. This provided support for the coach as well as an opportunity for sharing experiences.

Engagement with external training organisations was also found to be beneficial. It was often the case that sport-specific safeguarding training was not available. However, through the community mapping, people identified relevant sources of training. Even though such training was not specifically focused on the sports context, it was still found to be helpful and preferable to having no training at all.

For example, the European football club demonstrated a commitment to advancing the knowledge and skills of its employees by putting on regular safeguarding training for a range of its staff members. Training is tailored around the needs of particular groups and focused on issues such as conducting background checks or conflict resolution. This training is designed to supplement the training offered by the national Football Association, which staff are also encouraged to attend. A Safeguarding Officer observed:

> "When we put on training, they are way oversubscribed! It's an awareness session in which people are actively encouraged to make a contribution."

A coach at the club also said:

> "We have done a lot of stuff like training on dealing with violent people and we have gone on external training by our football association, so that's good."

Another significant contribution to the Club's safeguarding work is the positive and proactive attitude towards working with other organisations, both locally and internationally. This includes organisations such as the Police, social services, child protection agencies, other football clubs and local schools. The Club view their interactions with these organisations as opportunities to learn from experts in other fields. For example, working in partnership with the Police to understand international or domestic terrorism and using that knowledge to inform in-house training. This eagerness to work with and learn from partners and other organisations is highlighted in the following quote from the Safety and Security Training Manager:

> "We have had the opportunity to attend training in which we are alongside other organisations like social services etc. where we can also learn from them."

17.3 Case study: events, partnerships and advocacy

The case studies used in all of the other pillars have focused on a single organisation. This case study outlines the benefits of building networks in three key areas to show the breadth of impact: events, partnerships and advocacy.

17.3.1 Events

The organisation of events provide a clear opportunity for multi-agency working and the formation of networks. Such events may require the collaboration of a range of key stakeholders (e.g., the Police, transport, accommodation, health services etc.). One example of such a network approach was provided by an SfD organisation in Africa.

This organisation was tasked with the management of safeguarding during an international event which typically involves over a thousand children and young people. The organisation utilises staff in all key areas. Furthermore, the participating schools are asked to sign a code of conduct as well as to identify a designated safeguarding officer to act as a key contact. At the beginning of each tournament, a briefing meeting is arranged with representatives from all key stakeholders at which safeguarding is discussed. This meeting sets out all roles and responsibilities while also ensuring that everyone is aware of the possible risks to children and what should be done if any concerns are disclosed. If issues do arise then a committee is convened to discuss how it should be managed. Minutes are taken at each meeting to ensure an accurate record and to provide a point of reference.

Another example was provided by an elite football club. The quality of the Club's safeguarding procedures, particularly in hosting matches and events, has been recognised by many, including the local council. As such they have been deemed suitable to host a recent series of major non-sporting events, in which the demographic was an estimated 85–90% children and young adults. In order to do so they created an advisory group, engaging with Local Council, Child Protection Services, Police and expert Health Services Staff to put together a policy for the specific purposes of that major event. One of the most successful aspects of the safeguarding of those events was the development specified areas in which distressed children could seek assistance for a variety of reasons. These reasons were wide reaching from children who were separated from parents or friends, upset, sunburnt or simply needed to charge their mobile phones. This operation was also monitored and evaluated. A comprehensive independent report on the event found that there were approximately 40–50 welfare staff deployed for each event to manage the health and wellbeing of children in the designated areas and in the facility in general, which was operational until the early hours of the following morning. A member of the Match Day Staff said:

> "It worked fantastically well!"

17.3.2 Partnerships

Another opportunity for building networks was reported by organisations who worked through partnerships to deliver their programmes. These relationships can serve to strengthen the systems in place to safeguard children. The importance of this was highlighted by one International Governor who said:

> "You are only as good as your weakest partner."

One sports club gave examples of how they used partnerships at a range of levels. From a local perspective, the Club currently has a large number of players attending a local independent school. The Head of Safeguarding works closely with the school on an ongoing basis, while also working with the disciplinary panel of the school to ensure fairness is established when Academy boys have committed misdemeanours. While from an international perspective, the Club works with other football clubs and international child protection agencies to ensure the safety of children during international competitions. This is viewed as good practice and essential to the success of their international work. A Safeguarding Officer said:

> "We also have to ensure the safety of others too, especially when we come into contact with children from an international perspective, so it's about sharing good practice with partners too."

The International Football Programmes Manager highlighted how safeguarding is fundamental to their partnerships:

> "A lot of countries don't use the words safeguarding, but if we are there then we can't stray from our values."

The difficulties that may arise from working in different international contexts were identified by a Senior Coach at the Club who said:

> "We have a huge gambit and range of where we are (recruiting young players) from, we have a wide variety of cultures, levels of education etc. that are mixing together. So we have a wide range of issues that we have to look out for."

One such issue is that of people who pretend to be associated with the club. The Club's popularity is such that they are recognisable in many parts of the world. As such members of staff or representatives of the Club are likely to be given a great deal of respect and hence are in a significant position of power. One of the challenges that accompany this popularity is the increased likelihood that people may impersonate being a member of staff or a representative of the Club. In more recent times, the Club have been alerted to cases of people impersonating scouts in order to fraudulently obtain finances from parents who believe their child is set to sign for the Club. The Head of Safeguarding said:

> "We get emails all around the world from people saying our scout is arranging something and they are requesting $5,000, is this real?"

This was discussed as a concern for the Club, which may be approached by some parents after funds have exchanged hands already or by children who turn up to the training ground with false documentation, adamant they have the authority to train with them.

In working with external partners, the Club is clear about their requirements to ensure the programmes are safe for children. The Club's Global Safeguarding Policy clearly outlines the requirement for partners to have a clear line of accountability for safeguarding, at the senior board level, along with policies, protocols and personnel for the development of safe working environments. The International Programmes Manager explained:

> "We set quite strict guidelines on things like coach ratios and photography . . . if we are there we make sure the environment adheres to the standards we want and we have to make sure they know why. If things are not up to the standard we make recommendations for the next time, and if they are not applied then we won't work with them."

The Club will not provide charitable grants to Foundations that cannot demonstrate clear and effective safeguarding programmes and procedures. Opportunities are offered to develop these if they are not in place, with a six-month deadline.

17.3.3 Advocacy

The participants reported significant progress through advocating for the International Safeguards within their existing networks. This was acknowledged within this project through organisations working with their Virtual Learning Sets. Indeed, due to the work associated with the International Safeguards, the INF was awarded the Spirit of Sport Award at Sport Accord in 2015. This award honoured the INF's work in using sport as a tool to create change and improve the situation of communities around the world. Speaking on this award a member of staff said:

> "I like to think we won that on behalf of the whole international learning set because that was the basis for which the INF won that award.

We won that award acting as leaders in this field at an international level, really raising awareness of the project."

Having really bought in to the importance of safeguarding, and the International Safeguards in particular, the INF has made demonstrable attempts to go beyond internal influence and facilitate change in other sports. A member of staff at the INF explained:

"Our president is on the board of the association of IOC recognised international sports federations and she has had meetings this week. Within her council agenda she has requested that recognised bodies are to look at promoting the Safeguards to all 35 recognised sport, so the ones that sit just outside the Olympic games."

This staff member went on to say:

"So there again netball is taking a leading role and taking it to the board table to say that this is something that the adoption of the International Safeguards is something that all of the members of the IOC recognised sports should actually take on board, so we have lots of ways of communicating with our members but also communicating to the other international sports federations."

17.4 Summary

The present chapter discusses the eighth and final pillar, Networks. It highlights the importance of developing local, national and international relations with similar organisations who may collaborate and support each other's work. Challenges and barriers to building such networks are discussed, such as the sense of isolation that is often felt by individuals within sporting organisations, and cultural attitudes towards matters such as safeguarding children, which may differ heavily from that held by organisations implementing the International Safeguards. Examples of promising practice are presented, such as conducting community mapping processes to better understand the contexts and supportive services available. Representative examples are offered in relation to developing and delivering successful events, partnerships and advocacy.

References

Frost, N., & Lloyd, A. (2006). Implementing multi-disciplinary teamwork in the new child welfare policy environment. *Journal of Integrated Care*, *14*(2), 11–17.

Frost, N., & Robinson, M. (2007). Joining up children's services: Safeguarding children in multi-disciplinary teams. *Child Abuse Review*, *16*, 184–199.

H.M. Government. (2013). *Working together to safeguard children: A guide to inter agency working to safeguard and promote the welfare of Children*. London: HM Government.

Home Office. (2014). *Multi-agency working and information sharing project*. London: Home Office.

Chapter 18

Conclusions

This chapter reflects on the research questions addressed through this project and summarises the key findings. The researchers' reflections on completing this project are also considered. Topics to be explored through future research in this domain are also outlined.

18.1 Answering the research questions

The research questions which were derived from the project objectives were outlined in Chapter 6. These are now discussed in turn, with the key findings in each area being reiterated.

18.1.1 RQ1: Are the draft Safeguards appropriate for global adoption?

Broadly speaking, the principles underlying the original draft Standards were appropriate and there was clearly an unmet need for clear guidance on safeguarding across the wide range of contexts in which sport takes place around the globe. However, revisions were made to the draft Standards, based on extensive feedback, to optimise their appropriateness for global adoption. These developments were focused on four key areas.

Firstly, the title of the new concept was changed from the Standards to the International Safeguards for Children in Sport. This change was made in order to mitigate possible resistance to the name Standards. Secondly, rather than being overly prescriptive, the focus was on providing a framework. This served to emphasise that the International Safeguards allow for flexibility such that people can tailor implementation to the characteristics of the given context. Thirdly, the use of language was simplified throughout all of the International Safeguards. Clear and specific examples were given throughout to give people guidance on exactly what each criteria could look like in practice. The fourth and final change was the reduction in the number of elements from the eleven Standards down to the eight International Safeguards. All of the original topics were retained, they were just presented in a more condensed way with some aspects, such as the involvement of children, being embedded throughout the other International Safeguards as opposed to a separated element. The feedback collected through this research suggests that this updated version called the International Safeguards are now appropriate for global adoption.

18.1.2 RQ2: where are the participant organisations now and at the end of the pilot in relation to the safeguards?

Participants completed a self-audit at the start of the project in 2013 and again at the end of the project in 2016. It was clear that there was scope for progress across all of the Safeguards. The areas in which there was the least in place concerns the presence of procedures for managing safeguarding concerns and the availability of advice and support. These data were compared to assess any progress that had been made towards the International Safeguards. Looking at the organisations overall, progress was made across all of the International Safeguards as follows:

- Safeguard 1: Developing Your Policy – from 56% to 93%
- Safeguard 2: Procedures for Responding to Safeguarding Concerns – from 26% to 40%
- Safeguard 3: Advice and Support – from 33% to 40%
- Safeguard 4: Minimising Risks to Children – from 44% to 53%
- Safeguard 5: Guidelines for Behaviour – from 37% to 67%
- Safeguard 6: Recruiting, Training and Communicating – from 41% to 60%
- Safeguard 7: Working with Partners – from 37% to 67%
- Safeguard 8: Monitoring and Evaluating – from 37% to 53%

The most progress was made with respect to Safeguards 1, 5 and 7. The areas where there remains the most scope for improvement is the presents of procedures for managing safeguarding concerns and the availability of advice and support. Whilst improvements were made across all Safeguards, there remains scope for further progress to be made in terms of implementing and embedding these Safeguards. This project thus represents a significant step along the safeguarding journey. However, this data illustrates that the journey is not yet over and hence the journey continues.

18.1.3 RQ3: what profiles of activation do the various stakeholder groups demonstrate, and how does this change with the implementation of the Safeguards?

In order to assess change through the interview data, the concept of Activation States was used. This assesses people's voices, knowledge, feelings and behaviours related to safeguarding. These are evaluated on a scale from opposed through reactive to proactive. Overall, the Deliverers made progress at the individual level to be at least active across all Activation States. Particular progress was made in terms of knowledge (inactive to active) and behaviour (inactive to proactive). This shows that involvement in the International Safeguards project had achieved an important impact through developing these individual's awareness of safeguarding as well as having a clear impact on facilitating an increase in their behaviours related to safeguarding.

At the organisational level for the deliverers, at the start of the project, the modal response for both the voice and feelings categories was opposed. By the end of the project, the participants reported an active profile in terms of voices and feelings through describing a shared understanding of the importance of safeguarding children. Throughout the project, the organisational level for the Deliverers progressed from inactive to active with respect to both knowledge and behaviour categories. This qualitative data suggests that the Safeguards have contributed to changes not only with respect to people's knowledge and behaviours but also in terms of how people feel and talk about safeguarding within the participating organisations.

Overall, the Governors made progress at the individual level to be at least active across all Activation States. Significant progress was made in terms of knowledge (inactive to active) and behaviour (inactive to active). This shows that involvement in the International Safeguards project had achieved an important impact through developing these individual's awareness of safeguarding as well as having a clear impact on facilitating an increase in their behaviours related to safeguarding.

At the organisational level for the governors, progress was made across all areas. Voices progressed from opposed to reactive with feelings improving from opposed to active. Furthermore, knowledge progressed from inactive to active and behaviours improved from inactive to reactive. The research showed that the Safeguards have contributed to changes not only with respect to people's knowledge and behaviours but also in terms of how people feel and talk about safeguarding for those who support or govern organisations working with children in sport.

18.1.4 RQ4: what are the challenges and experiences of the participating organisations during the pilot?

Participants described a wide range of challenges throughout the project. However, there were also many examples of participation in this project being a positive, rewarding and worthwhile experience. The specific issues reported are discussed throughout the book. However, the eight CHILDREN pillars highlight both the potential challenges as well as the factors which could facilitate more progress towards the International Safeguards. The pillars are:

- Cultural Sensitivity – the need for flexibility within the Safeguards such that they can be tailored to the cultural and social norms of the context

- Holistic – integrating safeguarding into all aspects of an organisation as opposed to being an additional element
- Incentives – ensuring that there are clear reasons for individuals and an organisation to work towards the Safeguards
- Leadership – seeking and demonstrating strong support from those working in key leadership roles at the top and throughout an organisation
- Dynamic – the need to regularly review and adapt the Safeguards to maintain their relevance and effectiveness
- Resources – Supporting the implementation of the Safeguards with appropriate resources
- Engaging Stakeholders – Using a democratic approach which invites and listens to the voices of those in and around the organisation
- Networks – developing and maintaining networks with other related organisations

18.1.5 RQ5: what can be learned from selected case studies of the pilot experience?

A series of six case studies was conducted through collecting more in-depth data with targeted organisations. The key messages identified through these case studies were:

- Case study 1 (discussed in Chapter 10 – Cultural Sensitivity) – This focused on an international coaching deliverer and highlighted the importance of facilitating self-directed learning through helping people and organisations to find their own Safeguards. The benefits of adopting a pragmatic approach and of working to get the buy-in of people to take ownership of the Safeguards were also discussed.
- Case study 2 (discussed in Chapter 11 – Holistic) – This addressed the work of an International Governor. Effective collaborations were facilitated through promoting the development of a national policy, creating mechanisms for background checks, hosting a significant conference and building the capacity of partner organisations.
- Case study 3 (discussed in Chapter 12 – Incentives) – An international federation who works with member organisations around the world highlighted how these members were incentivised to work towards the Safeguards. This included strategies such as raising awareness, using and rewarding safeguarding champions and providing clear support to guide progress.
- Case study 4 (discussed in Chapter 13 – Leadership) – This focused on a European football club. It highlighted the need to gain genuine and demonstrated support from senior leaders in the organisation for the Safeguards. Leadership should be visible throughout having leaders responsible for safeguarding in all areas of the organisation.

The leadership should also be empowering through emphasising that safeguarding is not just one person's job, but it is rather part of everyone's job.

- Case study 5 (discussed in Chapter 14 – Dynamic) – This addressed the work of an international sport for development organisation. It emphasises that the journey towards the Safeguards takes time. This journey can be facilitated through having flexibility built into the implementation such that safeguarding can be tailored to the political and social norms of the context. The approach can be informed through periodic reviews and people can be supported by the provision of mentors to guide progress.
- Case study 6 (discussed in Chapter 16 – Engaging Stakeholders) – A sport for development agency explained the range of strategies used to engage with the children, parents and the broader community. This included open sessions to promote communication between all key stakeholders. Efforts to directly promote and protect children's rights also helped to facilitate further engagement from stakeholders when they could understand and see evidence of the positive outcomes of effective safeguarding.

18.1.6 RQ6: what should be included in an implementation guide for organisations seeking to adopt the Safeguards?

Based on this research, the implementation guides have been published. There are versions specifically for deliverer and governor organisations. It explains all of the Safeguards and gives clear examples as to how the pioneer organisations worked towards each Safeguard. The safeguarding journey was broken down into five steps:

- Step1: Foundation level (e.g., understanding the need for safeguarding)
- Step 2: The Self-Audit Tool (e.g., understanding the current status of safeguarding)
- Step 3: Developing your Safeguard (e.g., creating an action plan)
- Step 4: Implementing your Safeguard (e.g., promoting awareness and engagement with the policy or procedure)
- Step 5: Embedding your Safeguard (e.g., monitoring and reviewing practices)

A clear need for the implementation guides was emphasised to help people understand how their organisation can work towards the International Safeguards, irrespective of their current situation in relation to safeguarding. Initial feedback has already been received from organisations who are using and benefitting from these guides.

18.2 The seesaw model of safeguarding

These findings suggest that the International Safeguards are appropriate for global adoption, and when underpinned by the CHILDREN Pillars, enhance the proficiency of safeguarding within sporting organisations. Therefore, there is a reduced likelihood that children will experience maltreatment and its subsequent harm. In other words, the International Safeguards make a significant contribution towards shifting the balance of probability in favour of the protection of children from maltreatment in sport (as expressed in Figure 18.1).

18.3 Reflections

Inevitably, there are limitations associated with the approach adopted in this book which merit consideration. The authors of this book have reflected on their experiences of conducting this project. It is recognised that researchers are part of the social world that is being studied. Researchers bring their own beliefs, values and experiences (Matthews & Ross, 2010). Each of these factors have the potential to influence all stages of research from planning, through data collection and interpretation through to the way in which it is presented in a book. Rather than ignore or attempt to eliminate these factors, constructivist researchers seek to understand their biases that emerge from them (Denzin & Lincoln, 2005; Patton, 2015). For these reasons researchers engage in reflexivity, a process through which the researcher considers their role in the research process and how they contributed to the construction of knowledge (Sparkes & Smith, 2014).

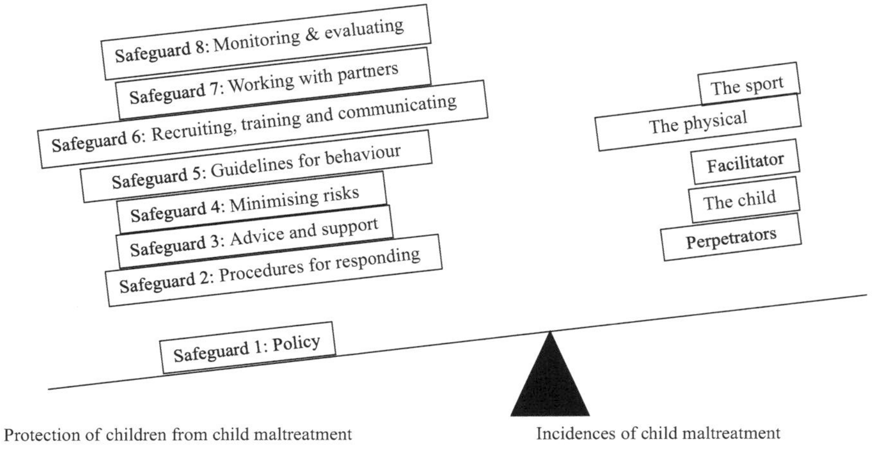

Figure 18.1 The seesaw model of safeguarding

It is generally held that a level of engagement within the contexts that one wishes to study is useful in enhancing the researchers understanding (Robson, 2002). Although the extent to which a social sciences researcher should be involved and engaged with the participants of their study is the subject of much debate within qualitative research literature (Cui, 2015; Southgate & Shying, 2014). This debate centres on the roles of researchers as insiders or outsiders, and the extent to which researchers should be involved or detached. Insiders should be understood as researchers who are studying groups that they have some degree of membership to (Cui, 2015). They share a broad sense of identification with the group, and are involved in its functioning (Southgate & Shying, 2014). Alternatively, outsiders should be viewed as researchers of groups with which they are not considered members of (Cui, 2015; Southgate & Shying, 2014). For these reasons outsiders are detached from the group, share little to no identification with the group and its functioning.

Amongst many of the debates on these topics, a pertinent consideration is the efficacy and ethics of adopting either style (Southgate & Shying, 2014). Many arguments have surfaced on either side of the debate, although it has also been argued that it is impossible for the researcher to be entirely one or the other during the data collection process (Naples, 1996; Spradley, 1980). Based on this, it has been suggested that researchers should strive for involved-detachment. This is the dynamic variation of involvement and detachment throughout various points of the research (Perry, Thurston, & Green, 2004). Our intention was to achieve this balance throughout the research, becoming involved where it assisted us to develop and maintain rapport, trust and respect, but distancing ourselves where we needed to be analytical and maintain our integrity and neutrality as researchers.

Throughout this three-year project, the researchers developed relationships with all of the participants and, in particular, those involved in the case studies. It should be acknowledged that at the start of these relationships there may have been concern from the participants with respect to the intentions of the researchers. For example, were we viewed as coming in to 'test' an organisation's safeguarding measures? Were we going to report back to a governor or funding organisation? Were we going to pass on sensitive information to the media? All of these points were covered in the initial meetings and ethics documentation. However, these concerns may have persisted and influenced the data. Similarly, at the later stages of data collection, rapport had been developed with the participants which may have biased the data. The researchers were cognisant of these risks and took steps to maintain trustworthiness throughout the project. However, such factors need to be acknowledged.

It should also be highlighted that this research has been able to achieve significant impact, both within and beyond the pioneer organisations. The research was built on fundamental principles which have subsequently been identified as best practice in facilitating impact. For example, Hanney, Greenhaldh, Blatch-Jones, Glover & Raftery (2017) identify three key strategies which are associated with achieving research impact on policy and practice. Firstly, there is collaboration with the end user to inform the planning of the study. This was certainly embedded in this project during the initial group meetings and online discussions through a philosophy of it being a co-produced project. Secondly, the project should be needs-led. The Safeguards project came out of a consensus of key organisations that there was a clear need for safeguarding in sport. Finally, there should be mechanisms in place for people to use the findings. This has been achieved through the International Safeguards being published along with the Implementation Guides. These strategies came about in a natural and organic way as opposed to being strategically planned. However, these characteristics do help to perhaps explain how this research has been able to achieve significant impact and the methods used can inform other researchers and end users as future projects are planned and conducted (Hanney et al., 2017).

18.4 Future research directions

Despite the significant body of work which has been conducted over the past 20 years, there remains a wide range of avenues for possible research. The vast majority of research on abuse in sport to date has focused on identifying and understanding:

1 The nature and prevalence of the different forms of abuse
2 The individual, relational and organisational risk factors for abuse
3 The experiences of those who have been abused

The significant contribution of the present research is the shift in focus from understanding abuse in sport to understanding safeguarding in sport. This opens up a variety of possibilities for future research. Some examples are summarised in Table 18.1, with ideas being considered for children, adults (e.g., parents, coaches and staff) and the organisational as a whole. Possible topics are identified with respect to the antecedents (e.g., before safeguarding), the nature (e.g., during safeguarding) and the outcomes (e.g., after safeguarding) of the International Safeguards.

Feedback on the implementation guide has been sought throughout the development of the various versions of these resources. However, there is now a need to evaluate the use of these resources by organisations on the ground through a piloting process. Research could be conducted to investigate how using the implementation guides can help an organisation progress towards the International Safeguards based on the collection of data from a range of sources (e.g., Self-Audit Tools, interviews/focus groups and organisational indicators).

Table 18.1 Ideas for future research

Stage	*Children*	*Adults*	*Organisation*
Antecedents	What makes children feel safe in sport?	What are stakeholders' perceptions of the Safeguards?	What is the current status of safeguarding in different organisations in relation to the Safeguards?
Nature	How can one effectively listen to children's voices when developing Safeguards?	How can one effectively gain the buy-in of all stakeholders in relation to the Safeguards?	How can one effectively work towards the Safeguards in different types of organisations?
Outcomes	How do the Safeguards impact: Children's experiences Children's well-being Children's performance	How do the Safeguards impact: Adults' experiences Adults' behaviours Adults' relationships with children	How do the Safeguards impact: Meeting organisational goals Reputation

The range of data collected through this research provides initial evidence of the significant progress that has been made across the International Safeguards and the associated benefits for children and the organisation as a whole. There is now a real sense of a global momentum around the International Safeguards. It is now important that future work is built on the platform created by the resources and networks which have resulted from this project to safeguard children in all sport contexts.

References

Cui, K. (2015). The insider – outsider role of a Chinese researcher doing fieldwork in china: The implications of cultural context. *Qualitative Social Work*, *14*(3), 356–369.

Denzin, N. K., & Lincoln, Y. S. (2005). *The SAGE handbook of qualitative research* (3rd ed.). London, UK: Sage.

Hanney, S., Greenhaldh, T., Blatch-Jones, A., Glover, M., & Raftery, J. (2017). The impact on healthcare, policy and practice from 36 multi-research project programmes: Findings from 2 reviews. *Healthcare Research Policy and Systems*, *26*. Retrieved August 30, 2017, from https://health-policy-systems.biomedcentral.com/articles/10.1186/s12961-017-0191-y

Matthews, B., & Ross, L. (2010). *Research methods: A practical guide for the social sciences*. Harlow, UK: Pearson Longman.

Naples, N. A. (1996). A feminist revisiting of the insider/outsider debate: The "outsider phenomenon" in rural Iowa. *Qualitative Sociology, 19*(1), 83–106.
Patton, M. Q. (2015). *Qualitative research and evaluation methods* (4th ed.). London, UK: Sage.
Perry, C., Thurston, M., & Green, K. (2004). Involvement and detachment in researching sexuality: Reflections on the process of semi-structured interviewing. *Qualitative Health Research, 14*(1), 135–148.
Robson, C. (2002). *Real world research* (2nd ed.). Oxford, UK: Blackwell Publishing.
Southgate, E., & Shying, K. (2014). Researchers as dirty workers: Cautionary tales on insider-outsider dynamics. *Qualitative Research in Organizations and Management: An International Journal, 9*(3), 223–240.
Sparkes, A. C., & Smith, B. (2014). *Qualitative research methods in sport, exercise and health*. London, UK: Routledge.
Spradley, J. P. (1980). *Participant observation*. New York, NY: Holt, Rinehart & Winston.

Index